Moonlight
on Linoleum

Moonlight
on Linoleum

A Daughter's Memoir

Terry Helwig

HOWARD BOOKS
A DIVISION OF SIMON & SCHUSTER, INC.
New York Nashville London Toronto Sydney New Delhi

Howard Books
A Division of Simon & Schuster, Inc.
1230 Avenue of the Americas
New York, NY 10020

In consideration of their privacy, the names and identifying details of some people
have been changed.

First Howard Books hardcover edition October 2011

HOWARD and colophon are trademarks of Simon & Schuster, Inc.

For information about special discounts for bulk purchases,
please contact Simon & Schuster Special Sales at 1-866-506-1949
or business@simonandschuster.com.

The Simon & Schuster Speakers Bureau can bring authors to your live event. For
more information or to book an event, contact the Simon & Schuster Speakers
Bureau at 1-866-248-3049 or visit our website at www.simonspeakers.com.

Designed by Davina Mock-Maniscalco

Manufactured in the United States of America

10   9   8   7   6   5   4   3   2   1

Library of Congress Control Number: 2011016818

ISBN 978-1-4516-2847-0
ISBN 978-1-4516-2866-1 (ebook)

For
Carola Jean, my mother,
and Amanda Jean, my daughter

Foreword

YEARS AGO, WHILE walking on a South Carolina beach with Terry Helwig, I had what turned out to be a propitious conversation. Close friends for over twenty years, we often walked the corridor of sand on Isle of Palms, talking about our lives and our work. On this October day, we were discussing the peculiar fact that many readers of my then recently published novel, *The Secret Life of Bees,* sometimes believed the story was based on my own childhood. They assumed that like my fourteen-year-old character, Lily, I had been forced to kneel on grits, had lost my mother when I was four, and had run away with the housekeeper to escape an abusive father. Of course, my childhood was nothing at all like Lily's.

After listening to my bemusement about this oddity, Terry said, "If I wrote the story of *my* childhood, it would be just the opposite. The story would be completely true, but no one would believe it."

We laughed at this little irony.

I knew the saga of Terry's childhood, which rivaled the sorrow and crazy-making adversity I'd invented for my own fictional Lily. Yet Terry had managed to arrive in adulthood with her soul beautifully intact, without a trace of victimhood, cynicism, or bitterness. Indeed, she was one of the most remarkable, loving, and utterly together persons I'd ever met.

Walking beside Terry that day, marveling at how such a mysterious transaction as that occurs in the human spirit, I almost missed the tacit suggestion in her comment: *If I wrote the story of my childhood.*

My pace slowed till I was at a standstill. "Have you thought of writing it?"

"I've thought of it," she said. "But—does the world really need another memoir?"

It was just like her to ask that question. It would not occur to Terry to write a memoir just because she could. In her mind, it needed to exist for a larger reason; it needed to be the sort of story that served something worthwhile; it needed to be needed.

"The world needs your story," I told her.

"I'll think about that," she said.

We can all be glad she did.

It soon became apparent that *Moonlight on Linoleum* had been lying innate, dormant, and fathoms deep inside of Terry for most of her life, waiting for the right culmination of time and realization. For years, I watched from the periphery as she worked on the book, laboring to render her story with unflinching honesty, bringing to it her indomitable humor and humility, and filling it with her deep and luminous vision of life.

The book is both a tender recollection and an unblinking portrayal of a heartbreaking yet heart-stirring childhood, one that unfolds among the little oil towns of the American West. The transience, privation, abandonment, abuse, anguish, and havoc in Terry's young world is, startlingly enough, met with equal portions of hope, dignity, resilience, ingenuity, funniness, and love.

The story reveals a family hovering on the unraveling edge of life: Carola Jean, a complex and unforgettable mother whom you may want to rage at one moment and hug the next; a good-hearted, oil-drilling stepfather, plus an array of other colorful men held in Carola Jean's thrall. Terry's five younger sisters fall under her tutelage, in the formation of an uncommon sisterhood that transmutes suffering into salvation. And at the center of it is Terry, a girl clinging to hope in the face of crushing realities, a girl determined to stay connected to her dreams, determined to save her sisters, as well as herself.

If I were asked to explain the statement I made on the beach that day when I told Terry the world needed her story, I could probably come up with a whole panoply of reasons for why it's true. But I will simply give you one. . . .

Remember that mysterious transaction in the human spirit that I marveled at where Terry was concerned? The one that allows one person to transcend life's hardships, becoming stronger, wiser, and larger in spirit, while another person succumbs to life's injuries, growing hardened, contracted, or stuck? Well, there are no explanations for that, there are only stories. The world needs *Moonlight on Linoleum* because it is just such a story. It is what redemption looks like.

—Sue Monk Kidd

Prologue

I COULD NOT FIND my mother's grave.

The caretaker thumped a large brown ledger onto his desk. "What's your mom's name?"

An easy enough question, except for those five or six marriages. *I should know her last name.* My face reddened as I stood momentarily speechless in the caretaker's office at Riverside Cemetery in Fort Morgan, Colorado.

"She might be under Carola Jean Vacha," I said. I remembered letters spelling THE VACHAS running vertically down a post on the front porch of her marigold-colored house before she died.

The caretaker's finger ran the length of the page. "Nothing under that name."

In the fifteen years since Mama's death, I had not been back. I was unsure what name had been etched onto her headstone. Come to think of it, I couldn't remember being consulted about a headstone at all.

"What about Carola Jean Simmonds?" I asked.

He shook his head.

"She married a lot," I offered. "How about Wilton or Redding?"

He raised an eyebrow and continued his search. "Here's Carola Jean Redding. Died April 29, 1974. Lot 398, Block 10," he said and flipped the ledger closed.

I followed him as he wound his way through a maze of weathered gravestones variously carved with lilies, roses, and angels. The graves didn't all look alike to him; he knew about lots and blocks. He reminded me of the ferryman on the river Styx, overseeing the dead.

When he came to a stop in front of a flat cement marker, barely larger than a brick, I was confused. Then I saw it: Mama's name crudely etched into cement. She had no headstone—only the plain dull marker the county had provided, which had begun to flake and crumble, surrendering to the surrounding grass.

She has a pauper's grave, I thought as I knelt and laid down the pink rose I had bought. I wrestled a clump of grass, trying to reclaim a corner of the marker. The cement felt cool to my touch. Wiping the smell of grass and dirt onto my jeans, I turned to the caretaker. "I know it's a little late, but what if I wanted to order a headstone?"

"People do it all the time," he said. He turned and walked away, leaving me to my thoughts.

* * *

I WAS forty years old, the same age my mother had been when she died. I stood at the juncture of the second half of my life, at precisely the place where Mama's footprints ran out. The years ahead of me would be virgin territory, unexplored by the woman who had ushered me into the world. The only thing I understood with any certainty was just how young Mama had been when she died.

During her graveside service fifteen years earlier, I had gazed up into the branches of a nearby tree, startled to see the juxtaposition of sunlight so near death. The beauty of pink blossoms punctuating the blue sky had taken my breath away. The colors of the world had never looked more vivid, my senses had never been more alive. It was as if death's razor had cut away the veil separating me from holy mystery, exquisite wonder blazing with sorrow.

Mama's casket had not yet been covered with earth. I had no idea then, being only twenty-five, what burial entailed. Mama's funeral was my first. My knees had buckled when I first saw her lying in the casket, her wax-like hands holding a single rose. The ink-blue bruise of ruptured blood vessels on her left temple, resulting from the overdose, had been camouflaged under a layer of caked makeup. Long sleeves hid the thick purple scars on the undersides of her wrists—scars that had been fresh wounds once, bleeding a river of red onto white sheets.

I had wanted to shield my younger sisters from the sight of Mama's blood that day, to spare them that memory above all others. That's how I summoned up enough strength to shove the dresser in front of the door, to rip the sheets into bandages, to shoulder the weight of Mama staggering down the hallway. I alone washed Mama's sticky blood from my hands. I had wanted it that way.

But now that I had a daughter of my own, I understood just how bereft I had been. Picturing myself as a young girl, flipping a crimson-splotched mattress, I wished I could have spared her, too.

FOR THE headstone, I selected a pinkish slab of granite and instructed the stonecutter to cut a single word for her epitaph: *Selah*.

The word *Selah* is an enigma, which describes my mother perfectly. Some think *Selah* refers to a musical instruction, meaning "a pause" or "stopping to listen." It may also have been used similarly to the word *amen*. Now that I was the same age as Mama had been when she died, I wanted to stop and listen to what her life had meant; I wanted to say amen to her, as if she had been a prayer.

The next thing to determine was Mama's last name. *Dare I change it to one of her earlier names?* After the funeral, her fifth or sixth husband, Lenny, only two years my senior, took all of Mama's old photographs, because he "loved her so." Lenny thought his year and four months with Mama trumped all the years my sisters and I had spent with her. I was even more offended when I learned, years later, that Mama's marriage to Lenny may have been null and void. Mama may not have been legally divorced from Tom. But Mama would have considered this legality nothing more than a pesky technicality, a minor inconvenience that had to be *negotiated*.

I was my mother's daughter.

I concluded that the legality of the name on Mama's headstone was a minor inconvenience that could be negotiated, so I chose the married name that my sisters and I loved best, the once-legal name that had defined Mama the longest, the name that belonged to a man I call Daddy, still to this day.

In addition to *Selah, Carola Jean Vacha* was etched into stone.

I invited the child I once was to have her say in these pages.
I am the one who came out on the other side of childhood;
she is the one who searched for the door.

My dad holding Vicki; Mama holding me

Emerson, Iowa

1950

"I LEFT YOUR DAD," Mama told me more than once, "because I didn't want to kill him."

She wasn't kidding.

Mama said she stood at the kitchen counter, her hand touching the smooth wooden handle of a butcher knife. In an argument that grew more heated, Mama felt her fist close around the handle. For a brief moment, she deliberated between slashing our father with the knife or releasing it harmlessly back onto the counter and walking away.

My sister Vicki was ten months old; I was two. Mama was seventeen.

By all accounts, Mama and Dad loved each other, even though Mama lied about her age. Mama told my dad that she had celebrated her eighteenth birthday; Dad, twenty-two, believed her. But the state of Iowa insisted on seeing Mama's record of birth before granting them a marriage license. Only then did Mama confess her lie. Dad broke down and cried. Mama was fourteen, not eighteen. Still, despite the deceit and age difference, on Wednesday, May 26, 1948, Carola Jean Simmonds and Donald Lee Skinner said, "I do." Mama's mother signed her consent.

Mama definitely looked older than fourteen. She had thick black hair that fell around her face, accenting the widow's peak she inherited from her mother. Her hazel eyes reflected not a shy, timid girl but a womanly gaze that belied her years. Physically, she was curved and full-bosomed. But she was not pregnant. According to my birth certificate, I came along a full eleven months after they married, proving their union sprang from something other than necessity.

Part of Mama's motivation may have come from her eagerness to leave home. Her older brother, my uncle Gaylen, witnessed the difficult relationship Mama had with their mother.

"This is hard to tell," he said. "When your mom was just a baby, I remember walking alongside her baby carriage with our mom. I must have been about eight. Carola was crying and crying and Mom got so mad. She stopped the carriage, walked to a nearby tree, and yanked off a switch. She returned to the carriage and whipped your mom for crying. I couldn't believe she was whipping a baby."

Uncle Gaylen fumbled for words, attributing his mom's state of mind to my grandfather Gashum's infidelity. "I think Mom took out all her frustrations on Carola," he said.

I wish I could scrub that stain from our family's history. I wish I could reach back in time, snatch the switch from Grandma's raised fist, and snap it across my knee. It might have made a difference. Mama's life might have taken a different turn.

She might not have been so desperate for tenderness.

By the time Mama turned fourteen, she had fallen for my dad. Instead of protesting when Mama asked to marry him, Grandma extolled my father's family, told Mama she was lucky to have him, and readily signed permission for Mama to marry. With the words "I do" uttered in the sleepy town of Glenwood, Iowa, Mama became the fourteen-year-old wife of a tenant farmer.

Around that time, Mama wrote a couple of jingles and sold them to Burma-Shave as part of its roadside advertising campaign. Mama liked to drive by a particular set of red-and-white signs posted successively along the highway near Glenwood. The words on the signs, which built toward a punch line farther down the road, were Mama's words, right there in plain daylight, for the whole world to see.

His cheek
Was rough
His chick vamoosed
And now she won't
Come home to roost
Burma-Shave

It's impossible to know which jingles Mama wrote, but all her life she loved the word *vamoose*.

DURING THE first year of their marriage, my parents moved into a house without running water, off County Road L-45 not far from the Waubonsie Church and Cemetery outside Glenwood. Dad, a farmer, loved the land and spent long hours plowing, planting, and tending the livestock. His mother, my grandma Skinner, lived four miles down the gravel road. Grandma Skinner had raised six children while slopping the pigs, sewing, planting a garden, canning, baking, and putting hearty meals on the table three times a day. I think Dad assumed all women inherited Grandma's Hestian gene.

But not his child bride, Carola Jean. She could write a jingle, but she knew nothing about cooking, gardening, cleaning, or running a household—not even how to iron.

"Your mom couldn't keep up with the house or the laundry," Aunt Dixie, my dad's sister, said years later. "If she ran out of diapers, she'd pin curtains or dish towels on you, anything she could get her hands on."

I doubt Mama knew what to do with a screaming colicky baby, either, one who smelled of sour milk and required little sleep. In a house without running water, I must have contributed to a legion of laundry and fatigue. The doctor finally determined that I suffered from a milk allergy and switched me to soy milk, which cured my colic, but not my aversion to sleep.

"In desperation," Mama recounted many times, "I scooted your crib close enough to the bed to reach my hand through the slats to hold your hand. Finally you'd settle down, but"—Mama would draw in a long breath here—"if I let go, you'd wake up and start crying all over again. You always wanted to be near me. Sometimes I cried, too."

Without fail, the next part of her story included a comparison between me and my sister Vicki, born fourteen months later.

"Now, Vicki was just the opposite," Mama marveled. "I'd have to keep thumping her heel just to keep her awake long enough to eat."

Mama's retelling of that story during our growing-up years made me feel like thumping Vicki, too, and it had nothing to do with her staying awake. I pictured Vicki sleeping peacefully and wished I had been an easier child. More than once I wanted to shout, *I can't help what I did as a baby!* But I held my tongue; I was good at that.

By the time Vicki joined our household, we lived in a former rural schoolhouse near Emerson, Iowa. It was here that Mama broke.

She was sixteen.

No matter how you do the math, the equation always comes out the same: Mama was little more than a child herself. The rigors of marriage, farm life, and two girls under the age of two finally came crashing down on her.

Mama had adopted a kitten, much to my delight and my dad's dismay. Dad did not want animals in the house. But Mama stood her ground; the kitten stayed. Mama loved watching it pounce on a string and lap milk from a bowl. She loved hearing it purr and worked with me to be gentle with it.

One afternoon, in the driveway, Dad ran over the kitten. Mama could not stop crying.

"He said it was an accident and he was sorry," Mama told

me years later. "But I never believed him." She jutted out her jaw. "He didn't want that kitten in the house."

I find it unlikely that my dad intentionally ran over a kitten. He had a reputation for being soft when it came to killing animals, even to put food on the table. But I do believe some part of their marriage died with that kitten.

When Mama found herself clutching the butcher knife, she said she thought about me and Vicki, what using the knife would mean, how it would carve a different course for each of us. I'll be forever grateful that Mama fast-forwarded to the consequences. She released her grip on the handle and chose divorce over murder.

I have only a single flash of memory of leaving Iowa.

I'm sitting on the plush seat of a train, the nappy brocade scratching my thighs. I'm not afraid, because I'm pressed against Mama's arm; I can feel the warmth of her against my side as she rocks rhythmically. She holds Vicki (who no doubt was sleeping). I repeatedly click my black patent shoes together and apart, together and apart, noticing the folded lace tops of my anklets hanging just over the edge of the cushion. The world is a blur passing by the train window. Clickety-clack. Clickety-clack. Watch your back. We are headed west to Fort Morgan, Colorado.

Vicki, me, and Mama

Fort Morgan, Colorado

WHY CAN'T I ask for money?" I asked. I was three at the time.

"Because it's not polite," Mama answered.

"Nancy does," I countered.

"I know," Mama said, "but only when Aunt Eunice is around."

Mama seemed to think this explanation made some kind of sense.

Much to my chagrin, whenever Mama and her sister, my aunt Eunice, had friends over, especially men friends, my cousin Nancy fetched her piggy bank. She sidled up to her marks, balanced her bank on one of their knees, batted her eyes, and asked if they wanted to drop some money into it, as if she were offering them a rare opportunity. Invariably they laughed at her spunk, dug deep into their pockets, and pulled out most of their spare change.

I knew a good thing when I saw it, which had prompted me to ask for a piggy bank, too. Mama's admonition that I couldn't ask for money seemed highly unfair. Why could Nancy ask? It aggravated me even more when Nancy shook her bank next to my ear so I could hear how rich she was.

I was five months older than Nancy. Neither of us had a daddy who lived with us anymore. Part of the reason Mama had headed west on the train to Fort Morgan was to be near her sister, Eunice. Mama's mother had also moved to Fort Morgan with her second husband.

Grandma could not have been thrilled with the prospect of her two divorced daughters and their children moving in with her and her husband. Maybe that's why Mama and Aunt Eunice rented the three-room, faux-brick, asphalt-sided house near the railroad tracks in town.

Turning the one-bedroom rental into two bedrooms required nothing more than Mama's nailing a white sheet to the wall and ceiling to block off one end of the living room. I envied Aunt Eunice and Nancy for being the lucky ones to sleep in the tent bedroom, while Mama, Vicki, and I shared the back bedroom. I liked when Aunt Eunice did not come home for days at a time because Mama let me sleep in the tent bedroom with Nancy to keep her company.

I remember a knock on the front door one morning. I followed Mama to see who was there and leaned against her leg. A man, whiskered and wearing clothes that looked too big, asked if we had any food to spare. I looked up at Mama to take my cue.

"Just a minute," she said and closed the door.

I followed her into the kitchen. "Mama, who's the man?"

"A hobo. Someone who rides the trains and doesn't have a home."

"Why doesn't he have a home?"

She opened the refrigerator door, hunched over, and pondered the empty shelves. Looking over her shoulder, she asked, "Should we fix him a mayonnaise sandwich, or a butter and sugar sandwich?"

I voted for the sugar and butter. One of my recent discoveries had been the sugar bowl, sitting smack-dab in the center of the kitchen table. If left alone, I fished a spoon from the silverware drawer, climbed onto one of the chrome-legged chairs, and pulled the sugar bowl toward me. I loved how the grains of sugar exploded into a thousand pellets of sweetness on my tongue.

Definitely a sugar and butter sandwich, sprinkled with a bit of cinnamon.

Mama made two sandwiches and stuffed them into a crackling paper bag. She started for the door and turned back to the counter. After a moment's hesitation, she grabbed the last orange out of a bowl on the counter and tucked it inside the bag, too.

I followed her back to the door to see if the hobo was still there. He was. He smiled when Mama handed him the bag.

"God bless you," he said.

Such a gesture might well be dangerous today, but in the early fifties, when doors were rarely locked and hopping trains a bit more common, nothing seemed out of the ordinary. What I felt that day had nothing to do with fear and everything to do with love for my mother. It may have been my first awareness of loving her, of seeing her outside of myself, of discovering a facet of who she was beyond being my mother.

Shortly after that night, I caught the flu. Propped on pillows in the back bedroom and old enough to know you did not soil the bed, I was mortified when I had diarrhea so bad I could not get up in time to run to the toilet. To add to my crime, I puked all over the sheets. A putrid smell filled the room as Mama hurriedly pulled off my pajamas and stripped the sheets down to the striped ticking on the mattress. I cried, certain I had angered her, but at a loss as to how to stop doing what I was doing. I could not even sit up without feeling dizzy.

Mama cleaned me up and it happened all over again. Between my gags and with snot running down my lips, I cried, "I didn't mean to, Mama. I didn't mean to."

Mama stopped her scurrying and dropped the linens. She wrapped her arms tightly around my hot body. "Of course you didn't mean to," she said. "You're sick. You can't help it."

To be held blameless while lying in diarrhea and vomit, to be treated with such tenderness in the most squalid of circumstances, filled me with euphoria. Mama not only understood; she loved me anyway.

After I got well, Nancy and I perched on a small ledge next to the house. Sitting shoulder to shoulder in our coats, we looked out over the neighborhood and the train tracks. It felt good to be outside again. The vapor of our words swirled around us.

Suddenly, Nancy startled me by crying.

"What's wrong?" I asked.

"I miss my mom," she said, wiping her tears with red knuckles. "I don't know where she is. Or when she's coming back."

It was true. Eunice had not been home. When she went on her drinking sprees, she sometimes disappeared for days, like the time she ended up at the dog races in Nebraska. I had been sleeping with Nancy in the tent bedroom for several days. I draped my bulky arm around Nancy's shoulder. Not knowing what else to do, I leaned my head against hers. We sat there, head to head, for a long while.

Eventually Aunt Eunice did return, showering Nancy with gifts and coins for her piggy bank. When Mama suggested maybe Nancy shouldn't ask for money, Aunt Eunice bristled and said, by God, she wasn't going to find fault with Nancy for passing around a little piggy bank. So it was that Nancy continued to jiggle her bank in front of anyone who came to sit in our living room.

Aunt Eunice and Mama tried to be there for each other, like two sisters adrift at sea, each trying to keep the other from going under. Maybe that explains why Mama did what she did. Maybe Mama was only trying to survive—to make life a little better for herself and for me. Maybe she thought she could still see me from time to time.

How does the conversation go when you offer to give away your older daughter?

Unbeknownst to me, Mama had offered me up to Wilda, a great-aunt by marriage. Wilda and her husband, Lyle, lived in Log Lane Village just outside Fort Morgan.

I have a picture taken at that age.

It is winter. Mama stands in a doorway, propping open a screen door with her left shoulder. Vicki and I stand outside the

door on a thin layer of snow and ice. I am not yet three, Vicki
is under eighteen months, Mama is close to eighteen years. All
three of us wear scarves tied beneath our chins. Vicki's scarf
looks oversized on her; she is without mittens and looks to be
teetering, trying to keep her balance. I look in the direction of the
camera with a quizzical expression, my bare hands tentatively
touching each other in front of my jacket. Mama wears a thin
smile and mittens that rest on either side of my shoulders. It's
impossible to determine if Wilda has already said no.

ONE OF Mama's favorite sayings was "Do not judge others until
you have walked a mile in their shoes."

Putting myself in Mama's shoes, which were most often white
moccasins molded in the shape of her size seven-and-a-half foot,
I see an eighteen-year-old girl with two children, one of them
still a baby, but a good baby, not much trouble. Her former husband is in Korea, drafted after their divorce; she has a sister who
disappears from time to time, leaving yet another child in her
care; she has no money, no high school diploma, and a mother
unhappy with the inconvenience of helping her out.

Mama may have questioned her ability, even her desire, to
raise two young daughters alone. I have no idea if Mama planned
to keep Vicki and give away only me. What is fact is that Mama
turned to a warm and capable woman, a woman who genuinely
seemed to care for her almost three-year-old daughter, a woman
who, perhaps, Mama wished had been her own mother.

Would it be so reprehensible to choose Aunt Wilda to be her
child's mother?

This is one of the miles I have walked wearing Mama's moccasins. I know other conclusions can be drawn, other miles walked. But I believe that Mama's offer to give me up did not come easily, that it exacted some price from her, that I was more than just a kitten needing a good home.

I wonder, though, if somewhere deep in my bones, I feared Mama might walk out the door like Aunt Eunice and never come back. Mama's willingness to let me go may have intensified my need to hold on. Most of my life, I clung fiercely to Mama. Grandma said I cried whenever Mama left and stopped only when she returned.

I hate to think how long I would have cried if Aunt Wilda had said yes. As it was, my fate was not to become the youngest of Wilda's daughters, or to grow up in Fort Morgan. My fate continued to rest with Mama, who found a job making malts and shakes at Yates Drug Store soda fountain on Main Street. Mama's wages did not afford much in the way of child care, so she left me and Vicki with her mother whenever she could.

One afternoon a young seismic driller, a doodlebugger named Davy from East Texas, walked through the front door of the drugstore. He walked across the black-and-white-checkered floor and eased himself onto one of the bar stools after a long day in the oil fields. Covered in dust, he wanted only to quench his thirst.

I suspect he looked up into the face of a raven-haired, hazel-eyed beauty and, like a duckling attracted to the first thing it sees larger than itself, he was imprinted with an irreversible attraction to Mama over which he had no control. Quite simply, she became north on his compass, the direction from which everything else followed.

Davy became a regular, stopping by each day after he finished work. He was a second-generation Moravian who loved to polka, spoke Czech with a Texas drawl, and yodeled decently. He had a thick shock of hair the color of corn tassels, and eyes the color of the summer sky in which the corn tassels blew. One of his front teeth protruded slightly, more of an asset than a liability because it drew attention to his easy smile. One could not notice him without also noting his muscled and lean physique shaped by the hard labor of working on a drilling rig.

Their courtship was brief. They married in a Moravian church in a sleepy town in East Texas where Davy's parents lived in a tin-roofed farmhouse.

I have two pictures of Carola Jean and Davy on their wedding day.

On the back of the first picture Mama's words, written in green ink, read, "Davy, me, and our witnesses in front of the church." Davy wears a carnation boutonniere and rests his left hand on Mama's back. He smiles so wide you can almost see his hope for a long, happy life with his new bride. The witnesses stand behind him and Mama on the church steps; they, too, smile widely. The only person not showing teeth is Mama. She looks at the camera pleasantly, her hands interlaced behind her back. She wears a dark-colored suit with a striped scarf around her neck, open-toed shoes, and a light-colored hat. An oversized mum-and-carnation corsage has been pinned onto her right shoulder. While beautiful, she does not appear to be radiant. Something seems to be missing.

On the back of the second photo, also in green ink, "Me at the place we stayed on our honeymoon. They were furnished in Indian design. Real cute." Mama leans against the back fender of a car, holding on to her purse and white gloves. She looks sophisticated, older than her nineteen years. Behind her stand individual white stuccoed rooms shaped like Native American

tepees; awnings extend from the windows. Mama's corsage
has been moved to her left shoulder; maybe she took it off to
dance.

No doubt the wedding celebration included kegs of beer and
polka dancing. This may have been the time Davy donned Mama's hat and sashayed around the dance floor throwing imaginary corn to imaginary chickens, calling, "Here, chickie, chickie.
Here, chickie, chickie."

It delighted me to learn that the man I came to love and call
Daddy wore a lady's hat and fed imaginary chickens. I'm sure an
eyebrow or two rose that night, not because Daddy wore Mama's hat but, more likely, because Daddy had married a divorcée
from Colorado with two little girls.

Daddy brushed our teeth at night and tucked us into bed; his
arms fit naturally around my shoulders and waist. He listened
to my stories about wanting to fly and laughed as I flapped my
arms and jumped off various chairs. He would say things like
"I'll tell you what, Squirt, if anybody's going to learn to fly, it'll
sure be you." If I had any complaint at all, it was simply that our
new daddy traveled away from home too often, looking for oil in
desolate fields in more states than any of us can remember.

Mama surprised me years later when she told me she didn't
love Daddy when she married him. To her credit, she had paused
for a long while after Daddy asked her.

Then she said, "But Davy, I don't love you."

Mama said Daddy told her, "That's okay. I love you enough
for both of us."

Imprinting is irreversible. I should know; Mama had imprinted herself on my soul as well.

Love was not unimportant to Mama; on the contrary, she
looked for it the way Daddy looked for oil. But Daddy was

Mama's one-way ticket out of Fort Morgan, a helpmate for her two girls, a good, fun-loving man who loved her fiercely.

Seventeen months after they said "I do," my sister Patricia Gayle pushed her way into the world in Harlingen, Texas. Patricia inherited Daddy's corn-silk hair and Mama's hazel eyes. She was a cheerful baby whom Vicki and I loved to hold, but even Patricia could not satisfy Mama's growing discontent at Daddy's long absences. Mama seemed to yearn for something that neither husbands nor babies could satisfy. More and more often, while Daddy worked out of town, Mama found babysitters for us and men for herself.

I realized other men slept in Mama's bed when I tiptoed into her bedroom one night and shook her awake.

"Mama, I wet the bed," I whispered.

Two shadowy lumps shifted.

"What?" Mama asked groggily.

"I had to go to the bathroom in my dream. I squatted down beside a tree. When I woke up, I was wetting the bed."

Only her shadowy lump got up and walked me back to my room.

"Is Daddy home?" I asked.

"No," she said, layering towels on the wet mattress. "Now go to sleep."

BEFORE OUR family of five fractured, I have a delicious memory of one rainstorm. Vicki and I had to be quiet while Patricia napped. Mama promised that if we would play quietly, she would make us fudge. I took the opportunity to show Vicki my wing collection.

My desire to fly had reached such a fever pitch that I had taken to catching butterflies and moths in the yard and yanking off their wings, carefully and guiltily storing them in a shoe box under the bed. I pulled out my treasure to share with Vicki.

"When I get enough of them," I confided, "I'm going to sew them onto my nightgown, so I can fly."

Vicki looked in my box of disembodied wings, unimpressed. "That's mean," she said, "taking their wings."

Her comment proved how little she understood me or my desire to fly. Did she think that I liked taking their wings? Exasperated, I shoved the box back under the bed. She followed me into the kitchen, where Mama measured sugar, cocoa, and milk into a pan.

After cooking the mixture, Mama dropped a small dab into a cup of water, turning it into a little ball with her finger. She poured in the vanilla, a fragrance that made me want to upend the whole sweet-smelling bottle into my mouth. Finally, Mama wrapped a towel around the pan and began to beat the fudge with the spoon, clinking against the sides of the pan until the liquid thickened into shiny chocolate.

"We might do this every time it rains," she said as she scraped and smoothed the fudge onto a buttered plate and licked her finger.

Could life get any better than eating fudge every time it rained?

"It needs to set," Mama said as she scooted the plate out of our reach on the counter.

Thankfully, Mama seemed to understand that waiting for fudge to set was akin to time standing still. She grabbed the chocolate-crusted pan, fished two spoons out of the drawer, and led us to the front stoop.

"You can sit here and lick the pan clean," she said. "The babysitter will be coming later." I squeezed Mama around the waist and sat down with Vicki.

The rain had stopped and left shiny pools on the sidewalk. The afternoon sun began to show, and a rainbow arched like a cat across the sky. Vicki and I talked about the pot of gold supposedly at the end of the rainbow and how we would like to find it. But, truth be told, we had our pot of gold right there between us. We painstakingly excavated all remaining chocolate from the sides of the pan.

We had no way of knowing then that three pans of fudge later we would be on our way back to Iowa, leaving Daddy, baby Patricia, and Mama. All Mama said the day she packed our clothes into the car was "You'd better say good-bye to your baby sister; you won't be seeing her for a while."

I cannot remember saying good-bye to Daddy. He must have been traveling.

Since it would be *a while* until Vicki and I saw Patricia again, we took turns holding her hand and running around the front yard; she giggled and tumbled and we all fell down together, rolling in the grass, laughing and cavorting like playful pups. That night, all three of us had red, itchy welts. "Chigger bites," Mama diagnosed, "from the grass."

Less than a week later, Mama dropped Vicki and me off in Iowa with our biological father, whom I no longer remembered. When you are six, *a while* does not sound all that long, unless you are waiting for fudge to set, or for your chigger bites to go away, or for your mom to come back and get you.

The dresses Mama sent Vicki and me

Glenwood, Iowa

MY HANDS SHOOK as I unpacked the black-and-white
Polaroid picture Mama had slipped into a five-and-dime
gold frame while packing our clothes. I rubbed my fingers
along the smooth metal, studying her face. Her hair had been
caught in motion, falling across her shoulders. I could almost

smell her scent, a blend of rose water and Evening in Paris.

The photograph had captured the physical trait I loved best about Mama: a slight gap, a diastema, between her two front teeth. The gap reminded me of the space between two piano keys on my toy piano, the one Mama had used to teach me to plink out the notes to "You Are My Sunshine."

I kissed the Polaroid picture before placing it carefully on the lace doily that adorned the dresser. I nudged the frame a little more to the left, so I could see Mama's face from the bed, pushed alongside the window next to the maple wardrobe where our clothes had been neatly hung.

"I'll come back for you," Mama had said several hours earlier, smiling and waving her hand, "at the end of summer." Then she jumped into the front seat of the car and the gravel crunched beneath her tires as she sped away. I watched the back of her head disappear into a cloud of choking dust.

A long, awkward silence followed as Vicki and I stood clutching our paper bag of possessions, waiting for a cue from Don, our biological father. The only memory I could conjure up of him involved my hanging from a porch rail and returning his wave from a tractor. That was it. I would have been two.

Once, Mama pointed him out to me in the photo album, in his army uniform, sitting next to me and Vicki and the two long-lashed, pink-cheeked dolls he had given us that stood over a foot tall. As I studied the picture, Mama said, without emotion, "That's your *real dad*. He came to visit you girls once in Colorado on his way to Korea."

At four, I don't think I fully understood what a *real dad* was, especially since I already had Daddy Davy. But at six, as I observed my real dad in the flesh, he looked a lot like his picture minus the army uniform. He wore jeans, a plaid shirt rolled up to his elbows, and white socks. His chocolate-brown eyes looked like mine, deep-set and a bit sad, like a cocker spaniel's. He looked like a giant to me then but, in actuality, he stood only five feet eight inches tall.

In order to keep my fathers separate, I decided to call him Dad and to continue calling Davy Daddy. One syllable, some DNA, and a thousand miles separated Dad from Daddy. As it would turn out, Daddy would always be one syllable more present in my life.

Vicki sidled closer to me. I noticed the cedar trees, blowing in the breeze, over Dad's right shoulder. A large garden flourished inside a chicken-wire fence. An arthritic dog limped up and nuzzled my hand with her wet nose. I stroked her neck, my fingers disappearing into the folds of her thick fur.

"That's Susie," Dad offered. He smiled and spoke softly, as if he were trying to calm a skittish calf. Something about his voice, tender and soft, put me at ease. I bent down and Susie licked my cheek. Vicki patted her head.

"Over there"—he pointed to a large elm tree—"I thought maybe I'd make you girls a swing. Would you like that?"

Vicki bobbed her head up and down. "Uh-huh."

I nodded. Swinging reminded me of flying. I had wanted to fly ever since I first dreamed about gliding effortlessly above the treetops. I had vowed to myself, right in the middle of that dream, to remember it. When I woke the next morning, I climbed onto a chair, spread my arms, and jumped. When that didn't work, I plucked my first set of wings off a butterfly.

The thought of swinging beneath the elm tree comforted me. I took a deep breath. Maybe there could be some goodness in this foreign landscape, after all, enough to hold us for a couple of months.

I glanced back down the country road. No car in sight. Just me, Vicki, and our real dad.

"Come on in," Dad said, holding open the squeaking screen door. Inside, a delicious aroma spilled out of the kitchen. "Oh my, that smells good," he said, smacking his lips. "Your grandma's killed a chicken for supper, and we're having mashed potatoes and gravy."

Just like in a fairy tale, Vicki and I entered the tidy white farmhouse, unsure of what lay ahead.

"THERE'S JUST one place you girls need to steer clear of," Grandma Skinner warned. "It's the quicksand hole down in the gully." She pointed her spatula toward the trees adjacent to the back porch.

"Once," Grandpa added, wiping strawberry jelly off his whiskers, "a horse and buggy fell in. Nothin' was ever seen of them again."

"Guy," Grandma scolded, "don't be filling their heads with nonsense. It's too small for a horse and buggy, but it's plenty big enough for two little girls. So steer clear."

"It used to be bigger," Grandpa whispered, and winked as Grandma turned her back to finish frying our eggs.

My mind began whirling like the old windmill near the barn.

After breakfast, with fingers that still smelled of bacon, Vicki and I edged our way down into the forbidden gully, slipping on dead leaves. Dappled sunlight shone in the undergrowth, and occasionally a bird flitted from tree to tree. Vicki and I poked around thickets and bushes until we finally came upon a smooth sandy patch. The top was flat and shiny, like Mama's fudge before it set. I picked up a large rock and plopped it in. It sank slowly in the quivering mud. We had found the quicksand.

Vicki followed suit with her rock. Again we watched it disappear. Then, as if it made perfect sense, I offered, "Let's make a sailboat and sail across it. And since you're littler than me, you'll have to ride it."

Vicki, whom Mama had dubbed Little Me Too, readily agreed.

We managed to keep our plan top secret. In the garage, against a back wall, we found an old wooden plank. I cut a sail from a piece of paper and then speared it onto a twig. We carried the plank into the gully, wedged the twig into a split in the board, and *voilà*, a sailboat.

We eased it carefully onto the quicksand. It didn't sink. "See," I said to Vicki. "Now step on the board." I held out my hand to steady her.

Vicki successfully maneuvered onto the plank. Everything looked good for the launch. But when I heaved the boat, Vicki promptly lost her balance and flopped into the quicksand. She began to swing her arms, keeping her head above the pea-soup water.

"Terry, look, I can swim, I can swim!" she hollered. What she did not see was that she was slowly sinking.

"Grandma, Grandma," I shrieked, scrambling up the bank.

I never again saw Grandma run faster than she did that day. Her apron flapped around her housedress; twigs and leaves shot out from under her feet.

"Grab the end of the stick," Grandma said, holding out a dead limb. "Hold on tight, honey. That's it."

Finally, Grandma marched a very muddy Vicki and a penitent me back to the house. "I told you girls to stay away from the quicksand," she scolded. "Terry, you're the oldest. You have to watch out for Vicki. She could've drowned."

I hung my head. I planned to write Mama and explain that I didn't mean for Vicki to fall in. But I didn't yet know how to print.

GRANDMA AND Grandpa took care of us while Dad worked days driving a tractor scraper for road construction. Most evenings and weekends Dad helped Grandpa with farm chores or courted his new girlfriend, Cathy, whose petticoats folded into beautiful bouquets of lace whenever she sat on the davenport. Cathy worked in an office at Mutual of Omaha in Omaha, Nebraska.

I think Dad sensed how much we missed Mama. He liked to play "patient" while we played "nurse," mainly because he could stretch out on the couch and close his eyes while we took his temperature, gave shots, and consulted each other about what to do next. Our favorite game, however, was "auctioneer." Dad delighted us by imitating an auctioneer at the livestock auctions.

"Ten-dollar bid, now. Who'll pay fifteen? Fifteen. Fifteen. Who'll bid fifteen? Fifteen-dollar bid, now. Who'll pay twenty? Twenty. Twenty. Who'll bid twenty?"

He continued in five-dollar increments until he tired and concluded with an emphatic "Sold to the little ladies in the front row," which of course would be me and Vicki, who wanted him to start all over again.

He taught me how to gather eggs and used our time in the henhouse to impress upon me the importance of multiplication tables, even though I was only six and had never been inside a classroom. Dad was particularly fond of math and, according to my uncle Gerald, had scored in the genius range on the army IQ test.

"Come fall," Dad said, "you'll be starting school. Wouldn't hurt to already know your times tables."

I stiffened. *Come fall? Surely Mama would be back for us by fall! How long could she stay away?*

Dad shooed a squawking hen off her warm eggs and continued his lesson.

"If you have two eggs in this nest," he said reaching into a wooden box lined with straw, "and you have two eggs in those two nests under the window, how many eggs would you have altogether?"

"Mmm." I wanted to please him, but I couldn't seem to locate the place in my brain that multiplied eggs and nests into numbers. I started to count the eggs on my fingers.

"Two times three is six," he said, tousling my hair. "You'd have six eggs altogether."

"I was just about to say that," I lied.

TRUTH BE told, farm life suited me, though I missed Mama fiercely. I loved to see the wind ripple across the undulating wheat fields, feel Grandpa's calloused hands squirting milk from a cow's teat, and kneel on the warm earth to marvel at the yellow-orange squash blossoms flaring into deep ruffles, like Cathy's petticoats.

Spending days in the garden with Grandma caused her to exclaim that I was "as brown as a berry and strong as a horse."

Maybe that's why I proudly bent one of her teaspoons in the kitchen. "Look how strong I am!"

Grandma paused from chopping cucumbers; her green eyes traveled from her bent spoon to my face. Then, clapping her hands to her cheeks, she exclaimed, "Oh my! You are *so* strong."

"Can I try, too?" Vicki asked.

After some weeks, most of Grandma's spoons stood at odd angles.

And when Mama finally sent a letter and forgot to mention when she might be returning, I called on my strength. That night I unfolded the letter to read to Vicki.

"Grandma already read it," Vicki said.

"Not this part," I told her.

I looked at the undecipherable squiggles and read aloud, not what was on the page, but what my heart most wanted to hear.

VICKI AND I joined Grandpa on a bale of hay in the barn, where dust particles danced and swirled in the sunlight streaming through the open door. We emptied our pockets to show him the rocks we had gathered earlier that day on the hill across from the windmill.

"Let me see that," Grandpa said, rising onto one elbow. His breath smelled like onions, which he routinely ate like apples.

I handed him my rock. Two barn cats sniffed the milk pail.

"See this here green stripe?" Grandpa observed. "This green could very well be uranium. Of course, we'd need a Geiger counter to know for sure and those don't come cheap. But if we found enough rocks with uranium in them—why, we'd be rich."

Rich sounded like a good thing to me.

"If you find any more rocks with green in them, bring them to me, okay?"

Grandpa's commentary fueled our imagination and curiosity. From that moment on, Vicki and I excitedly lugged every green rock we could scavenge back to the farmhouse. I also slipped my weekly dime allowance into the bottom of my sock drawer with the intention of buying Grandpa a Geiger counter, although I had not yet seen one at the five-and-dime store. It wasn't until Grandma noticed a growing pile of rocks by the back door that she became curious. That's when Vicki and I confessed to bringing home the rocks to help make Grandpa rich.

Always the pragmatist, Grandma marched into the barn and roused Grandpa from his afternoon nap on the hay. "Guy, I can't believe you are filling their heads with this uranium nonsense."

Then, turning to us, she said, "Girls, trust me, there's no uranium in those rocks."

Grandpa seemed almost as disappointed as we were.

Grandpa's belief in such things enlivened our ordinary existence and lessened the loss I felt. In Grandpa's world all things were possible, even waking up tomorrow morning to find Mama singing in the kitchen and making our breakfast.

After the uranium exposé, Vicki, Grandpa, and I kept our adventures to ourselves. When Vicki and I showed Grandpa how we went about finding baby snakes under rocks and leaves, he suggested that we not tell Grandma, as she wasn't particularly fond of snakes. And so it was that Grandpa began telling us tales, sometimes during our private picnics, of two heroines named Terry and Vicki who often saved the world. *Heroine* was added to my childhood résumé, right beneath *Can bend spoons and milk cows!*

IF THERE was an idyllic summer of childhood, it was that summer on the Iowa farm. Yet, if I had to choose a time when I felt the most forsaken by my mother, it was also that summer. Even back then, I was acutely aware of the paradox. On the outside, by day, I was like the morning-glory vine twining around the back fence. Every day opened to a life I loved on the land. I reveled in and relished the absolute freedom and abandon of being turned loose in Eden.

But then, each evening, after the sun set and the dinner dishes had been hand washed and dried, I became like the moonflower vine climbing up the weathered boards on the side of the garage. The moonflower opens its large fragrant blooms at night; they shimmer like moonlight and sweeten the night air.

I told no one about my sadness. Not even Vicki, who shared my bed. Vicki and I often helped each other fall asleep by twiddling each other's back. To us, twiddle was a light-touched tickle or scratch. Many times I asked Vicki to twiddle my back first because she would fall asleep, sparing me from twiddling her back, but also giving me time and space to think.

I would lie in bed remembering little things about Mama: the way she sniffed her food on her fork before putting it into her mouth; the funny way she sang "There's a hole, there's a hole; there's a hole in the bottom of the sea"; the feeling of her eyes on me, and what it felt like to look up and meet her gaze. I missed her smell, her laugh; I missed eating fudge on rainy days.

I evolved a ritual at bedtime before crawling into bed beside

Vicki. I held Mama's Polaroid picture to my heart. *I love you. Please come get us soon. I want to be with you more than I want to be anywhere else.* These were my prayers, my blooms that opened to the night. Then I pursed my lips against the cool glass and kissed her smiling face good night.

MY RECURRING nightmare intensified. The dream never varied:

Vicki and I stand alone on a train track. For reasons that only make sense in dream-time, we cannot step off the train track; the edges of reality do not extend beyond the railroad tie where we stand. I hear the whistle of a train in the distance. I look to see a black locomotive coming down the tracks. I am afraid. I take Vicki's hand and we begin to walk in the opposite direction, but the train is coming faster and faster. There is no way to outrun it. The whistle blows incessantly. My fear escalates as the train barrels toward us, looming larger and larger. I realize the only thing we can do is to turn and face our fate. I fold my arms around Vicki and turn my shoulder toward the train. This embrace does not seem futile in the dream. On the contrary, on some level, I seem to understand the importance of being held, knowing you are not alone, knowing that something, or someone, stands between you and whatever you fear.

I hold Vicki and wait for the train to hit us.

I would wake up gasping. I would reach across the bed to feel Vicki sleeping soundly beside me, and scoot deeper into the sheets, wishing I could wake Mama, wishing the sheets were her arms wrapped tightly around me.

In my dream, I held on to Vicki, the most precious thing I had to protect.

Mama did not come back for us that summer.

I do not remember anyone telling me why, or where she was, or what had happened to our sister, Patricia. I have no memory of Mama ever calling us on the wooden wall phone; I remember only the postman delivering a few cherished letters. Mainly, I remember kissing Mama's picture night after night, asking her to please come back.

While I had grown to love Grandma, Grandpa, and Dad, the face imprinted on me at birth was the face of my mother, the face in that Polaroid picture. If forced to choose between morning glories and moonflowers, I would have to choose the moonflower, even if it meant blooming in darkness.

BY LABOR Day, it was clear that we were staying. Vicki and I began our first of many two-mile walks to attend school together at Elm Grove, a tidy, white, one-room country schoolhouse complete with an outhouse, a water pump, and a wood-burning stove. Approximately one and a half dozen students, ranging in age from five to thirteen, took their seats in wrought-iron and wooden desks to learn under the tutelage and gentle guidance of Mrs. Cowden, enthroned behind an oak desk that paralleled an oversized black chalkboard in front of the room.

Sunlight spilled through the large windows as students shuffled in, whispered, and looked about, sizing up their classmates. The room smelled of chalk dust. An American flag dangled near Mrs. Cowden's right shoulder, while above her head the hands on the clock told the time, which I couldn't yet decipher. I studied the unfamiliar landscape and imagined that every child in the room had a loving mother at home, which left me feeling as empty and cold as the black potbellied stove in the corner opposite the flag.

Was Mama ever coming back?

I had turned Mama's picture over and decided not to kiss it for a week or more. But, one night, twiddling Vicki's back until she fell asleep, I imagined Mama being sad. I crept out of bed and looked at her picture in the moonlight.

"I'm sorry," I whispered. I reminded her that summer had ended and Vicki and I had started school.

The days grew into weeks. By the time the potbellied stove had been stoked and had warmed our classroom on a cold, blustery day in October, I had fallen in love with both school and Mrs. Cowden. Mrs. Cowden, whose hand had patted mine more than once, afforded me a gift equivalent to Prometheus's gift of fire to mortals. She taught me to read.

Through some magic of the brain, a stack of *Dick and Jane* basal readers, and something called phonetics, Mrs. Cowden and her bony forefinger helped me decipher lines on a page into words.

I was both insatiable and incredulous. "You mean to tell me I can learn to read every book in that bookcase?" I asked, pointing to the bookshelves at the back of the room.

Mrs. Cowden smiled and nodded.

In an instant, reading every single book became my mission. That mission may have dampened had I been standing in a library with rows upon rows of books. However, Elm Grove did not have a library, only the one bookcase. Mrs. Cowden had no need to arrange the books according to the Dewey decimal system. She sorted the books according to student height and ability. The younger, beginning readers looked for their books on the lower shelves, and each grade worked its way to the top.

Thankfully, Mrs. Cowden never put a cap on how high up you could read. She gave us carte blanche. Shortly after finishing the *Dick and Jane* series, I began reaching for books on the higher shelves. For me, who dreamed of flying, books were my magic carpet.

I worked very hard at penmanship and printed my first letter to Mama asking her when she was coming back. When no answer came, I found comfort and solace in reading books. When I read *Lassie Come-Home,* I cried through most of the book, wondering if I had the strength to keep reading. I longed to hug Lassie's neck and tell her I loved her, that I, too, hoped to find my way home to Mama someday. I felt the same way about *Black Beauty.* I loved the ending, when Black Beauty said, "My ladies have promised that I shall never be sold, and so I have nothing to fear; and here my story ends. My troubles are all over, and I am at home. . . ."

BY DECEMBER, the weather had turned frigid. Vicki and I traipsed back and forth to school through snow and mud puddles in black rubber galoshes that fit over our shoes. One afternoon, I spit out my gum—a dry, brittle weed that Grandpa had taught us to chew—near the mailbox. As usual, Vicki and I turned to walk up the sidewalk to the farmhouse. Just as I reached for the doorknob, the front door opened. My eyes widened. In front of us stood an older woman I had never seen before.

"Who are you?" she asked sternly.

"Terry and Vicki," I answered.

"Who?"

"Terry and Vicki!" Vicki shouted in her high-pitched voice.

"Nobody lives here by that name," the woman said.

I looked around to make sure we were at the right house. We were.

"We live here with our dad and grandma and grandpa," I told her.

Her next comment caused my stomach to turn.

"They don't live here anymore," she said. "I do."

That can't be, I thought. *Why wouldn't they tell us? Or take us with them?* Then I thought about Mama leaving us there and not coming back. *Maybe Grandma and Grandpa did move.* Instinctively, I curled my arm around Vicki's shoulder and turned my back to the woman.

"Come on," I told Vicki, who hung her head, "I'll take care of you." Still in our galoshes, we left the sidewalk and stepped onto the muddy road in front of the windmill.

"Wait!" the woman shouted, and started laughing. "I'm just teasing."

That is how I came to hate Aunt Mildred, my grandma's sister.

"It was so darling," Aunt Mildred later told Grandma, "when Terry said, 'Come on, Vicki, I'll take care of you.'"

I have no idea where I thought Vicki and I would go when we turned to leave the farmhouse, but it was within my realm of possibility that you could go to school one day and come home only to discover your family had moved without telling you.

Aunt Mildred had come that December to babysit us. Grandma and Grandpa had been offered a free ride to California in Uncle Owen's Buick to visit their daughter Helen. During Grandma and Grandpa's absence, Aunt Mildred, also a seamstress, made me and Vicki winter coats. While I did love the red wool muff Aunt Mildred made that kept my hands warm and made me feel like Shirley Temple, the cost had been to lose Santa Claus.

"You know Santa Claus doesn't really exist," she mumbled with a mouth full of straight pins as she tugged and pinned up the hem to my coat. "You're old enough to know that," she reasoned.

I wanted to pretend I hadn't heard her correctly. But, as Grandpa used to say, "You can't unfry an egg."

Still, Christmas was not a total disappointment. Aunt Mildred went back home and Mrs. Cowden finally acquiesced to my ardent plea to "Please, please, please let me be the angel in the Christmas pageant."

At the pageant, I saw Dad holding Cathy's hand. Evidently he had also asked for it. I later learned they were to be married. According to Dad, Cathy was to become our new mom. Unfortunately, I did not have a vacancy for that position. Everyone, except me, seemed to have forgotten that Mama was coming back.

AFTER THE wedding, Dad moved into Cathy's apartment in Omaha so they could remain near Cathy's office, thirty miles away. It didn't matter so much to me that Dad was gone because Grandma and Grandpa were the pillars of my well-being. On most weekends, Vicki and I visited Dad and Cathy in Omaha or they drove to Grandma and Grandpa's to see us. The majority of our days continued to fold unremarkably into one another, until the day I hugged a German shepherd.

At school, one finger raised meant you needed to pee in the outhouse; two fingers meant you might be taking a little longer to do your business. That day I raised one finger and Mrs.

Cowden nodded. I hated to go because I was in the middle of taking a spelling test with the third graders. Sometimes I forwent recess with my younger classmates to take the spelling test, even though I was a kindergartner and my score would not be recorded in Mrs. Cowden's book. Reluctantly, I put away my tablet and ran knock-kneed to the outhouse.

Once I had taken care of business, I decided to remain outside for the rest of our recess. Some of my classmates sat in a circle playing Duck, Duck, Goose, but several others had gathered around a tawny German shepherd wagging his tail in the school yard near the water pump. All dogs were Lassie to me. I approached the dog, kneeled beside him, and petted his head. He panted warm breath next to my ear and his wet, rough tongue licked the side of my cheek.

Then, without warning, the dog growled and lunged for my face, taking my mouth into his mouth. I reeled backward, unaware that he had torn open the entire right side of my bottom lip. Warm blood oozed from a ragged flap of skin.

In a senseless gesture, I cupped the blood in my hands, only to empty them and start over again. I did this over and over as I walked briskly into the schoolhouse, where Mrs. Cowden sat pronouncing the spelling words for the third graders.

I saw her face contort into a look of horror as she rose. Everything happened in slow motion. Mrs. Cowden flowed toward me like water, mouthing words I could not hear. I wanted to tell her it did not hurt, but words would not come out of my mouth. I felt only the warmth and thickness of my blood dripping through my fingertips.

Mrs. Cowden led me by the shoulders into the back room where we stored well water in a large earthen jug. She dipped a cloth into the cool water and pressed it against my mouth. I felt very still and calm, as if I were the eye of a hurricane, while Mrs. Cowden, the students, and the room swirled around me.

I watched Vicki jumping up and down crying and screaming, "Please don't die, Terry. Please don't die."

Mrs. Cowden rushed me out the door toward her car. She yelled something to the other children. I didn't hear what she said. My world was going black around the edges.

Vicki says she held my head in her lap while I pressed the bloody cloth to my face. Mrs. Cowden sped down the gravel road toward Grandma and Grandpa's house.

Grandma and Grandpa were visiting relatives and had asked Aunt Dixie, my dad's sister, to stay with us. Vicki and I loved Aunt Dixie and her two young daughters, DeEtte and Deanna. They peeked out the door that day when Mrs. Cowden lay on the horn. Aunt Dixie, covered in blood and feathers, rushed toward the car. She had just killed two chickens for dinner.

Mrs. Cowden told her I had been bitten, but she couldn't drive me to town because she had left the other children unattended at school. Aunt Dixie didn't know how to drive, so she asked Mrs. Cowden if she could at least drive us to the closest neighbor's house, which she did. On the way into town, in the neighbor's speeding car, I overheard something about *bleeding to death*.

Later that afternoon, I woke up in Dr. Harmon's office. My jugular vein had been spared by only an inch, and it had taken nearly two dozen stitches to piece my mouth back together. "You're a lucky young lady," Dr. Harmon said to me.

IT SEEMED to me that several good things could come from the attack by the German shepherd. Since my mouth was stitched closed and bandaged so tightly that only a straw could fit between my lips, breakfast, lunch, and dinner consisted of milkshakes—strawberry, chocolate, or vanilla. I estimated that I would not tire of this fare for at least twenty years or more. Thankfully, Grandma never thought of juicing carrots or watercress, although if Aunt Mildred had been around, she surely would have tried celery broth.

The first day after the attack, I reclined in bed, my back propped up by feather pillows. A glass of frothy ice cream and milk rested on a saucer by the bedside. I lightly tapped my fingers against the gauze and felt a slight pressure on my skin. The pain was sharp and hot.

Mama's Polaroid picture was on the dresser.

"Is somebody going to tell Mama that the dog bit me?" I asked Grandma as she tidied up the chenille spread.

"Why, yes, I reckon so," she said.

I was sure that once Mama heard how badly I had been bitten—that my *juggler* vein had been missed by only an inch and it had taken nearly two dozen stitches to sew my mouth together—she would put down whatever it was that kept her from jumping into the car and driving back to Iowa for me and Vicki.

I still remembered how Mama held vigil outside my oxygen tent when I was five years old. I had been with a babysitter all weekend. By the time Mama returned home from wherever it was she disappeared to from time to time, a cough racked my fevered body. Mama lifted me out of bed and drove me to the hospital. I had pneumonia. My memory was that having pneumonia was not so bad. Every time I woke up, I could see Mama's attentive face outside the clear plastic tent. She would reach in and squeeze my hand. I felt loved beyond measure; I could not help but smile.

That is why I was certain Mama would return once she knew about the dog bite. I thought it might take a week, two at most.

Mrs. Cowden stopped by to check on me and to bring me letters and drawings from all my classmates, even from the older kids who never paid much attention to me. Everyone basically repeated the same sentiments: *I'm sorry about what happened. Get well soon. I hope to see you again at school before it lets out.*

Mrs. Cowden pulled Grandma aside and told her that a boy named Billy had yanked the German shepherd's tail. The dog had reacted to this assault by biting the person closest to his mouth. Me.

In today's world, the dog might be quarantined and observed for rabies, but back then the general consensus was *If you pull a dog's tail, he's likely going to bite you.* No one seemed concerned about rabies or the dog attacking anyone in the future. He continued to run free.

After Mrs. Cowden left, I reread the letters, slurped my chocolate milkshake, and studied Mama's picture on the dresser. For a short while, I thought Billy might have done me a favor by pulling the dog's tail. But when the bandages finally came off and the puffy, swollen wound began toughening into a jagged red scar, I realized three things: Doc Harmon was not as good a seamstress as Aunt Mildred, Mama would not be rushing to my bedside, and Billy had done me no favor.

Another summer came and went.

THAT FALL, Mrs. Cowden talked to Dad and Cathy about my skipping first grade and entering second grade. She said I worked above my grade level and that Mama should have enrolled me in school before I came to Iowa. Mama's delay in sending me to school remains a mystery. She may have wanted me home to be a diversion for Vicki and Patricia, or perhaps a daily school schedule chafed against Mama's laissez-faire attitude.

Whatever her reasons, I skipped first grade and became a second grader at Elm Grove rural school. My second school year differed only in that my home life had changed. Dad and Cathy could no longer afford the Omaha apartment. Dad's farm and construction work was seasonal and Cathy was pregnant. The "glow of pregnancy" did not describe Cathy's experience. She never stopped vomiting and her knees often buckled beneath her, which is why she quit her job at Mutual of Omaha.

To accommodate two families, Grandpa and Dad, without consulting Cathy or Grandma, decided to create a three-room apartment on the second floor of the farmhouse, complete with a makeshift kitchen. Grandpa told Dad that he and Grandma would move upstairs to give Dad and Cathy enough room for me, Vicki, and our soon-to-be baby brother or sister. Cathy didn't want to move in and Grandma didn't want to move out. Grandpa and Dad built a door off the staircase to create a private entrance, which buffered the growing divide between Grandma and Cathy.

I didn't want Grandma to move out, either. Even though she'd be only a flight of stairs away, I'd miss the constancy of her rhythm in my life. Vicki and I often asked to spend the night upstairs in the same room with her and Grandpa instead of sleeping in our big bedroom downstairs. Grandma never said no.

Under the new arrangement, Grandma routinely opened her window and tossed Vicki and me pieces of candy as we stood on the sidewalk below on our way to school. And sometimes, if we were alone with Grandma, she whispered, "How are things downstairs with Cathy?"

When it came to being a stepmother, Cathy didn't get my vote, though she was a good mother to her son, our new baby brother, Lanny. The first strike against Cathy was simply the fact she wasn't my mother. The second strike was that she tried too hard to force me and Vicki to be model children to prove her competence as a stepmother. The third strike was her long list of rules and the spankings that followed if those rules were broken.

Our chores increased in size and number at first because Cathy's pregnancy was so difficult and later because taking care of a newborn required much of her time and focus. I went from believing I could do nothing wrong in Grandma's eyes to wondering if I could do anything right in Cathy's. We were spanked if our grades were less than A's, if we dirtied our shoes, made too much noise, or wasted food.

I fretted more than I ever had, fearing Vicki and I would get into trouble. On the way home from school one day, Vicki and I encountered the most dangerous of all beasts—the dreaded loose cow. The cow dawdled in the middle of the road, idly chewing her cud, a fugitive from a nearby pasture. Her long-lashed eyes studied us while her tail swished at the black flies trying to bite through her hard brown hide.

When she took several innocuous steps in our direction, Vicki and I dove between clumps of weeds.

"What should we do?" Vicki asked, crouching next to me.

I surveyed the surrounding area. "We'll just have to wait."

A red-winged blackbird flitted from post to post along the rusted barbed-wire fence. The red on her wings appeared and disappeared like the folding and unfolding of a fan. One option would have been to climb through the barbwire and walk through the field, but Cathy would be mad if we got our school shoes dirty. Better to wait.

My thighs hurt from squatting, so I plopped cross-legged onto the ground. The cow continued to gaze intently at nothing, her calendar evidently clear. Vicki had slipped into Neverland to build a house for her imaginary little people. Her miniature Habitat for Humanity project made use of grasses, leaves, and sticks.

Vicki would have welcomed my participation, but I had more pressing things to worry about—the cow, Cathy impatiently wondering where we were, dirtying our shoes if we did end up walking through the muddy field.

"I wish Mommy would come get us in the car." Vicki sighed.

I stared at her in disbelief. I knew she did not mean Mama. She meant Cathy. I threw down the stick I had been holding and lunged toward her.

"Don't ever call Cathy 'Mommy' again," I yelled, messing up the leaves in front of her. "She's *not* our mother!"

Vicki shrank away from me, crinkled her freckled nose, and began to cry. My reaction frightened her more than the cow. All she wanted was a mother waiting for her at home, a mother who would jump into the car and rescue us from our plight. Cathy was willing to become our *mommy,* but I couldn't allow Mama to be forgotten. My memory of her was all I had left.

WE SHARED good times with Cathy, too. She made us picnics, cooked with us, and fixed our hair. Many Saturday nights we drove into town as a family and Vicki and I were allowed to spend our dime allowance. I dreamed all week of what I would buy.

I walked up and down the candy aisle of the grocery store auditioning three of my favorite candy bars: Butterfinger, Hershey's, and 3 Musketeers. Then I picked up the Cracker Jacks box, studied the sailor boy and his dog, Bingo, and jiggled the box to garner a clue about the prize inside.

Cracker Jacks cost ten cents and candy bars five cents. More times than not, I chose the Cracker Jacks. They satisfied my sweet tooth and I liked the prizes (my all-time favorite being a tiny magnifying glass). Still, if I could delay gratification and save my dime for two weeks in a row, Dad generally threw in a buffalo nickel and I ordered the best treat of all—a frosty chocolate malt—at the hamburger joint. As I sipped the thick sweetness and looked across the booth at Dad and Cathy, I tried really hard to see Mama's face instead of Cathy's.

I could never give myself over completely to family life with Dad and Cathy. I feared that I, like Vicki, was forgetting Mama much against my will. Mama had begun to feel more like a ghost to me than a real person. And I had noticed, to my dismay, that Mama's Polaroid picture on the dresser had begun to fade.

I also suspected that Mama had begun to forget me and Vicki. The postman had delivered the proof. He brought two presents, one for me and one for Vicki. On Christmas morning, we raced to see who could rip open her package first, as if winning would prove one of us the better. I clawed the paper off in large sheets; a present from Mama was not to be dallied over.

I lifted the lid and sucked in my breath. Inside was a beautiful blue dress with a bertha collar trimmed in lace. I picked up the dress, swung in a circle, and held the collar beneath my chin.

The dress cascaded far below my knees. It took me a moment to figure out that the dress dwarfed me; it was at least two sizes too big. Cathy must have registered the look of disappointment on my face.

"You'll grow into it," she reassured me.

Sometimes, the unlikeliest things can blow out the flame of hope, like how tall you are in your mother's mind.

Me, Vicki, and our panda bear

Elkhart, Kansas

I TELL MYSELF IT was the haircut that caused me not to recognize Mama when she finally returned to Iowa for us. I was sprawled on the floor playing solitaire when a man and woman walked into the living room. I looked up briefly and then resumed shuffling the cards.

"Don't you know who that is?" Grandma asked.

I looked up again. The woman's hair was bobbed and she wore a maternity blouse like Cathy had worn during her pregnancy with Lanny. I couldn't place the woman . . . until she smiled. That's when I saw the space between her teeth and I suddenly recognized the smile from my Polaroid picture.

How can you study a face in a photograph for two years and not recognize that person when she walks into the room? How can you dream of running into your mother's arms over and over and then feel awkward when you finally stand in her embrace?

The shock of Mama returning seemed to encase me in a fog. Almost overnight, amid good-byes, promises to return, and packing whatever belongings Dad and Cathy would allow, the landscape of our lives changed again. Only this time Vicki and I climbed into the car and waved good-bye to Dad, Cathy, Lanny, Grandma, and Grandpa. Grandpa pulled out a red kerchief and swiped his eyes.

I'm not sure what Grandpa thought. Maybe he realized how much Mama's return meant to me, especially since he had lost his own mother around my age. Or maybe he realized we were growing up and embarking on an adventure beyond his windmill, beyond the farmlands of Iowa, beyond the reach of his embrace. Even though the three of us had never discovered uranium together, we had become rich nonetheless.

My allegiance would seesaw between the landscapes of my mother and father for a long time to come.

After turning off the farm road, we headed west toward Kansas. Fields of yellow sunflowers blurred past the open car windows. The air smelled of summer, asphalt, and adventure. My heart hummed with happiness. I had what I had been longing for—a space in Mama's life. Granted, Mama was almost two years late, and when it came to mothering, I was empty-bellied beyond words, but she had not forgotten. That fact alone made forgiveness spring from my heart.

I studied the two blue eyes glancing back at me in the rearview mirror. They belonged to Daddy Davy. I hadn't recognized him, either.

Court records show that Daddy divorced Mama on December 17, 1955; the judge awarded Daddy custody of our sister, Patricia, only two years old. Daddy moved Patricia into his parents' farmhouse in East Texas, where his parents and sister helped him care for her. He continued to work the oil fields.

Mama's whereabouts during this two-year period remain a mystery. Unencumbered by husbands and children, Mama could come and go as she pleased for the first time in her life. Yet, within seventeen months, she reconciled with Daddy, the man she professed *not* to love.

If love did not drive Mama back into Daddy's arms, what did?

On May 2, 1957, Mama and Daddy stood in front of the justice of the peace in Tucumcari, New Mexico, and vowed to love each other *until death do us part* for the second time. I don't know what Mama or Daddy wore, if they looked happy or sad, or where they went after the ceremony. There are no pictures of this wedding.

I do know that shortly thereafter Mama and Daddy drove to Iowa to pick up me and Vicki. Unbeknownst to us, Mama, Daddy, Dad, and Cathy had agreed that our visit would be temporary. Come fall, Vicki and I were to return to Iowa to resume school at Elm Grove. Dad and Cathy had talked to me and Vicki about coming back, but I had no idea Mama had agreed to return us at the end of summer.

Evidently, Mama and Daddy weren't so much pasting the family back together as they were bringing us to their home to *pay a visit*. Also, unbeknownst to me, Dad and Cathy had inquired about legal custody, which might explain why we had been instructed not to pack our toys.

If I had known then what the adults were planning, I might have flung myself to the ground weeping and kicking until everyone agreed I had survived without Mama as long as I possibly could. Anyone who had ever read Lassie knew that once she trekked a thousand miles to find Joe, her journey was over. She was home for good. Any other ending would have been too sad to bear.

So, upon our arrival in Kansas, when Daddy unloaded our belongings into their one-bedroom rental house, I moved in for good. I imagined we would soon pick up our three-year-old sister, Patricia, who still lived in Texas with Daddy's parents. I imagined life would return to the way things had been before Mama dropped us off in Iowa.

That night, when Mama slipped off her clothes and stepped into her nightgown, I discovered why she wore a full, loose blouse over her slacks. A fourth child grew quietly inside her expanding womb. We had a new baby brother or sister on the way. At the time, I didn't question *when, where,* or *how.*

VICKI AND I were digging in the dirt with spoons, trying to reach China, the day Mama came to the back door. Gray clouds boiled in the sky. A faint cast of green tinted the air.

"Time to come in," she said, pushing open the screen door with her hip and offering us a bite of her peeled banana.

I grimaced. "I don't like bananas."

"You don't?"

"Cathy made us eat black ones. They were awful."

"Terry got spanked," Vicki added, "'cause she threw hers away."

"Cathy spanked you?" Mama asked.

I nodded and Mama frowned.

The wind picked up. Mama grasped both of her elbows as she paced from window to window. Daddy was away wildcatting (drilling an exploratory oil well). Thunder rattled the windows.

"Logs are falling off the wagon in heaven," Vicki said, repeating what Mama had told us caused thunder.

I watched Mama watching the storm. Dad had been struck by lightning on the farm in Iowa after he and Mama first married. He didn't remember much about it, but the doctor surmised that his black rubber galoshes had saved him. Storms reminded Mama of opening the door that day to see him crawling in the mud toward the house, blood running from his ear.

Lightning flashed and thunder clapped. Mama jumped.

Someone pounded on the front door. It was our neighbor from across the street; her face looked like a puckered peach. She had taken a liking to Mama and probably felt sorry for her, a young pregnant woman with two girls, whose husband traveled a lot, new in town and living in the rental across the street, the one without a storm cellar.

"Why don't you and your girls come with me to the storm cellar?" the woman shouted, holding her flapping hood close to her face. "Might be a twister coming!"

Mama grabbed our hands and we trotted behind the neighbor lady toward a mound in her side yard. She and Mama lifted two wooden doors that folded out and away from each other. We climbed down cobwebbed steps leading into a dark hole in the earth. I was terrified of spiders and could almost feel them crawling on my skin. The old woman fumbled in the darkness, struck a match, and lit a kerosene lamp. The smell of sulfur filled the air as she shook out the match. She latched the doors securely from the inside by slipping a board behind two brackets. Then she let out a long sigh.

"We're safe now," she said.

The flame flickered, throwing long shadows across the mortared walls and earthen floor. It was cool and damp. I looked around. I had never seen anything like it. Fragments of light winked and glinted off the Mason jars filled with tomatoes, peaches, and pickles; the jars stood at attention in rows on the wooden shelves built against the sides of the cellar. The four of us settled onto creaking wooden crates around the lamp. I felt strangely comforted, tucked away from whatever danger raged above.

I liked the old woman and her cellar. She entertained us with stories about being a young pioneer girl and traveling in a covered wagon.

"My pa built a soddy with his own hands, he did. Nothin' but chunks of earth and prairie grass, cut and stacked like bricks."

Sitting there, I could easily imagine a house made from the earth. I reckoned how Vicki and I might build a sod playhouse instead of digging to China.

The word *panther* called me back to attention.

"Jumped right through the open window of the soddy. I could see him in the moonlight, slinking around the room. I was too afraid to cry out. I grabbed on to my sleeping sister like a June bug to a screen door."

"What happened?" Vicki whispered.

"He sniffed the air and must've decided I was too ornery to eat and hightailed it right out the window."

I laughed, not only because the old woman amused me, but because I felt happy. I was caught up in the archetypal undertow, present since the dawn of time, the one that compels humanity to sit around fires and tell stories.

I do not remember how Vicki and I found our way back into bed that night. Maybe we fell asleep in the cellar listening to more stories and wakened enough to stumble home. I only remember waking up later in the bedroom we shared with Mama and hearing her cry.

I tiptoed over to the edge of her bed and put my hand on her coarse hair. "Mama, what's wrong?"

She sniffed and turned my way. "Nothing, sweetie. You go on back to sleep."

"You still afraid from the storm?"

"That's it," she said. "The storm."

I now suspect Mama's storm had nothing to do with weather patterns and everything to do with the changing winds of her life. Once again she was alone and encumbered by pregnancy and children.

All I knew then was that my mama was crying. I comforted her the only way I knew how at eight.

"Want me to crawl in bed with you?" I asked.

She scooted over and opened the covers like a tent. I slid in beside her, snuggling up against her warm pregnant belly, like a June bug to a screen door.

"I love you," I said.

"I love you, too."

This is what I had imagined when I kissed her Polaroid picture good night.

"I'm going to miss you," she whispered.

My eyes popped wide open.

WOULD MAMA return us or keep us?

Once I knew that question was on the table, I immediately went to work to ensure the latter. I helped Mama around the house; I tried not to fight with Vicki, which required real restraint; and I scoured my mind for grievances against Cathy. I decided to let Cathy sink so that I might swim. Whenever I mentioned Cathy spanking us, I noticed Mama wrinkle her brow in disapproval. It wasn't that Mama didn't believe in spanking. To the contrary. I had experienced my share of welts and stings from her. But Mama didn't cotton to the idea of someone else laying a hand on her daughters, especially with any frequency. Mama seemed to grow more and more protective of me and Vicki whenever we told her of any unpleasantness in Iowa.

Yes, I sighed, we were spanked for getting our shoes dirty. Lots of times dishes waited for us in the sink to be washed when we walked home from school. I worried that I might not make an A. I had an awful dream, over and over, about a train running over me and Vicki. Sometimes Vicki gagged and couldn't eat her fried eggs so she had to hide them under the refrigerator. After the dog bit me, I waited for you to come. I kissed your picture and cried almost every night.

Toward the end of summer, Mama decided to keep me and

Vicki for the time being. We were to move with her and Daddy from Kansas to Texas. While I had been granted my heart's desire, my triumph was bittersweet. Sometimes, when I lay awake at night, I pictured Dad on the farm, sitting on his tractor, crying and holding on to my doll with the long brown curls, wondering why we never came back. I wanted to hug his neck and tell him I still loved and missed him. But how could I explain it? Mama was like air to me. Without her, I would die.

I didn't know then that I would never see Grandpa or Lanny again, or that Mama would forbid us to see or speak to Dad and Cathy for more than a decade. Years later, I came across an old faded letter tucked away that Mama had written to one of my dad's sisters, my aunt Betty.

Dear Betty and all,

Here are the girls' school pictures. This is something which I had vowed not to do, but the years soften most angers I guess. You have always been soft-hearted and were good to my girls. These are yours — please don't give them to Don. It takes more than the process of birth to make a father. I'm sorry, but I still feel he flunked the whole course. I realize he tried, somewhat, while they were with your mother. Had Cathy been kinder and more concerned with their welfare, he might still have them though I would never have signed any papers to that effect. They would have had to earn them — not barter for them like livestock. Nor bribe them. Do you think it kind that they were told they couldn't have their toys unless they came back? I'm so glad their love for me was stronger than their affection for their toys. I didn't have to bribe them. Legally, Don could have had them summers (I would have consented) if he had helped with their support. . . .

You know, I could fill a book with many of the things that went on while they were with Don. Many of them that I don't think he honestly knew about, but as a father, he should have found out. But to what purpose would this be now? Like pouring sand down a rat hole. So much for that. She'll never have another opportunity to lay a hand on them. Or, see them again. One of the reasons I won't stop by when we do go visit my brother.

As always,
Carola

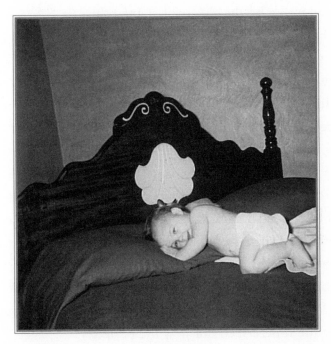

My baby sister Brenda

Amarillo, Texas

IT WAS EARLY August. According to Mama's calculations, her due date was still months away, sometime in January or February.

"Unless the baby is premature," Mama said.

That was the second time Mama had used the word *prema-*

ture. The first had been beside the Tilt-A-Whirl at the traveling carnival, with its thrilling electric lights, melodic notes, and sugary smells. I'd never seen a carnival or a cloud of pink cotton candy like the one Mama held for me as Daddy, Vicki, and I climbed into a bright blue oval-shaped car.

Mama, who looked to be growing a watermelon under her shirt, rubbed her belly and said, "I'll wait this one out. This baby might be premature as it is."

Her words hung in the air. Mama and Daddy exchanged glances, a momentary ripple passing between them. I didn't know then that Mama was trying to fit a nine-month pregnancy into a five-month time slot.

From my four-foot-tall perspective, the world of adults sometimes resembled a dark, deep lake, like the one that had tried to swallow me when I was only four years old. If I hadn't clenched my toes around a slippery rock and tiptoed like a ballerina back to shore, I might have drowned. I knew what it felt like to lose your footing and go under. *Precarious* is the word that comes to mind, and it described our new life perfectly.

Ever since returning from Iowa, I'd been trying to understand Mama's tears, Daddy's looks, and the way we bumped into one another as we tried to piece our family back together. I didn't always know how to act or what to say. I worried that Vicki or I might do something to make Mama sorry she had decided to keep us.

Upon our arrival in Amarillo, the four of us squeezed into a furnished one-bedroom duplex with a threadbare pull-out sofa bed in the living room. Mama bought a secondhand Singer that she set up on our red Formica kitchen table. She didn't know how to sew, but kept at it until one day she smiled and proudly held up a baby nightgown.

Part of the reason we moved to the Texas Panhandle was so Daddy wouldn't have to travel so many miles to the oil fields. Mama wanted his daily help and support. She said she needed him there to help when the baby arrived. Daddy came home most every night from the rig, unless a drill bit broke or someone lost a finger.

Most evenings, just as the sky turned crimson, he pulled up to the duplex in his grit-covered company pickup. More often than not he left his hard hat and work gloves on the passenger seat, stamped the dust off his steel-toed work boots, and clomped up the steps swinging his empty lunch pail. His sunburned neck and the layers of dust on his face and clothes gave witness to a long day in the field, which would begin again at dawn.

The family next door also had several children, so midafternoons, while Mama rested and Daddy worked, we piled into our living room or theirs to watch cartoons. Sometimes we played outside, but city living had reduced the size of my world considerably. No more roaming farm fields looking for uranium, baby snakes, or dinosaur bones. But city life had its pluses, too, like smooth sidewalks for bicycle riding, milkmen delivering jars of milk right to the front door, and melodious ice-cream trucks that gave you enough time to scurry inside for nickels and dimes to buy Fudgsicles and ice-cream sandwiches.

Evidently, religion, like milk and ice cream, could be delivered to your front door, too. I learned this when two Jehovah's Witnesses knocked on our door and Mama invited them in. A well-dressed man and woman handed Mama two magazine pamphlets: *The Watchtower* and *Awake!*

Mama tapped the rolled magazines against her palm as her eyes followed the man's fingers moving across his opened Bible. He read to her about a better world.

" 'God himself will be with them. And he will wipe out every tear from their eyes, and death will be no more, neither will mourning nor outcry nor pain be anymore.' "

Mama nodded. "A world without pain," she said wistfully.

When the man and woman stood to leave, they invited Mama to the Kingdom Hall and wondered if they might stop by again.

"Anytime," Mama offered.

She rose awkwardly from the couch, holding her protruding abdomen, and led them to the screen door. She said she had been meaning to buy a Bible. Mama particularly loved reading the Psalms.

One afternoon she worked with me, helping me memorize Psalm 23.

"The Lord is my shepherd; I shall not want."

Mama straightened suddenly and clasped her belly. "She's kicking," she said and placed my hand on her taut belly.

I smiled up at her. Beneath her cotton shirt, I felt a rolling sensation.

"I think we'll name her Belinda Fawn," Mama said. "That's a perfect name for a little one."

Without the benefit of technology, Mama seemed to know her baby would be a girl.

MAMA SOON entered the phase of pregnancy called nesting. School would be starting in a few weeks and Mama wanted her nest in order. She made dental appointments for me and Vicki, folded cloth diapers, and wrote out a to-do list.

"I should run errands," Mama said. "You girls want to see a movie?"

Vicki and I jumped up and down and hugged each other. We had seen only a few movies and had never gone to one by ourselves.

Mama gave us money, dropped us off, and said, "I'll be back when it's over."

The movie was well under way when Vicki and I entered the darkened theater with a bag of warm popcorn. After our eyes adjusted, we found two empty seats beside each other. Jerry Lewis and Dean Martin clowned on the screen, delighting us immensely, but we had missed most of the movie; it ended not long after we arrived.

As the credits began to roll, I nudged Vicki and whispered, "Let's go."

"But I want to see the beginning," she protested.

"We can't," I told her. "Mama will be waiting."

Vicki grudgingly got up and followed me outside.

We looked up and down the street. No Mama. Vicki and I looked at the billboard and smiled at the lady in the ticket booth. Five, ten, maybe fifteen minutes crawled by.

"I'm going to watch it again," Vicki announced and marched back into the theater.

I let her go, more worried about Mama's whereabouts than Vicki. Another fifteen or twenty minutes passed. I paced, looking continually up and down the street.

Maybe something's happened, I worried. *Could she have forgotten? Or maybe . . .*

My mouth started to quiver.

"Is somebody picking you up?" the ticket lady asked.

"My mom," I said. "She should've been here by now."

"Do you want to call her?"

I froze. I didn't know our phone number. Not even our address.

"We just moved," I said. "I don't even know our number."

"It's okay," the lady said. "I'm sure she'll be here soon."

I wanted to believe her. I wanted to believe it was impossible for Mama to drop us off and not come back. But I knew better, knew how easily the bottom could slip right out from under you.

I was near panic when I finally spotted our blue car driving down the street. Mama pulled up to the curb and saw me crying.

"What happened? Where's Vicki?"

I blubbered the whole story into her maternity blouse.

"What would make you think—"

Mama paused midsentence. I saw her eyes widen and a sad look cross her face. She drew me close to her and the baby inside of her; she smoothed my hair and kissed the top of my head.

THREE ITEMS remained on Mama's Nesting List: take me and Vicki to the dentist, buy us two store-bought dresses, and enroll us in school. I'd never been to a dentist, but the Butterfingers, 3 Musketeers, and Hershey's bars I had bought with my dime allowance in Iowa had all left their calling cards.

The only doctor I visited in Iowa was old Doc Harmon, when he sewed up my mouth. I didn't even see a doctor when Grandpa's car accidentally pinned my knee between the bumper and the garage while Grandpa swept the floorboards with his whisk broom and unknowingly bumped the gearshift. A pained look crossed his face as he quickly shoved the car into reverse and carried me inside to Grandma, whose diagnosis had been correct. I didn't need a doctor. By the third day, I hobbled out of bed, able to put a little weight on my swollen knee.

I wished my toothache would heal by itself like my knee, but Mama assured me only a dentist could make a cavity go away.

"Tell you what," Mama offered. "Vicki can stay next door and it'll be just you and me. I'll even hold your hand if you want me to, and afterward, I'll buy you a malt."

I couldn't remember ever going anywhere with Mama all by myself. Her offer seemed worth the price of a little pain. She came into the examining room with me and made small talk. I squirmed in the chair until the dentist entered the room and seated himself next to me. He looked remarkably like Captain Kangaroo.

"What happened here?" he asked and stroked my scar.

I blushed. I realized for the first time that others might breach the barrier of politeness to ask what had caused my scar. I rarely looked into a mirror and I'd all but forgotten about it.

"A dog bit me," I said shyly.

"That's some bite," he said. His eyes scrunched together as he also examined the scar from inside my mouth. The scar went all the way through.

"It was a German shepherd," Mama said. "We're lucky she didn't bleed to death."

"Did you bite him back?" the dentist kidded.

Later, as I slurped my malt, Mama studied me as if looking for the right words.

"You know, Terry," she said, "you have a beautiful smile. People respond to it."

I couldn't help but smile—often—after that. I love Mama still for introducing me to my smile. That was the kind of thing we talked about on our one-on-one dentist outings. I may have been one of the few children who actually looked forward to going to the dentist.

The Sunday before school started, Vicki and I kissed Daddy awake as he napped on the couch in his jeans and white T-shirt. We twirled round and round in our new store-bought dresses; Vicki called them our sister dresses because they were identical. Unlike the ones in Iowa, these dresses fit us perfectly.

"You look like twins," Daddy said. "You'll be the prettiest girls in school."

The next morning Mama strode into school with me and Vicki in tow. When the principal asked my last name, I was about to say Skinner when Mama interrupted, "Vacha. V-a-c-h-a."

I jerked my head up to look into her face; her eyes told me to *hush*.

V-a-c-h-a. I better remember how to spell my name, I thought.

Mama hadn't seen a lawyer; Daddy hadn't formally adopted us. But Mama never needed a judge or a sheet of paper to tell her what she could and could not do.

"Your dad lost his rights to you," she said later that day. "Davy is your daddy now."

And that was that. For all practical purposes, our natural father ceased to exist after that day. Vicki and I lived the rest of our childhood as if he had died. Mama never let us correspond, see, or hear from him again until I turned eighteen. Vicki and I kept the name Vacha until the day we married. Our school records, Social Security numbers, and medical records bore Daddy's last name.

I adored Daddy and didn't need a sheet of paper saying I belonged to him. Daddy's actions said it all. Never once did he indicate I was anything less than his eldest daughter, whom he loved and valued. Daddy's TLC did not depend on his DNA, nor did mine.

However, changing my last name to Daddy's was the easiest

part of going to public school. I experienced culture shock the moment I stepped inside the long corridor. It felt like another world.

"You don't know what a fire drill is?" one third-grade class-mate asked incredulously, as if I had just touched down from another planet.

On planet Iowa, Mrs. Cowden never instituted a fire drill, probably because our school was a one-room schoolhouse. I didn't know about the public-address system, either. At Elm Grove we stood and said the Pledge of Allegiance with Mrs. Cowden instead of listening to a crackling voice over the loud-speaker. Even the cafeteria required orientation.

In public school, I discovered, you couldn't take spelling tests with the older children; flush toilets replaced outhouses; and water spewed from fountains instead of a water pump, which was too bad because the fountain water tasted like chlorine. At Elm Grove, Mrs. Cowden would select a lucky student each morning to pump clear water from the well. It glistened in the sunlight as it bubbled over the earthen jug, held by one of the older boys.

I missed the constancy of Mrs. Cowden, the bookcase in the back of the room, and the rows of large windows looking out across the fields.

Since I didn't know anyone at public school, and Vicki's re-cess didn't coincide with mine, I often headed to the swings. One morning, as I pumped my legs back and forth, back and forth, picking up both speed and height, something marvelous hap-pened. As I swung forward, flying toward the sky, something deep inside of me kept going. It was as if I had been released from my body and soared above the playground, experiencing total exhilaration, total possibility. For a moment, I seemed to understand everything, even the darkest depths of the deepest waters. Nothing seemed over my head. I felt suspended. Loved. Loving. Vast.

And then I was Terry again, on the playground in third grade. Yet I felt changed, as if some part of me had momentarily stumbled into another dimension. I came away from that experience knowing that I was more than just a body. I was partly soul.

ON SEPTEMBER 6, 1957, only ten days after Mama's twenty-fourth birthday, and four months after Mama and Daddy remarried, Mama gave birth to her fourth daughter. If the baby had been smaller, Mama's assertion that she was premature might have been more plausible. But the baby weighed a whopping ten pounds and eleven ounces. Nor had Mama been reconciled with Daddy long enough to deliver his full-term baby.

Daddy chose not to count out the months on his fingertips.

Instead, he brought Mama and the baby home from the hospital and helped Mama onto the couch. Vicki and I crowded around the dark-haired cherub she held in the blanket.

"She's so big," Mama said, "the name Belinda Fawn didn't suit her. Meet Miss Brenda Annette Vacha."

Daddy tenderly took Brenda out of Mama's arms. "Lookie here," he said. Brenda had grasped his thumb.

Vicki and I marveled at her miniature nails. We kissed the baby moons rising above our little sister's nail beds. Later, Daddy fell asleep with Brenda in the crook of his arm. He made formula, fed her a bottle, and changed her diaper. Daddy once told me that every child deserves to be loved.

Brenda's arrival brought us together; I felt like we were truly a family. But, as it turned out, we were a family on the move. When Brenda was only three months old, Daddy came home and announced that the oil company needed him in southeast Texas, near Alvin. The bright side was that Alvin was less than a hundred miles from Daddy's parents, who were raising our sister, Patricia; her return would complete the missing piece to our family puzzle.

Mama checked me and Vicki out of school and told our teachers we were transferring to another school not far from Houston.

Yes, she agreed. It was a shame her girls had to change schools again so soon.

We packed up our school dresses, Brenda's baby items, and the Singer sewing machine. Brenda slept on the backseat between me and Vicki. Daddy whistled at the steering wheel as we turned onto Highway 87 toward the Gulf of Mexico. Mama stared off into the flat plains ahead.

Me, Vicki, and Patricia "performing"

Alvin, Texas

THE HONEYMOON ENDED as quickly as it began. Mama's and Daddy's angry voices woke me in the middle of the night.

"It doesn't take three hours to buy a loaf of bread," Daddy said.

"I'm with them all day," Mama fired back, "and all week when you're not here. I need a break."

"At the bar?"

"I stopped by for a few minutes after the store."

"The store closed hours ago."

"Leave me alone," Mama said.

Daddy did. Everything quieted down.

Mama went to the *store* two or three times a week. During the day, when Vicki and I attended second and third grade at Alvin Elementary, Mama stayed home to watch the baby, and three-year-old Patricia, who had returned to live with us. But frequency was not the issue with Daddy. He couldn't understand *why* Mama needed to go to the store in the first place, especially if she wasn't carrying grocery bags when she returned. I didn't understand, either. I didn't like to hear them arguing. I'd taken to wishing Mama was pregnant again so she'd stay home in the evenings the way she had in Amarillo.

It's hard to define "normal" when you're a kid. Is normal what happens to you most of the time? *Normally, Mama stayed home.* Or is normal what *should* happen to you? *Normally, a new mother doesn't hang out in bars.* Or is normal based on some measure of right and wrong? *It isn't normal for a married woman to hang out in bars without her husband.* At that age, I thought "normal" was whatever the adults around you did.

I didn't think it *abnormal* for Mama to be daubing on lipstick and fluffing her hair in the mirror before leaving the house in the evening. But when I saw her primping, I'd feel the bottom dropping out from under me. I knew Daddy would be sad and angry.

If I asked her, "Where're you going?" she'd most often answer, "Timbuktu," which meant none of my business. In my world, *Timbuktu* was a normal response.

One morning, after another one of Mama and Daddy's arguments, I woke to the smell of bacon. Daddy normally cooked breakfast on the weekends. Always an early riser, he had gone out early and brought home the fixin's for breakfast, which included bacon, eggs, and syrup for pancakes. It must have been payday. He also bought a newspaper; it lay open on the kitchen table.

He hadn't shaved and his blond stubble made him look tired. I heard him up with Brenda during the night. I hugged him around the waist and told him I loved his pancakes, which was true. But my main reason for hugging him was because I thought he might be sad about Mama. I also told him I was hungry enough to eat four pancakes, maybe more, which made him smile. He began measuring flour and baking powder into a mixing bowl.

Daddy knew his way around a kitchen both at home and on a ship; he had been a cook in the navy. I watched him pour ladlefuls of batter into the sizzling cast-iron skillet and adjust the flame.

I opened the comic pages and smoothed out the crackling newspaper. I leaned in close to have a good look. I wanted to figure out why a boy at school had been calling me Dick Tracy.

The name-calling started after I caught him and another boy offering a girl a quarter at recess if she would climb up the slide a second time. What she didn't realize was that both boys planned to stand below her and peep again underneath her dress. The stretched-out elastic on her underpants had stopped protecting her privacy many washings ago.

"I don't think you should," I advised the girl. She looked

from me to the boys. The boys laughed nervously and ran off. Later, one of them called me Dick Tracy.

In the comic pages, the police detective Dick Tracy outwitted numerous villains. I wondered if the boy had meant I was a good detective, but that seemed way too generous coming from someone caught in the act of *peeping*. More probable was that the scar on my mouth made me look like Dick Tracy. His square jaw was accentuated with deep lines around his mouth.

"Do I look like Dick Tracy?" I asked Daddy.

"What?"

"A boy at school called me Dick Tracy."

Daddy poured himself another cup of black coffee from the percolator on the stove. He brought his steaming cup over and set it down on the other side of me and slipped into his chair, looking at me.

"I'll tell you what. If that boy thinks you look like Dick Tracy, he either needs glasses or somebody's been putting something in his milk," Daddy said. "Now, if he had said Brenda Starr, that's another story!"

Daddy was still shaking his head and muttering "Dick Tracy" when he rose to clean off the kitchen counter, tossing the eggshells into the trash. He bent down and picked up something from the floor.

"Well lookie here," he said.

"What?" I strained to see.

He held up a wiggly cockroach. I recoiled. Mama hated cockroaches; she said they signaled filth and poor living conditions. In Mama's world, the only good cockroach was a dead one. She drummed into our heads the importance of keeping the kitchen spotless and putting food away in tight containers. Unfortunately, she couldn't control the habits of previous renters or the warmer climate in southern Texas, which favored the survival of *Periplaneta americana.*

I had never studied a cockroach up close, so I cautiously approached the squirming insect trapped between Daddy's fingers. Two hairlike antennae waved in the air. After a few moments, Daddy wordlessly took his free hand, fished a match out of the matchbox, and struck it on the side of the gas burner. He slowly moved the flame beneath the abdomen of the cockroach. Just as it lifted its abdomen, trying to avoid the heat, Mama walked into the room. She immediately assessed the situation.

"Stop that this instant!" she yelled at Daddy. "If you want to kill it, fine, but don't you dare torture the thing. That's cruel and heartless." Daddy threw the cockroach to the floor and squished it beneath his loafer.

"I can't believe you were torturing it," Mama scolded.

"It's only a cockroach," Daddy defended. "You despise the things."

"Cruelty is cruelty," Mama answered.

The lowly cockroach would be one of my first lessons on human decency. I am an expert witness when I say Daddy wasn't a cruel man. I saw him cry many times when he was touched, proud, happy, or sad. I saw him climb trees to rescue kittens, fix a leak in the neighbor's faucet, and look under the hood of a stranded motorist's car. I think Daddy thought what I had thought up until that moment: something as lowly as a cockroach didn't merit human decency. If you're going to kill something, what difference is there in how it dies?

Mama's answer to that question would have been *suffering.*

It was Mama's low tolerance for suffering and cruelty that caused her to turn her fury on Grandpa Vacha.

In early June, we piled into the car and drove past colorful fields of Texas bluebells on our way to Grandma and Grandpa Vacha's farm. We planned to stay a few days, and by some miraculous stroke of good fortune, Mama decided I could stay an extra week by myself after the rest of the family returned to Alvin. I could hardly contain my excitement. I missed so many things about farm life: the animals, the freedom, the closeness to the land.

Back then, Grandma and Grandpa Vacha's farm was self-sustaining. They planted, harvested, canned, butchered, and smoked their own meats. They looked to the *Farmer's Almanac* for weather forecasts and planting tables based on the moon's phases. They were second-generation Moravians who lived a *normal* life based on the *old ways*.

However, their normal looked nothing like ours, which may have caused some of the disharmony between Mama and Grandma. Mama called Grandma's admonitions old wives' tales and Grandma said things like "a stitch in time saves nine" when she noticed Mama had not mended our clothing properly. Sometimes they sounded like two guinea hens gabbling. Unfortunately, one or the other usually ended up in tears.

When we first arrived, everything went smoothly.

"*Jak se máš?*" Grandpa asked, which was Czech for "how are you?" Grandpa wore his familiar shorts, cowboy boots, and safari helmet. When we hugged him, he playfully poked our belly buttons and called them our *pupiks*.

Since it was Saturday, Grandma and Grandpa changed into their "town" clothes and we drove to the county courthouse square to socialize with the other farm families gathered in town. Grandma joined the women fanning themselves and gossiping beneath the shade trees on the courthouse lawn. Across the street, Daddy and Grandpa joined the men, clacking down their dominoes to play a game of Moon or 42. Mama watched Brenda while Vicki, Patricia, and I practiced turning cartwheels near the gazebo bandstand. Intermittently we all sipped RC Colas from chilled bottles that wept in the heat.

Afternoons like that made me wish our family could live that way forever.

Back at the farmhouse, Grandpa disappeared into a small pantry that I nicknamed his money room. Cigar boxes, tins, and glinting jars lined the shelves, making the pantry look like an old-time general store. Inside every container were bills, silver dollars, half-dollars, dimes, and buffalo nickels. Grandpa came out of the room with a five-dollar bill for each of us. I thanked him and carefully tucked mine into my special purse. Back home, unless Mama needed it, I would push it into the slot of my piggy bank.

Grandpa had lost faith in institutional banking during the Great Depression. His solution had been to dig a hole in the dirt floor of his detached garage and wedge in a widemouthed jar to hold his big bills. I remember a $10,000 bill, but maybe it was only a $1,000 bill. (Grandpa leased the mineral rights to his land, converting his revenues into high-denomination bills, which the US Treasury circulated until 1969.) After securing his money in the jar, Grandpa covered the area with a large sheet of plywood stained with oil leaks from his car. He locked his vault by parking his car on top of the plywood.

Grandpa had just locked his vault when he discovered his young hunting dog had dug beneath the fence of the chicken coop and killed a chicken. Mild-mannered Grandpa picked up the dog, two paws in each hand, and slammed his body to the ground. The dog yelped and lay there, its breath knocked out of him. Mama shrieked for Grandpa to stop.

Grandpa bellowed at the dog in Czech. Then he yelled to Mama in English, "Farm dogs have to be taught not to kill livestock!"

"No animal deserves to be treated that way," Mama insisted.

Grandma and Grandpa must have struggled to reconcile Mama's concern for their dog with her seeming lack of concern for their son. Grandma never approved of Mama's divorcing Daddy, or her decision to send her children away for two years. Grandma and Grandpa had been the ones to take care of Patricia when Vicki and I were sent to Iowa.

Grandpa was, by nature, a peacemaker just like Daddy. So, a few hours after the dog incident, he came out of his small bedroom off the back porch, acting as if he and Mama had not argued. Mama and Grandma, on the other hand, gave each other a wide berth. Both seemed relieved when it came time to say good-bye.

But Grandma cried when she hugged Daddy. Tears formed in Daddy's eyes, too, as he pulled away and said they best be going.

Thankfully, Mama didn't renege on her promise to let me stay the week with Grandma and Grandpa. For a whole week, I would be immersed in their wonderful world.

While Grandma and Grandpa talked on the porch, I wandered toward a lone oak tree, dripping in Spanish moss, not far from the barn. I climbed onto a wide branch listening to the whir of grasshoppers. Sitting there felt like the most natural thing in the world. I felt so at peace in those giant arms. In between leaning my back against the bark and jumping down to rejoin Grandma and Grandpa in the kitchen, I fell in love with that tree. It would become the single most important icon of my childhood.

* * *

AFTER I returned home to Alvin, Mama sat me down and told me that my grandpa in Iowa, Grandpa Skinner, who had talked about striking it rich on uranium, had died. My aunt Betty wrote to say Grandpa had said good night to Grandma and never woke up. He died in his sleep of a heart attack. It was normal, Mama said, for older people to die. I sadly scrawled the date of Grandpa's death into the white Bible Grandma Skinner had sent to me. *Guy Raymond Skinner died October 9, 1958.*

I paused when I recited my prayer that night: "Now I lay me down to sleep. If I should die before I wake, I pray the Lord my soul to take."

Mama had found a Kingdom Hall and the Jehovah's Witnesses again, or they had found her. She spent a fair amount of those early days in Alvin studying and reading her Bible. However, when I asked her what happened to people when they died, she did not flip open her Bible; rather, she pointed to a boiling pot on the stove.

"See the steam coming off the potatoes there?"

Steam wisped upward toward the kitchen cabinets.

"It's a little like that," Mama said. "When we die, our body stays but our spirit rises like the steam."

It made sense. Hadn't some part of me, unconnected to my body, soared upward in Amarillo on the swing that day? I silently watched the steam rising from the potatoes, wondering where Grandpa's spirit went. Wherever it went, my love followed him there.

* * *

ONE NIGHT, after we had moved into our second rental house in Alvin, Daddy shook me and Vicki awake in the bunk bed, mumbling something about seeing the moon. Vicki preferred the warmth of the covers, but I managed to pull myself up and out of bed. The wood floor felt cool to my bare feet.

Daddy led me out of the house and halfway down the rough cement sidewalk. He knelt down beside me and scooted me in front of him. My gaze followed his finger.

"Lookie there," he said.

I looked up to see a star resting on the tip of the crescent moon. Daddy called the star Venus.

"You may never see them so close together again in your lifetime," he said. I heard the awe in his voice.

Never again so close together.

The bright star and the crescent moon etched themselves on the wall of my mind. That night Daddy wakened me not only from my bunk bed but also from my tiny world beneath a single roof. I looked up into the grandeur of a greater scale. I felt infinitesimal, the night sky felt immense, and Daddy stood somewhere in between. I don't think either of us realized that he and I, standing together in the night, mirrored the proximity of Venus to the crescent moon.

I would later come to know Venus as the morning and evening star, twinkling at dusk and dawn. I also learned that Venus took its name from the Roman goddess of love and beauty whom the Greeks knew as Aphrodite. Aphrodite had no childhood; she was born adult, nubile, and infinitely desirable. Though she married, she was frequently unfaithful to her husband.

Infidelity seemed to be one of Mama's weaknesses, too. After Daddy began working out of town again, Mama looked for ways to feel loved outside the Kingdom Hall. One of them was Chief.

I think Mama met him at the edge of the sea near Galveston at the café where she worked.

I have a picture of Mama sitting in front of an adding machine in the café's office. The café was one of Mama's attempts to "better herself" and help bring in some much-needed money for the family. Our utilities had been turned off a time or two, and Mama had taken to throwing our unopened bills into the trash.

Mama thought that she and a girlfriend could manage a small café. I don't know the particulars of their arrangement, but Mama and her friend kept the books, waited on customers, cleaned tables, and cooked if the short-order cook didn't show. Mama took me to the café some weekends to help clear tables and wash dishes.

In the alley behind the restaurant, Mama discovered Trixie, a starving kitten foraging in the garbage can. We brought her home, and I made it my mission to make up for all the bad that had ever happened to Trixie. I slipped her extra bits of food and spent endless hours entertaining her with twine. At night, she curled into a ball against me. I buried my face into her fur, breathing in the musky scent of milk. When I whispered "good kitty," she nuzzled her nose against my chin. Sometimes she groomed me as if I were a cat, too. I loved the feel of her sandpaper tongue.

After some time, Trixie became pregnant. Mama warned me I might wake one morning to find a bed full of kittens. Neither of us could have imagined what actually happened. I opened my eyes to see a half-eaten kitten, still wrapped in its opaque birth sac, dangling from Trixie's mouth. I shrieked and ran for Mama.

Mama removed what was left of the dead kitten and helped Trixie deliver three live kittens. Afterward, Mama found me in the living room, my knees drawn up underneath my chin. She sat down beside me and rubbed my arm.

"She didn't know how to be a mom," Mama said. "Remember how scrawny she was when we brought her home? She didn't have a mom for very long. She just didn't know any better," Mama reassured me. Which was why, days later, when Trixie opened her mouth to lift one of her kittens by its scruff, I panicked.

"Trixie's eating her kittens again!" I screeched.

Mama assured me Trixie was now being a good mother. Mama cats carried their kittens in their mouths when moving them to safety. However, I soon discovered just how hard mothering was. Trixie's mammary glands became infected and necessitated a stay at the vet's office. In Trixie's absence, Mama and I fed the kittens warm milk and honey every three to four hours from two baby-doll bottles we borrowed from Patricia. The pug-nosed kittens mouthed the hard tip of the plastic bottles, dribbling more milk down their fur than into their bellies. But they thrived. We nestled them into the folds of an old bath towel, inside a cardboard box, which we set next to the warm oven.

The vet finally called to say Trixie could come home. Mama clicked the receiver into the cradle and said, "Terry, I don't know how we're going to pay the bill. They won't let her come home unless we do."

"I have money," I said.

I walked into the bedroom, grabbed my white piggy bank, and brought it to Mama. She nodded and we hammered it open. It held change and two five-dollar bills Grandpa Vacha had given me. Mama counted out some of her tips from the café. Together, we pooled enough to bring Trixie home.

Having Trixie back was worth every penny. I soaked up the sight of her and the kittens sleeping in a jumbled pile of tails and paws. We had two boys and a girl pouncing on one another and chasing their tails until it was time to give them away. It was terribly lonely that first week without the kittens.

It was during this time of grieving that I woke to see Chief climbing out of Mama's bedroom window, either because Daddy had come home sooner than Mama expected, or because Mama awoke to hear noises in the driveway that she attributed to Daddy. In actuality, the noises Mama and Chief heard may have been two men trying, unsuccessfully, to repossess our Ford.

I had never seen anyone climb out of June Cleaver's window on *Leave It to Beaver*. Something had begun to feel off-kilter to me. I loved Mama and I loved Daddy, but I disdained the middle place between them where Mama opened the door to her bedroom or used her window for escape. I longed for Mama to become less like Aphrodite and more like Hestia, the goddess of hearth and home.

If only Mama were more like other mothers or my grandmothers.

This longing would grow into a quintessential thorn that pierced both Mama and me.

NOT LONG after Chief climbed out the window, I went to school, the same as any other morning, except that Trixie had been taken to the veterinarian again.

Toward the end of the school day, during choir practice, a woman from the principal's office walked in and asked me to follow her. I nervously wondered if I had done something wrong. The principal asked me to take a seat. Evidently, Mama had called and said I was to check out of school immediately because we were moving.

I looked at him in disbelief. "We're moving?"

"That's what your mom said," he said. He handed me a fist of papers and said I could check out of school as soon as I turned in my library book.

"It's at home," I told him.

He frowned and looked over the top of his glasses. "You should have brought it to school with you."

"I didn't know we were moving."

He shook his head and told me to drop the book off at school before we left town.

I came home to find Mama crying in front of a man who had a wad of money in his hand.

"Fifty-five dollars!" Mama exclaimed. "That's it? Fifty-five dollars for all the furniture in this house?"

"Take it or leave it, lady," the man said, unmoved by her tears.

"It's highway robbery," she said, grabbing the money from his hand.

Clothes, dishes, knickknacks, everything Mama wanted to take had been tossed into bags and boxes. Brenda played near a pile of discarded items in a corner of the living room. Patricia saw me, dropped her baby doll, and ran up to hug my waist.

"Help me get this stuff into the car," Mama ordered. "We're leaving."

"Where?" I asked. "Where're we going?"

"We're moving to Ozona, where Davy is. We have to move fast."

That's all I knew. We had to leave town fast. Apparently our creditors were closing in.

As we pulled out of the driveway, it hit me.

"Mama, what about Trixie?"

Mama looked at me as if she had been waiting for this conversation to play out. "The vet won't give her to us unless we pay the bill. We don't even have enough money to buy groceries, Terry. We can't get her out. And even if we did have the money, the vet's office is closed for the night."

I felt a physical pain in the area of my heart and a knot so tight in my throat that it caused me to moan, "No."

"I'm so sorry," Mama said; tears filled her eyes. "I'm sure the vet will find her a good home."

I pictured Trixie peeking from a cage and buried my head in my hands. I knew what it felt like to wait for someone to come for you.

My baby sister Joni

Ozona, Texas

OZONA WAS THE only town in Crockett County's three thousand square miles of rugged terrain. A statue of Davy Crockett stood in the town square.

In Ozona, Mama was suddenly pregnant again. It comforted me to see her reading in her bed most evenings, a paperback resting on her big belly. Pregnancy had a way of tethering Mama closer to home; she spent less time in Timbuktu and more time bent over the Singer sewing machine.

A threadbare blanket of calm settled over our family. No one came to take our car, maybe because Daddy traded it or made good on the back payments. Our slate had been wiped clean again: new town, new rental house, new electric company. Clean slates came easier before the age of computers and the Internet. A body could pretty much pick up stakes, drive to a small town in the middle of West Texas, and begin again. Neighbors were not unduly suspicious of newcomers; the oil and ranching industries afforded a fairly respectable way to enter and leave town. Some neighbors were downright generous, offering us boxes of clothes they no longer wore. It felt like Christmas every time we opened one of those boxes.

Still, despite people's generosity, I began having another recurring nightmare.

Everything seems normal as I take my seat in the classroom. The teacher asks us to open our books and start reading. As I open my book, I look down and discover that I'm not wearing shoes. I'm barefoot. This mortifies me. I try to figure out how to slip out of the classroom.

The dream surely reflected my struggle to find solid footing as I moved from one town to another. I had become the perennial new girl at school, walking into classrooms where children had known one another for years. Instead of feeling sure-footed, I felt barefooted. My shoes remained at home. And where was home? I had already moved eleven times.

*   *   *

IN THE fall, Mama gave birth to Joanne. Joni, as we came to call her, had Daddy's corn-tassel hair and sky-blue eyes. One smile from her and you were willing to do whatever it took to amuse her: stand on your head, play peekaboo, imitate every animal sound in the barnyard. Even sing a lullaby, which for me was nothing short of courageous. I had issues about my singing voice. I couldn't carry a tune, and the music teacher at our new school gave me ample opportunity to prove it.

Joni's arrival brought the usual care of a newborn, with night feedings, dirty diapers, and lost sleep. To keep from going under, Mama enlisted me. With the birth of Joni, I morphed from being Vicki's playmate into Mama's little helper.

Mama taught me how to give Joni a bottle and change her diaper; sort laundry into piles of darks and lights; light the gas oven with a match; polish our shoes for school; and watch over Patricia, who had just started first grade. I was ten, Vicki nine, and Brenda not quite three.

Like any novice, I made my share of mistakes.

"Something's wrong with the corn bread," I complained to Mama the first time I followed a recipe and lifted my pale, thin corn bread from the hot oven.

Mama stuck a fork into the pan and broke off a piece; she sniffed it and popped it into her mouth.

"Tastes like cake," she said. "How much cornmeal did you use?"

"I forgot cornmeal," I said, clasping my hand over my mouth.

"Guess we could call it 'Accidental Cake,'" Mama teased.

We served it anyway, along with a pot of steaming pinto beans, for supper. Daddy chewed his piece politely and said it was not all that bad, actually. He never was a very good liar. Vicki crumbled the cake into her beans and stirred them into mush, smiling at me in between delicate bites. She wanted to please me. I think Vicki missed being playmates.

I missed her, too. When Mama allowed us to play outside together, we headed for Johnson Draw, a wide gully that cut through the center of town. But time and circumstance had begun pulling the gates of our childhood closed; the entrance to our Narnia would soon be overgrown.

I felt swallowed by the grown-up world, like I had slipped into a pair of Mama's dress-up shoes and could never take them off again. Remnants of my former self lay in Johnson Draw, where Vicki and I played Tarzan for the last time; on Avenue D, where I stopped surreptitiously buying nickel Hershey's bars at the corner grocery; in the Caverns of Sonora, where I seized Patricia's hand to keep her from touching the helictite butterfly formation instead of reaching out and touching it myself.

Mama had begun asking me to stay home from school occasionally, once or twice a month, to help with the babies, especially if she had one of her migraines. The notes Mama wrote for my excuses were exactly the same.

To whom it may concern,
Terry was absent due to the fact she was ill.

Sincerely,
Jean Vacha

I WAS an eager student and didn't like missing school. Learning new things satisfied my curiosity and opened me up to a world that lay beyond Crockett County and even the United States, which had grown from forty-eight to fifty states—a fact our schoolbooks didn't yet reflect.

I never knew when one of Mama's headaches might strike, and they could be sorely inconvenient. The morning I was supposed to go on a field trip, Mama staggered into the kitchen, where I was buttering a piece of toast for Patricia's breakfast.

"I've got a splitting headache," she said, lowering herself onto the kitchen chair.

I knew she wanted me to stay home. But instead of asking me outright, she wanted me to say something like "Do you need me to stay home?" There was less guilt that way. But I couldn't say it. Not on that day.

"Oh, Mama, I can't stay home today," I said, choosing my words carefully. I wanted to go on that field trip more than I had wanted anything in a long time. "We're supposed to go to the movie set. Remember? For our field trip."

Mama closed her eyes and rubbed her left temple.

I continued to pack my sack lunch, acting nonchalant, as if there were no question about my going. "We're supposed to bring our lunch to eat *on location.*"

Mama sighed and rose from the table. "Suppose you shouldn't miss your field trip," she said finally.

She teetered down the hall into the bathroom. I heard her rattling more pills in the pill bottle. Then I heard her gagging.

"Vicki Lee," she called out.

My gain was Vicki's loss. Vicki, only nine, started staying home, too.

I said good-bye to Vicki that morning and walked Patricia to school, carrying my autograph book and my sack lunch. Patricia looked longingly at my newly pierced ears. She had no idea how much they stung. Only days before, Mama had poured Kahlúa into three glasses of Coca-Cola to steady everyone's nerves. After a few effervescent sips, Vicki and I began to giggle and barely minded that Mama pinched our earlobes between clothespins until they numbed and turned white. She unflinchingly pushed a threaded needle through our fleshy lobes as if she were sewing on a button. She knotted the loop of thread and told us to move it back and forth twice a day for the next several weeks, and to keep our ears clean. Gold studs were a luxury we couldn't afford.

Getting ready for the field trip that morning, I cleaned my ears with alcohol-soaked cotton balls and forwent my ponytail, allowing my hair to fluff into a lion's mane to hide my ears. No other girls had strings dangling from their earlobes. At school, my classmates and I noisily boarded a bus that sped through the arid terrain toward Brackettville, Texas. We were on our way to see John Wayne, who was directing, and starring as Davy Crockett in, the movie *The Alamo*.

Crockett County had been named for Davy Crockett. Even though Mr. Crockett had been born in Tennessee, he valiantly fought and died at the Alamo. A granite statue of him stood on the south end of Ozona's town square, where we sometimes wandered after the double feature let out at Adwell Theatres. His famous words had been engraved in the stone statue: BE SURE YOU ARE RIGHT, THEN GO AHEAD. My problem was I never knew for sure if I was right.

On the movie set, John Wayne sat atop a lift, behind the camera, directing. I shielded my eyes from the sun as I observed him. He wore a faded kerchief around his neck and animatedly pointed at the men on horseback riding toward the camera.

I clutched my autograph book and smoothed my hair as I scouted for other movie stars. We couldn't approach John Wayne, but Frankie Avalon, who played Smitty, captivated me with his warm smile as he steadied my autograph book on his knee. Whenever I looked at his fluid signature, angled across the page, I felt fluttery inside.

I loved the Texas landscape and its people. I liked mesquite-fired barbecue and the big sky that lit up with a million stars at night. I liked the Texas twang I heard when others spoke, a twang I began to hear in my own speech. I liked the cowboys who wore boots, shiny belt buckles, and sweat-stained cowboy hats. And, like Mama and Daddy, I came to appreciate the way a country-and-western song could reach down inside your heart and put music to the trouble you felt within.

On the long ride home from the field trip, I felt unspeakably happy and grateful that I had spoken up. Meeting a movie star face-to-face seemed like the most implausible possibility in the universe—especially my universe. Our entertainment consisted of grilling hamburgers on an oil drum cut in half and welded to-gether to make a barbecue grill, pitching horseshoes in the sand, and churning homemade ice cream. Yet I had Frankie Avalon's honest-to-goodness, authentic autograph to prove just how close to him I had stood.

I decided not to brag to Vicki about getting the autograph, at least not right away. I'd been plain lucky and I knew it. Standing up to Mama was like defending the Alamo. The odds of winning against her or Santa Anna were about the same.

Weeks later, after I had bragged to Vicki about Frankie Ava-lon's autograph, I walked Patricia to her first-grade classroom. When her teacher saw me, she signaled for me to wait. Her heels clicked rapidly on the floor as she approached me.

She sidled up to me and lowered her voice. "Did you know Patricia's been wearing red lipstick in school?"

"No, ma'am, I didn't," I said.

"I didn't think so. You best tell your mom."

Which was exactly what I did when I got home from school that afternoon.

Mama soundly scolded Patricia for sneaking into her miniature Avon samples. Evidently, Patricia had been slipping into the restroom after I dropped her off at school and daubing lipstick on her lips, none too evenly, as it turned out. Mama said sneaking would not be tolerated in her house. Luckily, Patricia was spared the switch, but I doubt that relieved her any.

Her lipstick fetish had likely stemmed from feeling left out. When Mama told Patricia she was too young to have her ears pierced, Patricia folded her arms across her chest and stuck out her bottom lip, which quivered slightly.

Patricia was, quite literally, the classic middle child who bridged the span between *the babies* (Brenda and Joni) and *the older girls* (me and Vicki). Patricia lacked an exclusive membership in either of the clubs. If she wanted to sit on Mama's lap, rarely vacated by Brenda or Joni, she was too old. If she wanted her ears pierced like me and Vicki, she was too young. There seemed to be no *just right*, except maybe in a tube of red lipstick.

Patricia also developed the peculiar habit of sleepwalking. Since Mama had put me in charge of Patricia, I kept an eye on her day and night. She held a prominent place in my psyche, though she seemed unaware of this. She often withdrew into herself. In addition to her being a middle child, her particular history probably exacerbated her feelings.

On the Vacha farm, she had been an only child, fussed over by Aunt Lillian and Grandma and Grandpa. Because I remembered Patricia as a baby, before Vicki and I went to Iowa, I assumed Patricia remembered me, too. But she didn't; she had been too young. She had no memory of Vicki and me holding her hand or of running through the yard laughing and tumbling into the grass. When she returned to live with us, we were strangers to her—even Mama.

Patricia decided to teach us a lesson by running away. She walked to a nearby park and sat on the swings until dark. Frightened and thinking we would surely be worried, she came home and found all of us going about business as usual. None of us had even missed her.

If I could step back into the river of time and wade toward Patricia's silhouette sitting alone on that park swing, I would crouch next to her and say, "Sister, we've been looking everywhere for you. Please don't ever scare us like this again. Our family would be bereft without you; you are loved beyond measure." Then I would pull out a tube of coveted red lipstick, roll it on her lips, and guide her home.

ONLY A few weeks after Mama pierced my ears, I cut the foul-smelling, pus-encrusted threads from my infected ears and discarded them into the trash. I would not, as I had hoped, be wearing glinting, pierced hoops like Mama. Mama admitted that thread had probably been a bad idea; gold would have healed better. She assured me my ears would be fine—hole-less, but fine.

Before my earlobes healed completely, Mama called me into her bedroom and broke the news that we would be moving again.

"On Monday, I want you to tell the teachers that you, Vicki, and Patricia will be checking out of school," Mama said, holding Joni's bottle. "And bring home everybody's report card and records so we can take them with us to Colorado."

I arrived in Ozona in the middle of fourth grade and was leaving in the middle of fifth. Vicki, Patricia, and I were about to become *new girls* again.

Moving to Ozona midyear was challenging because, by then, most girls had found their friends' group. The one exception had been a lonely skinny girl in my class with glasses as thick as cola bottles. Sadly, I had been the only one to show up for her birthday party.

As far as I could tell, this move would differ from our clandestine move the previous year. No one was chasing us. Daddy merely needed us to be closer to his work in Colorado. Still, I continued to worry about owing people money, especially since I knew that men came under the cover of darkness to repossess things that weren't paid off. I still witnessed a number of unopened bills burning in the trash barrel in the backyard. It troubled me, shamed me, actually, to realize that Mama didn't even bother to open them.

When I finally voiced my concern to Mama, she stated matter-of-factly, "Well, you can't squeeze blood from a turnip."

Mama didn't seem unduly concerned by the bills or our impending move. Maybe she didn't mind moving back to Colorado. Mama had penned her feelings for the Rocky Mountains in a poem she titled "Home."

I've found a place
On God's green earth
That is to me
Of priceless worth

Its meadows, leas,
And gladed vales

Its waterfalls
Like maiden veils . . .

A pine tree stands
Amid this grace
Its shadows seem
To pattern lace . . .

My heart is there
I shall return
Amidst the flowers
Among the fern

To my mountain home
Of azure skies
In wooded hills
My contentment lies

"COME ON," Daddy said. "It'll do you good." He wanted to take Mama dancing. He reached out to twirl her around.

I didn't mind when Daddy joined Mama in Timbuktu. He kept the poachers away.

Mama finished bathing Joni in the kitchen sink, smeared a little petroleum jelly on her fingertips, and fashioned Joni's hair into a single curl on top of her head. We all loved that curl cresting like a solitary wave on the ocean.

"Well, I best get ready," Mama said. She handed Joni to me, wrapped in a towel. "Will you diaper her for me?"

"Why do we have to move so often?" I asked sourly, taking

Joni from her. I had begun to feel nervous about walking into a new fifth-grade classroom.

"I complained because I had no shoes, until I met a man who had no feet," Mama said in a singsong voice.

It wasn't the first time I heard Mama say that. I abruptly turned my back on her and carried Joni into the bedroom. No wonder I never told her about my nightmares of showing up barefooted in school. I heard Mama setting up the ironing board in the living room to press the blouse she planned to wear dancing.

I laid Joni on the bed, pulled her up by one ankle, and scooted a diaper underneath her. When I lifted the baby-powder tin to sprinkle her bottom, an inane thought passed through my head.

I wonder if this would fit into my mouth.

Evidently the neurons in my brain, firing or misfiring, needed a diversion from the thoughts of moving again. Joni contentedly sucked on her toes, so I opened my mouth wide. Wider even to force the tin of baby powder in between my teeth. Joni's eyes grew large. My mouth stretched so taut over the top of the metal tin that I could not smile back at her.

Satisfied with my experiment, proving, I guess, that I had a big mouth, I tugged on the container. It didn't budge. I yanked harder. Still nothing. My gag reflex activated and made breathing more difficult. I began to panic.

I hurriedly picked up Joni, still bare-bottomed, and ran into the living room, where Mama stood pressing her shirt. She looked up from the ironing board completely perplexed. I ran toward her, carrying Joni, with the large container of baby powder dangling from my mouth.

"Ough. Ough." I coughed and pointed to my throat.

Mama quickly set down the iron and laid Joni on the couch.

"What on earth?" she asked, as she tugged on the container wedged between my teeth. She couldn't pull it free. Finally, she wrenched the tin sideways and slipped it from my mouth. My jaws ached and my teeth tingled.

"Whatever possessed you—" she asked.

"I wanted to see how big my mouth was," I answered, realizing fully how lame and ridiculous it sounded.

Mama's disbelief turned into laughter. She folded over. I started laughing, too. We held our stomachs and laughed until tears ran down our cheeks. I remember the sound of Mama's laughter, warm as corn bread fresh from the oven.

Unshaken by my lapse of good sense, Mama left me to babysit while she and Daddy went dancing. I was to sleep in her and Daddy's bedroom, which doubled as Joni's nursery; the crib had been pushed against the wall in the corner of the room. Mama wanted to make sure I heard Joni when she woke up for her nighttime bottle.

I doubt Ozona, which claimed to be "The Biggest Little Town in the World," had a live band playing locally, but Mama and Daddy could Texas two-step to almost any song playing on the jukebox. In the stillness of the night, I pictured Mama and Daddy dancing together, Daddy leading and Mama following.

Soon enough, Joni fussed in her crib. I lifted her into bed with me to give her a bottle. Her wide eyes looked into mine in the lamplight; she stared at me as if I were a full moon. The rhythmic sounds of her swallowing filled the room. I leaned forward and kissed her fuzzy forehead. Then, ever so softly, I began to sing to her.

My foot in the stirrup, my pony won't stand;
Good-bye Old Paint, I'm a-leavin' Cheyenne.

*   *   *

BEFORE WE left Ozona, Thanksgiving fell on the wrong side of payday. We couldn't afford to buy a turkey.

Daddy didn't apologize; he merely bought a package of ground hamburger meat and molded it into the shape of a meatloaf turkey, complete with drumsticks on the side and a meatball for a tail. Mama was in bed with another migraine, so Daddy prepared the meal. He opened up several cans of creamed corn and made mashed potatoes and macaroni and cheese.

Mama, wearing Daddy's pajamas, gathered with us around the kitchen table. Daddy placed the meat-loaf turkey on a platter and lowered it onto the table beside the other steaming bowls. The seven of us bowed our heads and Daddy offered up a simple prayer. He thanked God for our family, for our food, and for the opportunity to be together.

A carful of girls—Patricia, me, Joni, Nancy (who came to live with us),
Brenda, and Vicki

Grand Junction, Colorado

LIKE TUMBLEWEEDS BREAKING free from their roots, we rolled across the Texas highway toward New Mexico and western Colorado. None of us knew we would be adding yet another child to our family in Grand Junction—not a baby, either. Mama had her tubes tied after delivering Joni; she didn't plan on giving birth again. As Patricia put it to one of our neighbors, "Our mama was spayed."

Daddy hitched a large orange U-Haul trailer, crammed to the ceiling with our belongings, to the back bumper of our Ford Fairlane. He and Mama speculated whether the Ford could handle the almost one-thousand-mile trek to Colorado without breaking down.

"Maybe with a lick and a promise," Mama teased.

"Colorado or bust," Daddy added.

The trailer hitch rode so low it scraped against the pavement when we pulled off the highway to take a photograph in front of the state-line sign reading: WELCOME TO NEW MEXICO "THE LAND OF ENCHANTMENT." The seven of us unfolded out of the car, grateful to stretch our legs. We squatted behind some bushes, hiding from the occasional motorist, and peed rivulets into the bone-dry earth. Before we folded back into the car, we gathered around the sign, looked at Daddy's camera, and said *cheese*.

Just as the road sign promised, New Mexico was a land of enchantment. Our route took us through grass plains studded with yucca plants, dense forests of pines, and the Sangre de Cristo (Blood of Christ) Mountains, which glowed a deep red at sunset. We traveled within a hundred miles of the White Sands Missile Range near Alamogordo, where, fifteen years earlier, the first atomic blast had stunned the world. We drove through Roswell, where a flying saucer supposedly crashed on a nearby ranch two years after the atomic blast.

Traveling through the countryside in 1960 provided an education all its own. History, geography, anthropology, folklore—all of it came to life outside our window. We sometimes drove in silence down the highway that curled like a ribbon toward the horizon, taking in the splendor of the ancient landscape.

If I had to pick a single painting to represent my childhood connection to the big-sky country of Texas, New Mexico, and Colorado, I would choose Georgia O'Keeffe's *Ladder to the Moon*. It evokes what I felt when I gazed into the distant horizon or tilted my head to marvel at the starry heavens. Driving through big-sky country back then, I noticed how infinitesimal a particular problem like moving seemed when set against the backdrop of creation.

I was still feeling this expansiveness when we pulled into a motel, its red VACANCY light blinking. I looked around and spotted the swimming pool. Daddy opened the car door, got out and adjusted himself (a habit that drove Mama crazy), and went inside to the registration desk.

Daddy had been given a modest expense account to move us, so the whole family could do something we rarely did—eat in a café for breakfast, dinner, and supper, plus stay in a motel with a swimming pool.

Could life get more luxurious than a motel with a swimming pool?

We pulled on our bathing suits while Daddy lifted the hood of the car and tinkered inside. He unscrewed the radiator cap and added water. The needle had been riding close to hot all day. So had we. The Ford didn't have air-conditioning.

DADDY WAS both tour guide and teacher. He ferreted out unique opportunities on our travels with the same finesse he had for locating oil trapped between layers of sediment. If there was a mummy, a ghost town, or a two-headed rattlesnake display within a hundred miles, Daddy thought it worth a side trip.

Both Mama and Daddy had an intrinsic curiosity about life, which led Mama to ask Daddy if he would drive us through one of the nearby pueblos. Mama said she had always wanted to do this *more than anything*. Daddy loved to grant Mama's wishes. He beamed when he came back to the car with directions from the gas-station attendant.

"There's one not too far off the road up yonder," he told her.

We found the dirt road and drove toward the village. Mama was electrified by it. She sat up tall in the front seat and told Daddy to slow down. She pointed out an American Indian man wrapped in a colorful striped blanket leaning against an adobe wall on the second floor of the pueblo.

We drove by so slowly that my eyes met his. He seemed to see all the way inside me. His gaze was so intense, I had to look away. Suddenly, I felt we didn't belong there, that we were intruders. But Mama felt different. She said she wouldn't be surprised if our family tree included an American Indian. She didn't have any genealogy records or charts, just a *hunch* that her thick coal-black hair originated from genes that weren't European.

Mama had more than her coal-black hair in common with the American Indian man wrapped in the blanket. Her gaze was every bit as intense. Whenever Mama's eyes locked on mine, it seemed she could tell my every thought. That kind of scrutiny caused me to look away. I didn't like anyone seeing my raw seams or knowing my thoughts—not until I had figured them out for myself.

*　*　*

MOST EYES followed our passel when we walked into the cafés along our route. Tables generally had to be pushed together, a booster and high chair located, and seating arranged to make sure an older child or adult sat next to a younger one to help with cutting, napkins, and spills. Patricia always wanted mashed potatoes and gravy, Brenda loved "girl" cheeses, and my favorite meal was a hamburger with French fries. And, if the budget allowed, a chocolate malt to top it all off.

I loved hamburgers so much that I decided to order one for every meal on that trip. Mama, feeling particularly jolly, had no objections. She even interceded on my behalf several mornings, asking if the breakfast cook would serve me a burger instead of eggs.

"Yes," Mama admitted to the waitress, the request was a bit unusual, but maybe the waitress could ask the cook if it was possible. Mama might then share that she too had some experience working in cafés.

"It never hurts to ask," Mama told me.

She was right. I became known within our family as Wimpy, Popeye's friend who loved hamburgers. I was also the family poison tester. If the other girls ordered chocolate malts along with me, I devised a way to procure a few extra sips.

"You know," I whispered, "sometimes you have to be very careful with malts because it's easy for people to put poison in them." When alarm registered on the younger ones' faces, I offered, "Would you like me to taste yours and make sure it isn't poisoned?"

They would gratefully scoot their drinks in front of me; I would take a long, slow draft, smack my lips, and give it my nod of approval before going on to the next one. If I was feeling particularly naughty, I might say the malt tasted a little funny, which, of course, required a second sip. My sisters quickly wised up, but for a shooting-star moment, I was their hero, willing to sacrifice myself in order to save them.

Nearing the end of our trip, we chugged up the San Juan Mountains into Durango, Colorado; our Ford struggled mightily to pull the U-Haul trailer and seven bodies to an elevation of 6,512 feet. Daddy teased that we might need to get out and push the car the rest of the way to the motel.

Mercifully, it was the end of our driving day. I climbed out of the car and spread my arms, like the bald eagle flying overhead that Daddy had pointed out earlier. I inhaled the crisp mountain air. I had never seen a prettier place on earth. No wonder Mama loved it so. Nestled in a valley, Durango looked like a picturesque mining town, with a narrow-gauge railroad running between it and Silverton. The historic buildings lining Main Street made me feel as if we had stumbled into the Wild West.

Later, I climbed into bed with Vicki and Patricia.

"Tomorrow," I told them, "we drive on the Million Dollar Highway."

"Why's it called that?" Patricia asked.

"'Cause it's made out of money," I said.

"Nuh-uh," Vicki said and turned over to go to sleep.

Truth is, I wasn't lying entirely. One story says the Million Dollar Highway cost a million dollars a mile to build; the other story alleges that the fill dirt for the highway contained a million dollars' worth of gold ore. I liked the latter story better. When we stopped for breaks or to admire the vistas, I looked alongside the road to see if I could spot a gleaming nugget of gold. Grandpa Skinner had taught me well.

Our travels ended the next afternoon as we drove into Grand Junction. The Ford, dust-covered and bug-splattered, had made it. The Utah state line lay twenty miles to the west, where Daddy would end up working in the fields for weeks at a time. A semi-desert landscape surrounded us. In front of us was the largest flat-topped mountain in the world, the Grand Mesa.

Grand Junction lay in the valley between the mesas. Daddy and Mama located a tidy little rental house near enough for us to walk to our new school. But before our closets had a chance to get messy, Mama and Daddy moved us into yet another rental near the outskirts of town. It was far enough away that Vicki, Patricia, and I had to transfer to our third school that year.

Instead of feeling disappointed, I surprised Mama with my enthusiasm. She didn't know I was happy to be leaving my fifth-grade teacher. He scared me. He had never done anything to me, never touched me, but several times he stood so close I could feel his body heat. I started shaking once and couldn't stop until he backed away. When I felt his eyes following me, I wouldn't look at him, because his gaze never felt teacher-like.

I practically skipped into my classroom in the new school. I liked my teacher immensely and buckled down to learn Colorado history, which had nothing to do with Davy Crockett and the Alamo. It wasn't until two weeks later that my teacher said something about *you sixth graders.*

Confused, I raised my hand. "Is this fifth or sixth grade?" I asked in all earnestness.

"Sixth," the teacher said, looking surprised.

Then I looked surprised. "I'm a fifth grader," I told her.

She raised her eyebrows and quickly led me into the principal's office, where we untangled the misunderstanding. Afterward, I walked behind the principal into a new class of fifth graders when I overheard someone whisper, "She's the new girl."

As the new girl, I didn't know if I would have time left in the school year to make a new friend. But if I did make a friend, I wanted to invite her to play at our wonderful new house, which was the second reason I didn't mind moving. When I saw the house for the first time, I could not believe our good fortune. '

From the living room, your eye traveled to the treed backyard, sloping to a small stream, perfect for wading. The bedrooms were filled with light and breezes. Off the living room, in a sunny corner, was the most special alcove I had ever seen. Mama called it the library.

A *library*. It sounded like something Frankie Avalon might have in his house. Mama was an avid reader, yet we had only a handful of books, which filled little more than half a shelf. But still, I loved our library. A pair of floor-to-ceiling windows flanked the bookshelves, and sunlight streamed into the room.

I twirled round and round in the sunlight, thinking, *We could live happily ever after here.* I felt certain that whatever ailed our family could be cured under that very roof. Mama's headaches and visits to Timbuktu, Daddy's absences, our transience, all of it could be healed just by living in such a perfect house.

That first month, sprawled on the library floor, I was inspired to write a work of fiction that I unabashedly called *The Lost City of Enchantment*. I still have the yellowed, lined paper scrawled in pencil. The opening line reads "It was a nice day in May."

I wanted to believe the Lost City of Enchantment existed, that it could be found if only one looked long and hard enough. It was a beautiful, magical place where trials were overcome, orphans found homes, and people stayed in one place.

Mama snapped a black-and-white photograph of our family during this time, in our backyard, not far from the creek. I cherished this photograph because it marked a time when I still believed in enchantment.

We pose in front of a tree, probably one of the cottonwoods.

Vicki and I wear identical pleated skorts. As usual, Vicki's hair is coiffed perfectly; mine looks as if it's been combed with an egg beater. Vicki looks French, with her petite features and dark hair. Patricia, looking more like Mama than any of us, has her left hand resting lightly on Daddy's shoulder. Daddy sports a crew cut; I think he smiles at Mama instead of the camera she is holding. I surmise he is glad to be home for the weekend. His white T-shirt, with rolled-up sleeves, tucks into his jeans. His gold wedding band glints on his left hand as he props Joni on his lap. I hold Brenda. My gaze travels off into the distance; maybe I am thinking how much I love this place.

THE DAY I learned we had to move again, I couldn't catch my breath. My dreams of living happily ever after in our glass-slipper house shattered to the floor.

"Why?" I cried as I sank to my knees. "Why?"

Our house with the library was to be sold instead of rented.

"Can't *we* buy it?" I wanted to know.

But, of course, we couldn't. We barely had enough money to pay rent. From that day forward, I longed for us to buy a house of our very own, one that couldn't be snatched away. I yearned for something sturdy and solid, made from bricks and mortar, something that could withstand all the huffing and puffing of life.

Suffused with melancholy, I again helped pack up our belongings. When I opened one of Mama's drawers, I came across a new item—diet pills.

Mama began to pop the diet pills, both to feel good and to lose weight, though her twenty-six-year-old figure still turned heads. Amphetamines hadn't been banned yet for weight loss. Doctors still prescribed them, unaware that continued use could make their patients paranoid and that withdrawal could trigger depression. In addition to the amphetamines, Mama was now taking barbiturates for her migraines. Her moods began to yo-yo. She became as hard to predict as the weather.

When Daddy was out of town and Mama in one of her *fogs,* I learned to fend for myself. And, being the oldest, I learned to fend for my sisters, too. Because if I didn't, who would? It was around this time I came to realize a hard truth. Once your sisters begin looking up to you as if you really could save them from being poisoned—as if you know a way out of a dark cave—there's no going back. You'll draw your last breath trying to find that door to the Lost City of Enchantment, because you can't bear to let them down.

OUR NEXT rental was short a library, but it did have, much to Patricia's delight, a playhouse next door as well as a playmate Patricia's age. These same neighbors also owned our rental house and had a daughter my age and a son four years older. Janet became my best friend and her brother, Landon, my first crush. Janet wrote in my autograph book (the same one that Frankie Avalon signed), "You are a very sweet girl who likes a boy named Landon, a dumb brother."

After we arranged our clothes in new drawers and closets, summer arrived. Mama seemed to perk up. One weekend when Daddy came home, Mama drove herself across the Rockies to visit her mother and her sister, Eunice, in Fort Morgan, Colorado. When Mama returned from her visit, she carried yet another box of clothes into the living room with my cousin Nancy in tow.

"Terry, you remember Nancy?"

I nodded. I remembered both Eunice and Nancy and our time together in the house with the tent bedroom, almost eight years earlier.

"Nancy's going to stay with us for a while," Mama said.

I studied Nancy. She was five months younger than I and about thirty pounds lighter. She looked like a beanpole with Bette Davis eyes. And she didn't look happy.

I cleaned out part of a dresser drawer, where Nancy stacked her underwear.

Later, Mama called me into her bedroom and told me to sit down.

"Eunice isn't doing well," Mama said, fingering the beads on her white moccasins. "She's drinking more and I'm worried about Nancy. She spends six days a week with the babysitter."

I couldn't understand why Aunt Eunice started drinking so young. I remembered a graduation photograph of her as class valedictorian. Why would a young woman as beautiful and smart as Aunt Eunice begin drinking so destructively by the time she graduated from high school?

Eunice, Mama said, had been blamed for causing their father's death. Their mother had asked Eunice to babysit Mama, but Eunice refused. So their mother stayed home while their father went out. Later that night, their father fell to his death.

Instead of comforting Eunice, Grandma accused her. "If you had watched Carola like I asked, your dad would still be alive," she said. "I wouldn't have let him ride on the running board of that car."

Aunt Eunice was twelve and Mama two.

Liquor had been Eunice's river of forgetfulness, her Lethe in Hades. Drinking helped her forget, but the cost was her competence, her daughter, and her health. I worried that Mama waded in those waters, too. But the day Mama brought Nancy into our house, she was clearheaded and determined to help.

It couldn't have been easy for Mama to trump her older sister. Mama told me Eunice had been good to her as a child, hugging and holding her the way I cuddled Brenda and Joni. Mama had given me Aunt Eunice's middle name, Eilene. Eunice, in return, had given Nancy the middle name Jeanette, a longer version of Mama's name, Jean.

Nancy had not wanted to give up Sundays with her mother to stay with us that summer, but the painful reality was that we lived too far away for her to see her mother with any regularity.

It probably didn't help that Nancy and I crashed broadside right away.

Mama had just proclaimed me old enough to watch the girls by myself, which allowed Mama tremendous freedom and numerous visits to Timbuktu, though Joni was still a baby. Mama had taken to writing out a list of chores to be completed in her absence, in addition to my babysitting. A typical list might read:

Rinse dirty diapers in diaper pail
Wash darks and whites, don't forget bleach in whites
Fold and put away clothes
Iron my blue blouse
Put on pot of beans
Sweep kitchen floor
Take out trash

I oversaw and delegated the different chores among Nancy, Vicki, and me. Everything had to be crossed off the list before Mama came home. Frankly, having Nancy around made things easier; we had one more pair of hands. But no one appreciated that Mama had made me foreman of the crew. I didn't relish the position myself, but my qualifications were indisputable. I was the oldest.

One afternoon I observed Nancy ironing Mama's shirt differently from the way Mama had taught me to iron.

First, you iron the collar, then the shoulders and behind the neck. Then you iron the sleeves so the shirt doesn't wrinkle while you're ironing the sleeves. Lastly, you iron the sides and back of the shirt.

Being foreman of the crew also included quality control.

"Want me to show you how to iron the sleeves without wrinkling the shirt?" I asked.

"I know how to iron," Nancy informed me.

I put my hand on the ironing board. "Mama likes her shirt ironed a certain way."

If Nancy and I had hair on the backs of our necks, it would have bristled as we circled each other like two animals, trying to establish who was alpha.

"You better move your hand off the ironing board," Nancy insisted.

"Or what?"

"Or I'll iron it."

"You wouldn't."

"Try me."

I kept my hand firmly planted on the ironing board.

Nancy glared at me. "You asked for it," she said and drove the iron into the underside of my wrist.

A searing pain shot through my flesh. I jerked my hand off the ironing board. Nancy's brazenness stunned me; I think it stunned her, too.

"Wait until I tell Mama," I threatened and turned on my heels. I strode into the kitchen and tore off an end from the aloe plant, our cure for scrapes and burns. I blew on the aloe's sticky coolness on my skin, trying to soothe the pain, then gave the kitchen a good mopping to help soothe my pride.

When Mama came home, I debated outing Nancy, but something about Nancy's pluckiness impressed me. I decided I could always tell on her later.

Slowly, Nancy and I began to forge an alliance. She may have been impressed that I kept my hand on the ironing board or that I kept my mouth shut—about not only the ironing but another incident, too.

We were lying on the bed late one evening talking together, looking out the window, and listening to the crickets. Suddenly, a light went on in the house next door. Janet's brother, Landon, the one I had a crush on, came into his bedroom and shut his door, but he neglected to pull down his shade. Getting ready for bed, he pulled his T-shirt off and began to unbutton his jeans.

"We can't look," I told Nancy and lowered my eyes.

"Why not?" she asked and stared straight ahead.

I watched her watching him. I never looked up.

One thing I came to learn about Nancy: she wasn't about "making nice." If a pink elephant walked into the room, Nancy pointed out where it stood. She spoke her mind and asked difficult questions. As the ironing incident proved, she didn't shy away from confrontation. She was skinny but had chutzpah.

At the end of that summer, Mama and Eunice came to a major decision. Nancy's stay would continue indefinitely. Our rental house now teemed with six girls under the age of twelve. That fall, Nancy and I enrolled in the same sixth-grade class.

Nancy, Vicki, and I were close enough in age that we began to view ourselves as comrades contending with forces larger and more powerful than any one of us. Maybe that's the void we filled in Nancy's life—she had us seven days a week. But she still missed her mom.

Without Mama home to referee, we older girls threw our share of hissy fits. Vicki liked to bite, I used my strength, and Nancy used her fingernails. But when we heard Mama's car pull up outside, we immediately forgot our differences. We grabbed our dust cloths, brooms or mops, and busied ourselves with the chores not yet crossed off the list. Mama usually entered the house unaware she had put an end to one of our brawls. Every once in a while we tattled on one another, like the time I asked Mama what I should put on my bite.

"What kind of bite?" she wanted to know.

"A human bite," I answered, throwing Vicki to the lions.

But 95, maybe even 98, percent of the time, we played on the same team, often covering for one another and genuinely enjoying one another's company.

It became our habit to pile onto the same bed, like a litter of kittens, in a tangle of casually draped arms and legs. Joni and Brenda liked to romp in the center of our circle. We were their human playpen. One afternoon, our conversation turned to Dusty Dinton, Mama's apparent boyfriend. Mama first brought Dusty home and introduced him to us while Daddy worked in Utah. After the introduction, Dusty began showing up at our house a good bit when Daddy was out of town.

"Don't say a word to Davy about Dusty," Mama ordered.

I didn't want to hurt Daddy so, of course, I didn't mention

Dusty. I didn't realize then that not telling Daddy might hurt him even more.

However, Mama couldn't force us to like Dusty.

That afternoon on the bed, we decided to secretly call Dusty the White Urp, our version of Wyatt Earp, the frontier marshal who joined in the famous gunfight, along with Doc Holliday, at the O.K. Corral in Tombstone, Arizona.

"White Urp was here again last night," Nancy said.

We pantomimed sticking our fingers down our throats as if to make ourselves throw up.

Dusty played in a band called Dusty Dinton and the Troubadours. His band sang country-and-western songs and Dusty played the guitar. I couldn't pick out Dusty from a lineup today, but I remember he looked like a cowboy.

More than once, he brought his guitar to the house, placed the guitar strap over my shoulders, and showed me how to arrange my fingers on the frets and strings to play various chords. The day I strummed a tune, with Dusty's fingers guiding mine, I slipped and started to like him. Which, of course, was betraying Daddy. I handed the guitar back to him and ignored him the rest of the day. But withholding my affection proved difficult.

My biggest slipup came when I babysat for Mama's friend JoAnn. Mama had left a note on the kitchen table detailing everything that needed to be done before she came home. Before I could cross off "Fold the laundry," JoAnn came to pick me up. I instructed Vicki and Nancy to fold the clothes while I was gone.

Later at JoAnn's house, the phone rang. It was Dusty.

"I just wanted to warn you," he said. "Your mama's coming over and she's hoppin' mad that the clothes weren't folded when she got home."

Evidently, Vicki and Nancy hadn't gotten around to folding them.

But why would Mama drive to JoAnn's house? I couldn't leave the children until JoAnn returned.

"Why's Mama coming here?" I asked.

"She aims to give you a lickin'. I just wanted to warn you."

Dusty sounded genuinely sorry; it was his version of a courtesy call.

Too soon, I heard a car door slam. Mama barged through the front door waving a hairbrush in her hand and yelling. She came at me with the brush and struck me across my arms, legs, and buttocks. I hardly recognized the woman in front of me.

"When I tell you to do something, young lady, you sure as hell better do it," she yelled. "Do you hear me?"

"Yes, ma'am," I answered, but I wouldn't give her the satisfaction of seeing me cry, even if it prolonged the spanking. The only control I had in that moment was to withhold my tears, so I did. I knew Mama would turn on Vicki and Nancy if I told her that I asked them to fold the clothes while I was gone. I decided to deal with them later. Right at that moment, I couldn't wish Mama's wrath on anyone.

After she spent her rage, she let go of the brush and sat there shaking and breathing hard.

"I'll see you at home," she said finally and left.

JoAnn's five children, all under the age of ten, had been listening in the next room. They wanted to know what I had done wrong and if the marks on my arm hurt. I told them not to worry, that my mom was mad about some clothes, and that the marks didn't hurt all that bad. When JoAnn dropped me off, she said she was sorry; one of the kids told her what had happened.

Dusty asked me if I was okay when I got home. I nodded and headed for the bedroom, climbed into bed beside a sleeping Vicki, and cried myself to sleep.

JOANN AND Mama met that summer at the Lori-Li Lounge on Highway 6, where Dusty and his band played. Mama and JoAnn forged a friendship while drinking and dancing with the patrons of the Lori-Li and the Tivoli.

Right away, I understood Mama's affection for JoAnn. She was vivacious and funny and had lived most of her life in Texas. She had a drawl as sweet as honey and could coat any curse word with her accent so as not to jar your ear or morality. This was fortunate, since she could not utter a sentence without the interjection of one or two expletives. Something as benign as going to the grocery store might translate into "I drove to the store and forgot the damned grocery list sitting on the counter. Shit, if my head wasn't screwed on, it would fall off and scare the hell out of somebody." Years later, when JoAnn turned her life over to Jesus and became a born-again Christian, I actually missed her colorful language.

But before JoAnn became a Christian, she packed a pistol in either her purse or glove compartment for protection. Once she came out of a bar to find someone rifling through her glove compartment; luckily, she said, the pistol happened to be in her purse. She drew it, aimed it at the man, and warned, "You damn well better have a good excuse for being here."

JoAnn fired the gun into the air just to teach him a lesson. JoAnn's target practice consisted mostly of firing her gun into the air.

Between them, Mama and JoAnn had eleven children. Sometimes we packed a lunch, piled into two cars, and drove up to the Grand Mesa for a picnic. When Mama and JoAnn were in charge, I was off duty, free to wander on my own. I relished those rare moments of solitude.

After the whipping at JoAnn's house, we had arranged just such a picnic.

"Where's Terry going?" Brenda asked.

"Leave her be," Mama answered. "She'll be back in a bit."

Mama seemed back to normal and willing to grant me some time to myself.

I wandered away from the group and discovered an outcropping of flat red rocks the size of foundation slabs, overlooking the valley below. I admired the expanse, wishing I could wake to see it every morning. I began to imagine what a dream house would look like, built there on the mountainside.

My footsteps became the blueprint. The straight lines I walked between the flat rocks and pinyon pines laid out the bedrooms, one for each of us. A large flat rock became a step-up living room. And over to the left, where two slabs came together, that was my library.

THAT DECEMBER, after Mama talked JoAnn into taking classes with her at Mesa College, she and JoAnn received their high school equivalency diplomas. In a celebratory mood, we all gathered in front of JoAnn's television set to watch *The Wizard of Oz*. We piled pillows and blankets onto the floor between bowls of popcorn and a plate of fudge. It was one of those rare golden moments when everything seemed right with the world. I felt secure, all of us watching Dorothy in her ruby-red slippers carrying Toto down the yellow-brick road.

I felt hopeful after Mama earned her GED. I thought things would be different. But her visits to the dim-lit, smoke-filled Lori-Li continued. However, Mama's nights listening to Dusty Dinton were apparently numbered.

ONE SATURDAY morning, the smell of bacon and the sounds of Mama and Daddy talking in the kitchen reached us in the back bedroom, where we had all piled onto a single bed. Unexpectedly, Daddy appeared at the doorway. He leaned against the doorjamb, holding a spatula and crying.

"What's wrong?" we asked, alarmed and in unison.

Daddy sagged onto the edge of the bed. The spatula dangled toward the floor.

We huddled around him. He struggled for words.

"Your mom wants a divorce," he said finally.

Divorce. The word tolled like a death knell drowning out the rest of what Daddy said.

Then I heard him say, "Maybe you girls could talk to her. Tell her we're a family. Maybe she'd listen."

I didn't want to lose Daddy. But what could I say that I hadn't already? Daddy was unaware of the conversation I had with Mama after I walked in on her and Dusty in the bedroom one morning. Mama's shirt was unbuttoned and her bare breast shocked me. Angry and disgusted, I turned and left the room. I don't know what I thought happened between them, but seeing it *in the flesh* bothered me greatly.

Mama buttoned up and followed me into the living room.

"You should've knocked," she said.

"What's wrong with Daddy?" I asked, flopping onto the couch.

"He's a good man," Mama said. "Maybe even the type I would want to grow old with, but I'm a long way from a shawl and a rocking chair, Terry."

That's what she always said when she felt I was judging her. *I'm a long way from a shawl and a rocking chair.*

While I never said anything about a shawl and a rocking chair, I did wish, more than anything, that Mama would be more like Janet's mom. Janet's mom didn't have boyfriends. She could be found, most nights, perched on a corner of her couch. She washed the family's clothes on Tuesday, baked cookies, and made supper every evening. Janet and Landon washed and dried the dishes after supper, which seemed more than fair. I never told Janet, but it comforted me to know that her mom was next door.

Janet shyly asked me once who the man who came to our house was. She said some neighborhood kids had been calling my mom a "playgirl." I didn't know the exact definition of a playgirl, but I felt certain Janet's mom had never been called one. It didn't matter much to Mama what people called her. She never put much stock in what the neighbors thought. If she caught them spying on her from behind their curtains, she stopped, smiled, and waved vigorously in their direction. This embarrassed me beyond belief.

"Well, they deserve it," Mama said as their curtains quickly fell into place again.

If everybody in the neighborhood knew about Dusty, it wasn't a huge leap to assume Daddy knew, too. But I wasn't about to bring up his name. Just in case. I gave Daddy a hug and told him I would definitely talk to Mama.

He rose and walked out of the bedroom, still gripping his spatula. Nancy, Vicki, Patricia, and I sat shell-shocked on the bed. Brenda and Joni, oblivious to our tears, played peekaboo under the sheets.

Daddy and Mama talked privately off and on throughout the morning. Before I had a chance to approach Mama, Daddy came in with red eyes but looking much happier. He told us we didn't need to talk to Mama after all. She had changed her mind, he said, and now we'd all be moving with him to Fort Stockton, Texas. That's how I learned we would be moving.

Daddy drove ahead without us because he needed to get the rig set up in Fort Stockton. Mama and the rest of us were to follow, retracing our steps through the Land of Enchantment—only this time, with Nancy aboard.

Mama always knew Daddy would be loyal to her as long as she stayed with him. He would do anything for her, except stay in one place. The nomadic life of doodlebugging was the only work he knew. He was good at it, too. A finer driller would be hard to find. Oil companies were paying good wages to seismographic drillers with the skills and expertise Daddy was acquiring, especially since hundreds of thousands of acres awaited exploration in the Southwest. Unfortunately, setting down roots in a particular place was never part of Daddy's job description.

Providing for his family was another matter, however.

Daddy willingly turned over his paycheck and his heart to all of us; he gladly accepted the role of husband, father, and provider. He loved Mama, despite her indiscretions, and he loved us, too, pure and simple.

Mama, age 27

Fort Stockton, Texas

L OOKIE HERE," DADDY said proudly, sliding open a cabinet door the size of a shoe box. "It's a spice cabinet."

Daddy tried desperately to win Mama over, but Mama was having none of it. "How could you do this without asking me?" she huffed.

Daddy's boyish grin disappeared. "I thought it would be easier. Just tape the cabinets shut, hook up the trailer hitch, and that's that. Nothing needs to be packed."

Mama would learn, sooner than she realized, just how easy it was to move a trailer.

"Can we even fit in here?" Mama asked.

"You know, I've been thinking," Daddy said, seemingly relieved that Mama was open to conversation. "I can raise the beds for storage underneath, put cabinets here in the hall, maybe take down this wall." He thumped the paneling.

We followed Daddy down the narrow hall of the ten-by-fifty-foot, three-bedroom M-System trailer house. Daddy had purchased the trailer before Mama and all of us girls arrived in Fort Stockton. It didn't take us long to explore five hundred square feet of paneling and linoleum, soon to become our new home on wheels.

Despite Mama's reaction, Daddy patted the kitchen door-jamb proudly. He had never owned a home before. Mama sat on the sectional, her head buried in her hands.

In the end, Mama stood up, sighed, and signaled that we should start unloading the U-Haul. Somehow we squeezed our belongings into the green-and-white trailer, parked in a trailer park at the edge of town near West 17th Street alongside a dozen or so other trailers.

Better Homes and Gardens likely never ran a spread on trailer houses or trailer parks, but a tour of our trailer would have begun with the metal-grate steps that led to our front door. Mama and Daddy's bedroom lay to the right of the front door, just off the living room. Their bedroom had just enough space between the double bed and the walls for two bodies to stand on either side. A plain square mirror hung over a two-foot-wide built-in dresser, just off the foot of the bed, next to a small closet.

Outside their bedroom, two sets of louvered windows allowed light into the living room, sparsely furnished with a tan Naugahyde sectional set atop spindle legs. Either end of the sectional could be interchanged with a cushion or a wooden-top side table. The living room opened directly into the kitchen, where the sink and stove lined a side wall, next to a small window. Across from the stove, Daddy placed the long picnic table and two benches he had built so all of us could sit together for meals. We added two chrome chairs to the ends and Mama camouflaged the picnic table with a rectangular piece of oilcloth.

Chili powder, garlic salt, onion powder, sage, poultry seasoning, ground mustard, and cinnamon filled the tiny spice cabinet Daddy had been so proud of when he first showed Mama the trailer.

A narrow hallway led to the back of the trailer. The middle bedroom couldn't have been bigger than six by eight feet. Daddy eventually removed one wall and built oversized bunk beds for Brenda, Joni, Nancy, and Patricia. They paired up, two in each bunk. Two clothes drawers pulled out from beneath the raised closet.

After Daddy removed the wall to the middle bedroom, Patricia fell backward off the top bunk one morning while making her bed; she had leaned back, thinking the wall still stood behind her. I happened to walk by at that very moment, caught her squarely in my arms, and hefted her back atop the bunk, almost without breaking stride.

Outside the middle bedroom, our washer hummed almost continuously in the corner of the hall. It marked the entrance to the only bathroom, which was so small you could touch the sink, the toilet, and the tub at the same time. Eight toothbrushes stood erect in a ceramic mug.

The back bedroom, the largest, with a long built-in dresser and equally long mirror, went to me and Vicki. Mama may have wanted me to be close to the girls in case they needed something, or she may have wanted the back bedroom to be our hangout, which it became. All six girls, along with Freckles, a wirehaired terrier puppy Daddy brought home, and Midnight, my newly found black stray cat, would pile onto the bed to talk, play pitch, do homework, or watch a small television placed catty-corner on the edge of the dresser.

One afternoon, lying on the bed in the back bedroom talking to Nancy, I raised my arms in the air and moved them rhythmically. "Did you know you can feel the vibrations of the drums beating in Africa?" I asked Nancy.

"No, you can't," Nancy said dismissively.

"It's true. In the books I've been reading about Africa," I went on, "it says they use this special wood that sends vibrations around the world. I can feel them right now." I held my hand very still.

Nancy paused at this because I had, indeed, been reading books about Africa, tomes actually, some of them five hundred or more pages. I had inexplicably become obsessed with Africa. I wanted to know about its jungles, plains, people, and animals, and about the archaeologists, explorers, doctors, and plantation owners who lived there, such as Karen Blixen, Mary and Louis Leakey, David Livingstone, and Albert Schweitzer.

I longed for adventure, to explore unexplored places, to stand beneath an acacia tree and scan the horizon for lions, elephants, and horned rhinoceroses.

Somehow, someday, I will go to Africa, I vowed to myself. It was as if my life depended on it. I extrapolated that if a twelve-year-old girl living in a trailer park in Fort Stockton, Texas, could find her way to Africa, why then, anything might be possible!

"Really. If you raise your hand like this, you can feel them," I said. I tapped out a beat with my hands in the air.

"I know you're teasing," Nancy said. "I'm not going to raise my hand."

"Fine," I said and haughtily left the room. Still, I waited outside the door, peeking in to watch Nancy. I sensed she might be curious. I clomped my feet as if I had walked down the hall into the kitchen. Sure enough, Nancy furtively raised her hand into the air.

"Ha," I said as I bounded back into the room and pounced onto the bed, "fooled you."

I liked to tease Nancy partly because she was gullible and partly because I loved to laugh. But on some level, I was also jealous of Nancy.

She and I had been enrolled in the same sixth-grade class in Grand Junction, Colorado. When we transferred to the new school in Fort Stockton, they had only one opening in their upper-ranked sixth-grade class. Nancy and I had similar grades, so we took a placement test to see which of us would *win* the open slot in the higher-ranked class.

Nancy won.

That she had been placed in the higher-ranked class irritated me the way a scratchy label in a new shirt pricks your back. Without thinking, you reach back to scratch where the label rubs, or you find yourself making up stories about African drums.

DUST STORMS blew through Fort Stockton with some regularity. The arid landscape, dotted with prickly pear, yucca, and desert grasses, tested the fortitude of even the hardiest inhabitants, especially in the early years. The historical marker at the Old Fort Cemetery in the center of town attested to the hardships of frontier life. It pointed out that no headstone was erected for a person over forty. That statistic sobers me more now than it did when I was twelve. At twelve, I considered Mama old at twenty-seven.

If not for millions of barrels of oil, Fort Stockton might not have lived long, either. Hundreds of pump jacks sat atop the Permian Basin, one of the most prolific oil-producing areas in the United States. The pump jacks looked like giant donkey heads nodding up and down, drinking up the oil trapped between the world's thickest rock deposits of the Permian geologic period. The caliche blowing around in the dust storms probably harkened back to the evaporation of an ancient Permian sea.

One day toward the end of the school year, I suggested to Nancy that we pick up our pace and hightail it home before the dust storm hit. Getting tackled by a West Texas dust storm burned your eyes, stung your lungs, and left grit on your teeth. No matter how tight the seal around a door or window, a fine layer of silt usually found its way inside by the time the dust storm subsided. If the winds blew particularly hard, the dust could sandblast a car and leave permanent damage.

The storm still loomed in the distance when we stepped onto the gravel road that ran alongside our trailer. However, something unexpected waited for us up ahead.

What on earth? I wondered.

A colossal bus loomed in our driveway. The bus rivaled the size of our trailer. Nancy and I forgot about the dust storm and studied the bold script on the side of the bus.

"Oh, no!"

I stopped in disbelief, reeling as if falling backward from a top bunk with no one to catch me.

How could Mama allow it?

Mama might as well have rented a billboard that said "I am unfaithful to my husband." Right in broad daylight, in letters at least a foot high, the writing on the custom bus read DUSTY DINTON AND THE TROUBADOURS. No doubt the bus had already turned every head in the neighborhood.

I wondered if Mama assumed no one would tell Daddy or if she just didn't care. I cared what the neighbors thought. I cared if Daddy found out. I cared that Mama had a box of letters from Dusty hidden in her closet and that he had been writing to her since we left Grand Junction.

We girls suspected Mama had been hiding something. Five hundred square feet does not allow much room for secrets. Our suspicions led us to stand on the foot of Mama and Daddy's bed and snoop in the closet, after Mama had left for the week-end to visit Juárez, Mexico, a border town on the Rio Grande about 250 miles away. It did not take us long to discover the shoe box full of letters under a pile of Mama's clothes on a shelf in the closet. We looked at one another and the contraband let-ters; Daddy was out of town working and Mama would not be back for another day.

Mama had left me *to hold down the fort* with the explicit instructions that if we needed anything at all, I was to summon our neighbor Rose, in whom Mama confided. I didn't think it particularly unusual to be left with the girls; I had been babysit-ting for over a year. It didn't matter much if Mama was five miles or two hundred and fifty miles away; the chores and responsibili-ties at home were about the same. If Daddy called, I was to tell him that Mama was not home, which was the truth. Under no circumstances was I to tell Daddy she had gone to Juárez.

I knew Mama would be furious if she caught us reading her letters, but getting caught seemed highly unlikely. We had plenty of time to read them before she returned. Without hesitation, we shook the letters out of their ragged-edged envelopes and took turns reading White Urp's professions of love.

After our snooping, we cooked supper. Our usual fare consisted of fried potatoes, corn bread, and a ham hock simmering with pinto beans. Depending on where payday fell and what had been stocked in the trailer before Mama left town, we might prepare our favorite meal—Mexican food. Under the best of circumstances, five or six darkened avocados would be resting in a bowl on the kitchen counter.

Our neighbor Rose taught Mama and us how to make beef enchiladas, and guacamole with a mortar and pestle. Rose knew how to make corn tortillas that rivaled those sold at the Comanche Tortilla and Tamale Factory in town, but an hour of cooking could be saved if we bought ready-made tortillas.

When we cooked enchiladas, Vicki, Nancy, and I stood in a line between the stove and kitchen sink, assembly-line fashion. One of us flash cooked the corn tortillas in oil; another dipped them into a skillet filled with tomato sauce and chili powder; and, finally, one of us filled them with meat, cheese, and onions, setting aside a few without onions for Patricia and Daddy. We rolled the enchiladas jelly-roll fashion and tucked them side by side on a cookie sheet. The trailer filled with a delicious aroma as the enchiladas cooked and bubbled for twenty minutes in the oven. They became one of our family's favorite meals.

*　*　*

WE HAD big news to tell Mama when she returned home from Juárez.

A funnel cloud had touched down and whirled in the field across from the trailer park. The sky turned a grayish green and everything grew still. Rose pounded on our trailer door. She told us girls to hurry over to her trailer because she didn't like the looks of the sky. I hefted Joni onto my hip and we all ran barefoot across the yard to Rose's trailer, even smaller than our own.

Rose's two sons, four and five, stood on the couch looking out the picture window at the vacant field where the new high school was to be built. Our eyes fixed on the dark gray funnel cloud that dropped from the sky and moved across the field like a giant top, spinning a vortex of dust, wind, and debris. We had no storm cellar to run to, no basement to hide in, not even a bathroom or closet large enough to hold all nine of us. So we held our collective breath and waited.

When I fretted about the future, Mama used to sing the song "Que Sera, Sera" as a way of saying that no one knows what lies ahead. We were no match for a tornado that could crush trailers, uproot trees, and lift cars into the air. The only thing I knew to do was surrender to our fate, whatever that might be.

Que Sera, Sera.

The funnel cloud churned parallel to the trailer park in the open field and then disappeared as quickly as it had come. Nothing in our vicinity had been touched; we had been spared. In a matter of minutes the danger had passed. We stood there a while longer, holding on to one another.

*   *   *

MONTHS LATER, on the day of the approaching dust storm, Nancy and I weren't worried about tornadoes. We walked past Dusty's gigantic bus into the back door of our trailer. We purposely chose the back door because we didn't want to say hi to Dusty or any of his Troubadours.

Mama strode into the back bedroom.

"I won't have you being rude," she scolded as she waved her finger toward the living room. "I want you to march right in there and say hello."

I trudged in and said hi. Instead of asking *Why don't you leave Mama alone?* I asked, "Why do you have a bus?"

Dusty smiled and slapped his knee. "Isn't it great? We're on tour!"

The dust storm finally hit.

Hours later, a fine layer of silt covered the linoleum floor just under the living-room door. Dusty's bus had pulled out. I secretly hoped it had been sandblasted.

I don't think Daddy found out about Dusty's visit or his letters. But he did find out when Mama went on a road trip with two cowboys. All hell broke loose.

DADDY WRENCHED the trailer hitch until it thudded onto the ball mount of the truck. I grasped his hand, slippery with sweat and grease, and tried to pry it from the winch, hoping to dissuade him. "Please, Daddy! We can't just leave. She won't know where to find us."

He jerked his hand away as if my touch stung him. "I don't give a damn. She should have thought of that before she took off." Then, pointing his finger toward my nose, "And you should not have lied!"

"I don't know where she is, other than what she said, honest. She was taking Nancy to visit her mom, that's all she said."

"And the men in the car?"

I looked down at the chalky white patch of caliche. I had omitted the part about two men being in the car. But how could Daddy know that? He was drilling a hundred miles away.

He slammed everything into the back of the truck: our rusted bicycles, the oil-drum barbecue grill, the metal steps leading up to the trailer house. I had never seen Daddy this angry. Veins bulged near his temples, his eyes narrowed to slits. He stopped and looked at me over his shoulder, sweat saturating his white T-shirt. "Get inside and finish making supper."

"But—"

"You heard me. I'm gonna teach her a lesson she won't forget. We're leaving in the morning."

I knew he meant it. That night would be our last in Fort Stockton, Texas. And unless Mama came home in the next twelve hours, which was unlikely, knowing Mama, she would be driving up to an empty trailer space, with no forwarding address.

I climbed into the trailer and slammed the door behind me. The fan of the swamp cooler whirred in the ceiling; the evaporating water felt cool against my hot cheeks.

"What was Daddy hollering about?" Vicki yelled from the back bedroom.

What should I tell them?

I walked into the bedroom to see Vicki twisting a rubber band around Patricia's braid.

"My hair's gettin' braided, too," Brenda piped up. She was playing with Joni on the bed, next to Vicki and Patricia.

I slumped onto the chenille spread, following its ridges with my finger.

"We're moving," I said, trying to sound nonchalant, willing my eyes not to water. If any crying was to be done, it would have to come later, after everyone else had fallen asleep.

Vicki's head jerked up. "Where?"

"How come?" Patricia wanted to know, turning her head sideways, one braid in, one braid out.

"I don't know. But we're leaving tomorrow."

"Without Mama?" Vicki asked.

"That's what Daddy said," I told her, "but I'm sure Daddy will tell her where we're going."

In fact, I was not sure at all.

EARLIER THAT week, Mama walked into the back bedroom, where I was folding laundry on the bed. "I'm putting you in charge of the girls for a few days," she announced, picking up some of Nancy's folded underwear and stuffing it into a brown bag. "I'm taking Nancy to visit her mother in Colorado.

"Hand me that," Mama said, pointing to her black bra on top of a pile.

I tossed it more forcefully than necessary.

"Watch it, Teresa Eilene."

She glared into my face and I felt my cheeks grow hot. I knew to keep my mouth shut. Mama couldn't abide sassing. Not long ago, she had slapped me across the face; the memory of her stinging handprint was a powerful deterrent.

Doors and drawers slammed as Mama packed. She and Nancy scurried down the trailer steps, carrying their bags. I followed them outside, Joni slung across my hip. That is when I saw them—two men, waiting in the car. I had never seen them before.

"I should be home before your dad gets back into town. But," she said, looking me squarely in the eye, "if he asks, you tell him we took the bus."

Then, pulling away, she leaned her head out the window and yelled, "You girls need anything, ask Rose."

I stood there watching the car disappear out of the trailer park. In a matter of minutes, Mama had packed up and said good-bye, as if the trip had come up unexpectedly, over a beer at the bar.

Mama went to visit Eunice in Colorado. That's what I told Daddy when he came home sooner than we expected.

Daddy had come home early because the company wanted him to work in a new location. Under ordinary circumstances, he might have decided to commute a little farther rather than move us again so soon; we had been in Fort Stockton little more than six months. But in light of Mama's latest escapade, he planned to teach her a lesson. As he told her when he first showed her the trailer house: *Just tape the cabinets shut, hook up the trailer hitch, and that's that. Nothing needs to be packed.* We were about to discover just how fast our house on wheels could move.

I mixed up some leftovers for Midnight, whom I had not seen all day. I opened the trailer door and began calling, "Here, kitty, kitty, kitty. Come on, Midnight. Here, kitty, kitty." I squatted to look under the truck. No sign of him. I put his food on the floor and closed the door.

Vicki and I washed and dried dishes while Daddy cleared the counters. Everything had to be put away before Daddy could tape the kitchen cabinets shut. Vicki cleaned off the top of the built-in dresser in our bedroom. Patricia helped Brenda pull a nightgown over her head. After I settled Joni into bed, I opened the trailer door; Midnight had not come back for his supper.

I called again. Then I turned to Daddy in the kitchen as he ripped off a piece of duct tape and slapped it across the cabinets to keep the doors closed.

"What if I can't find Midnight?"

Daddy looked up; his face softened. He seemed to know what I was asking.

Would you leave without him, too?

"Go on out and look for him. We'll finish up here," he said.

I closed the door behind me.

"Here, Midnight. Kitty, kitty."

I saw Rose through her trailer window, rapped on her door, and slipped inside. Everything came tumbling out. I told Rose that Daddy aimed to move the trailer without Mama knowing; that I feared Mama might not come looking for us; and that on top of everything else, I couldn't find Midnight anywhere.

Rose was making tortillas in her cast-iron skillet, filling the kitchen with the scent of corn flour. She wiped her hands on a dish towel and laid her hand on my shoulder, trying to reassure me. She told me Mama would find us somehow, and that if I didn't find Midnight, she would take care of him for me, but she thought she had seen him under her trailer, asleep in an old tire.

I hugged her, told her thank you, and said I would miss her.

"I'll miss y'all, too," she said and kissed me on the cheek. "Good luck."

Back outside, I squinted into the shadows under Rose's trailer. Sure enough, I spotted Midnight folded into the tire.

"Thank goodness I found you," I whispered.

I still remembered leaving Trixie at the vet's in Alvin. Many memories haunted me during this time. I would lie in bed at night repeating, *I'll be so glad when I forget this. I'll be so glad when I forget this.* Sometimes it worked. Most of the time, I still remembered things, but I began to forget how badly they hurt.

I gathered Midnight under my arm and backed out from under the trailer. Like it or not, he was headed for a new home. I wished my perennial wish—that we could live in a brick house, a solid, sturdy home (maybe even with a library) that couldn't be moved from one day to the next.

I rubbed a cramp below my navel; I had started my period during Mama's absence. I bled into a Kotex pad hooked onto a sanitary-napkin belt, just like Mama. A sliver of thought, like the slimmest crescent, began to wax in me. How many more similarities would I share with Mama as I matured? I desperately wanted to travel to Africa someday, but never via Timbuktu.

Me, seated on Grandpa's tractor

Ozona, Texas
Revisited

I HELD JONI AND sat in the front seat, where Mama usually
sat. Two men studied me through the open window. They
looked from me to Daddy pumping gas and back at me.

They think I'm his wife, I thought. *I'm twelve and they think I'm his wife and Joni's mama.*

I stared straight through them. I didn't care what they thought. I didn't care about anything. I didn't care about our destination or how long it would take us to arrive. I sat there mute and in a state of shock. Maybe Mama felt the same way when she was fifteen with me on her lap, only the man pumping gas *was* her husband.

In a sense, we'd all been sucked up into a tornado and spun into a new land. When the spinning stopped and the air cleared, we found ourselves not in Oz but in Ozona, where we had lived fourteen months earlier. Vicki said she reckoned Mama would show up sooner or later.

I attribute Vicki's nonchalance to the fact that she wasn't the oldest sister. For better or worse, I had been a buffer between Vicki and the world since the day she was born. Even in my dreams, I stepped between her and whatever locomotive barreled toward us. But Vicki was right. Mama and Nancy did somehow find us.

When Nancy and Mama didn't see the trailer, they stumbled into their own version of *The Twilight Zone.* Bewildered, Mama rapped on Bud and Rose's trailer door. Rose told them what happened and offered to put them up for the night. Rose bedded her boys on the floor and Nancy climbed into the top bunk, leaving the bottom one for Mama, who stayed up to talk with Rose in the kitchen.

In the midst of Mama's questions and confusion, Nancy overheard Mama tell Rose she didn't expect Eunice to live much longer. Eunice had cirrhosis.

That night, Nancy lay in the dark and cried silently for her mother.

In the morning she and Mama set out after us.

Mama appeared contrite in the beginning, as she and Daddy sorted through the wreckage of their differences, trying to piece their relationship back together. Their détente, however, failed to lessen my vigilance. I found myself constantly monitoring the weather patterns of their marriage. I took note of their interactions the way a farmer might analyze cloud formations to determine if the calves should be rounded up, or in my case, my sisters.

THE THING about both life and weather is that seasons come and go. Sometimes a really fair summer can make up for a really harsh winter, which turned out to be the case for us that summer in Ozona. There's a Texas expression—walking in tall cotton—which means that times are good. Cotton plants grow tall when everything aligns just right—the sunshine, the rainfall, and a lack of pests. That's what happened that summer; we walked in tall cotton, both literally and metaphorically.

One evening Daddy walked into the kitchen at the end of a dusty week, dropped his pile of soiled work clothes on the linoleum floor, and looked at Mama hopefully.

"Want to take the girls camping this weekend?" he asked. "I came across this perfect spot on the Pecos River, not far from the rig."

Mama bit her lip.

"Oh, could we, Mama?" I begged.

Mama looked from me to Daddy.

"It'll remind you of the Colorado River," Daddy said, upping the ante.

"Please," I said.

Mama let out a sigh. "Okay," she conceded, "it might do us all some good."

The next morning, Daddy happily yanked blankets and spreads from the beds, rolled up the cotton rug Mama had purchased in Juárez, and tossed clanking skillets, pans, and utensils into a cardboard box, which he loaded into the trunk of our car.

We had no sleeping bags, no tents, no shiny red Coleman stove. Mama wrestled the top rack out of the oven. "Our cooking stove," she announced.

Impressed, I raised a thumb of approval that seemed to please her.

Daddy dug through a five-pound sack of potatoes. "Phewee," he said, wrinkling his nose, "there's a rotten potato in here."

"And it's you," I said, grabbing a squealing Brenda around the waist and nuzzling her neck.

The simpler choice would have been to haul the trailer to the river rather than empty it into Daddy's pickup and the Ford. After countless armloads, we older girls, wearing cutoff jeans and dime-store flip-flops, helped the younger ones aboard. We formed a caravan: Daddy and a couple of girls in the pickup; Mama and the rest of us following in the Ford.

Our wheels hummed along the hot pavement as we drove southwest on a farm-to-market road that turned into dirt at the county line. The nearest town to us on the Pecos River would be Pandale, now listed as a ghost town. Pandale was reachable only by unpaved roads. A weathered sign posted outside the lonely general store read PANDALE, TEXAS/POPULATION VARIES.

That morning, with windows down and hair flying, we sped through the wilderness dotted with mesquite, desert willow, and scrub oak. The only signs of civilization belonged to nodding pump jacks, grazing cattle, and rotating windmills, which filled the stock tanks with precious water, enabling livestock to survive in uninhabitable land. Even the wild mule deer and pronghorn antelope drank from the stock tanks, increasing their herd size, which made for good hunting.

Daddy slowed the pickup and pulled off to the side of the road. We followed suit. He left his truck door open and walked toward us.

"What's wrong?" Mama yelled, sticking her head out the window.

"Lookie there," he said, leaning in toward Mama on the driver's side.

We all strained to see. Daddy's eyes were as sharp as a hawk's cutting circles in the sky. He had spotted a tarantula. Shivers went up my spine. The tarantula was the size of Daddy's fist. It lumbered near the edge of the road, strumming the air with its front legs.

Daddy pointed out several more. It was too early for the fall migration of mating tarantulas, but they were more active than usual. Storm clouds had likely produced a gullywasher, causing them to seek drier ground.

It was no secret that spiders scared the *bejeezus* out of me.

However, from the safety of our car that summer afternoon, I found Daddy's arachnology lesson fascinating. I watched the tarantulas with curiosity until Daddy hopped back into his pickup and drove off in another cloud of dust. We continued to bump along behind him on what looked and felt like a rutted wagon trail. A fine layer of grit began to coat my teeth. Daddy's brake lights winked on and off as he slowed down and abruptly sped up again.

"He's probably lost," Mama said. "One of his shortcuts!"

I smiled. Daddy had a reputation for shortcuts. Not very

good ones, either. Some of his shortcuts added as much as two hours to our drives. But that day, Daddy seemed to know exactly where we were headed. He zoomed over a cattle guard with us in close pursuit.

Suddenly a loud thumping noise filled the car. The steering wheel began to shimmy.

"Hells bells," Mama said, "I think we blew a tire."

Daddy barreled ever onward in the pickup, bouncing like a bucking bronco down the road, unaware that our old horse had thrown a shoe. Eventually, he realized we had fallen behind and he turned around. Flat tires, bathroom stops, missing a turnoff, nothing (except maybe Mama driving off to Colorado with some strange men) ruffled Daddy's feathers. He good-naturedly unloaded the entire trunk of supplies onto the side of the road and ferreted out the spare tire and jack.

He rolled the spare hand over hand. "You girls oughta look for arrowheads over yonder." He nodded. "I found one last week."

After changing the tire and repacking the trunk, we finally reached the banks of the Pecos River, an oasis in the midst of parched land. Sunlight broke into a thousand shimmering diamonds on the water. The river had carved a shallow canyon through layers of rock. Rock shelves, a dozen shades of charcoal, overhung the water. Cedars and scrub oaks lined the top of the canyon walls, their gnarled roots gripping the thin soil and rock to keep from tumbling into the river.

We drove out onto large slabs of bedrock almost as smooth and flat as concrete. I stretched my arms into the blue sky and turned my face toward the sun. I loved Daddy for finding this place, secluded from the outside world.

Daddy immediately started unpacking. He hefted the ten-gallon orange plastic water cooler down from the back of the pickup, its contents sloshing inside. The cooler, covered with dust, left a dark imprint on his white, sweat-soaked T-shirt just below his chest.

Vicki carried armloads of blankets from the trunk; Nancy helped Mama unload the food; and I unfolded Joni's playpen, where she was to sleep. Brenda and Patricia played games of patty-cake with Joni on the rug that Daddy had unfurled on the rocks.

"Davy, you sure we're safe from critters?" Mama asked. She leveled the oven rack onto a pile of river rocks.

Daddy dabbed the sweat from his forehead onto the sleeve of his T-shirt. "I'll tell you what," he answered, "we're pretty much surrounded by water. Whatever's out here would have to know how to swim."

Our camp rested atop the bedrock, surrounded by the river on all sides. The path we had driven across, lined with mesquite bushes and sage, narrowed and became interspersed with rivulets of water that led to our rock island.

"This here water will keep most everything away," Daddy reiterated, "except maybe cottonmouths."

"That's a comforting thought," Mama answered. "You girls hear that?"

"Yes, ma'am," we chorused.

"Snakes can swim?" one of the girls asked.

"Yes siree," Daddy said.

"How come they're called cottonmouths?" Patricia wanted to know. Patricia was our little zoologist. She had introduced me to my first horned toad, resting placidly in the palm of her hand.

"Their mouths are white inside, like a cotton boll," Daddy said. Then, as if remembering Patricia's penchant for lizards and such, he warned, "Don't be messing with any moving in the water."

After we unpacked, Daddy slipped his pocketknife into his front jeans pocket and rested his fishing pole, complete with an orange bobber, over his shoulder. The pole dipped up and down as he and Mama walked away. In addition to fishing, they planned to cut green tree branches to roast our hot dogs and marshmallows.

"Maybe we'll have us some rainbow trout instead of hot dogs for supper," Daddy said. He winked and slid his free hand across Mama's shoulders.

I watched as he and Mama walked out of sight. The weather forecast looked good; I had high hopes that the two of them were on the mend.

Joni napped in her playpen. I glanced her way periodically to make sure she still slept. A while later, I did a double take.

An enormous, hairy tarantula stood poised on the pink blanket no more than ten inches from Joni's face. Mercifully, Joni still slept. Little patches of perspiration clumped her blond hair into ringlets around her face.

Where was Clint Eastwood when you needed him?

I knew Joni might wake any moment.

"We've got to get Joni out," I told the girls.

We gathered and quickly formulated a plan. We decided to drop a large rock on the tarantula *after* I removed Joni. We couldn't risk accidentally dropping the rock on Joni or missing the tarantula with Joni so close by. Mustering all my courage, I reached into the playpen with the speed of a striking rattlesnake, grabbed Joni, and snatched her up into my arms.

Joni fussed, but, unbelievably, the tarantula didn't move. Not even a shiver. I quickly passed Joni off and we moved into Phase II of our plan.

Vicki hefted a large rock into my hands, which had begun to tremble slightly. I carefully positioned the rock above the unsuspecting tarantula, praying I wouldn't miss. If the tarantula jumped on any part of my flesh—*Had Daddy said they could jump?*—I would faint, never mind being bitten. I held my breath and dropped the rock.

Bull's-eye!

"We did it," everyone cheered.

When Mama and Daddy returned to camp, Daddy figured the tarantula must have hitched a ride when we stopped to change the flat tire and unloaded the contents of the trunk onto the side of the road. He felt certain we didn't have to worry about any more.

THAT EVENING, Daddy dredged fresh-caught trout in cornmeal and tossed the filets into a cast-iron skillet crackling with bacon grease, which we stored in an old Folgers tin. Mama covered potatoes in foil and buried them in the ashes at the edge of the fire until they were done and the foil had turned black. Daddy sat on the cooler and the rest of us atop blankets, savoring the sweet taste of trout and licking butter that melted over the sides of the potatoes.

Later, while toasting marshmallows, we heroines basked in Mama's and Daddy's astonishment and admiration as we told and retold how we had rescued Joni. Firelight lit our faces and our laughter traveled out into the night. Afterward, we settled onto our pallets for the night.

I lay outstretched on my back, my head cradled in my hands. I felt the firmness of the bedrock beneath my blankets. Some of the girls slept in the back of the pickup, but I preferred to be near the campfire, trusting that Daddy was right. There were no more tarantulas about. I luxuriated in the rare feeling of solitude. Embers glowed in the fire. A night symphony played within the canyon: the plangent howls of coyote harmonizing with chirping insects and rippling water.

My body ached from riding the rapids earlier that afternoon. I bumped against the rocks for so long that I wore a hole in my cutoff jeans. We older girls sat on our butts with our feet pointing downstream. Much to our delight, and Mama's chagrin (Mama had dreamed more than once that I had drowned), we shot through a chute of rapids flowing briskly over large stones. Laughing and sometimes coughing up mouthfuls of water, we lined up, over and over, for another ride.

Lying there, I felt slightly dizzy, as if I were still bobbing in the water. But when I looked up to see a million stars staring back at me, my full attention turned to the night sky. *Could anything be more beautiful?* The Milky Way looked like a veil tossed across the horizon.

As if on cue, a falling star flared across the sky. I gasped when I saw another and yet another. I stopped counting when the number reached into the teens. I had unknowingly stumbled upon the Perseid meteor shower, which peaks in August every year. Meteor after meteor hurled itself against the night sky. It was magical. I lay there enraptured. My mind stopped clamoring. Worry, longing, bewilderment—everything quieted. I became nothing other than a portal for amazement.

With the stars still falling all around me, I vowed to remember that night forever. I decided to fireproof it in my memory by painting a picture, much like Van Gogh's *Starry Night,* onto the canvas of my mind.

There would come a time, when summer passed and other winters came, that I would lie awake, beneath the tin roof of our ten-by-fifty-foot trailer, and summon up that picture of an infinite universe, spinning with stars and wonder.

THE NEXT few weeks in Ozona were punctuated with trips to the swimming pool south of town, next to the rodeo arena; Daddy's company barbecue, where he pounded spikes into the sand to play horseshoes with the other drillers; and quiet evenings with Daddy and Mama at home. The only disruption to our harmony came when Daddy asked, as he did most every year, where we wanted to go for vacation.

The vote was always the same. Seven to one to go to Grandma and Grandpa Vacha's. We saw them only once or twice a year and missed them terribly. Plus, to us, their farm was a veritable Disneyland. Thankfully, Mama didn't veto our vote.

As we drove down the two-lane highway toward Grandma and Grandpa's farm, I tried to cheer Mama up with a riddle, like the sphinx of Thebes.

What has four wheels, nine heads, twenty legs, and eighty moons?

Nobody guessed the answer: our family riding in the car—six children, two adults, and a wirehaired terrier named Freckles, which accounted for one of the heads and four of the legs. The moons totaled the number of moons in our fingernails.

The taller we girls grew, the tighter the squeeze into our Ford. The hot drive without air-conditioning tested everyone's patience, especially Mama's. Her switch extended the reach of

her arm and drove home her message—*I told you to stop it*—
with stinging clarity.

Suitcases on the floorboards leveled the backseat into one
large bed. Seat belts never crossed our minds. Mama and Daddy
decided to travel at night to lessen the number of bathroom stops
and to mollify our endless bickering.

Seven hours later, we turned off the highway to take the back
road to the farmhouse. It could hardly be called a road. Our
bumper hit one rut so hard Daddy thought we might lose the
oil pan. In the darkness, our headlights lit up a fallow field of
weeds and sent rabbits scurrying. Finally, we discovered a slim
path of mashed-down weeds made by Grandpa's tractor. And
then we saw it, the porch light slicing through the darkness, its
warm glow guiding us past my favorite oak tree and, finally, to
the farmhouse.

Grandpa opened the screen door yawning and waving.
Grandma followed with her permed curls slightly askew. The
dogs kept barking until Grandpa hushed them in Czech. Open
arms welcomed us onto the wooden porch that hugged the farmhouse.

I loved that porch. Grandpa had recently repainted the floor
a shiny gray, the pillars white, and the ceiling a light blue to
mimic the sky. The porch swing hung from rusted chains outside
the windows of the back bedroom.

Just inside the bedroom stood two iron beds, pushed against
either wall, where Mama, Daddy, and the younger girls would
sleep. My bed was to be the couch in the dining room. Vicki and
Nancy were assigned to the attic with its feather bed and a trunk
of yellowed Sears catalogues.

I marvel that Grandma and Grandpa welcomed our herd
for two weeks. Nine heads, twenty legs, and eighty moons had

a way of upsetting the status quo. On the first morning, Vicki and Nancy, trying to be helpful, tossed their chamber-pot pee out the attic window onto the tin roof. Trouble was, Grandpa had carefully guttered the roof to collect rainwater into a large holding tank beside the porch. Not only did their *night water* contaminate the rainwater, but it smelled ripe in the noonday sun. Grandma suggested, none too gently, that from then on they bring the chamber pot downstairs in the morning so it could be emptied properly.

For reasons no one understood, Brenda and Joni decided to use one of the window screens as a cheese grater. Grandma fussed over that screen like a mama bird and kept repeating, *Jezis Maria, Jezis Maria!*

Then I cornered one of the farm cats underneath the porch, convinced I could befriend him like I had my stray, Midnight. But the wild tom had other ideas. He clawed five bleeding lines down the side of my face. *Jezis Maria,* Grandma cried as she ran for her rubbing alcohol and iodine.

And so it went.

Grandpa didn't pray so much to Jesus and Mary. His mild oath included the word *prdel,* which loosely translated to *my ass!* Over the years we picked up a few Czech words because Grandpa and Grandma never bothered to leave the room to talk privately. They merely switched to speaking Czech, which always made me wonder which one of us had done something wrong.

For the most part, however, Grandma and Grandpa spoke English, laughed, loved, and fed us. The screened-in porch, with its massive oak table and assorted chairs, was where we took our noon meal, the most substantial of the day. Two pie safes, originally made to safeguard the baked goods from critters, lined the porch walls.

After setting out the food, Grandma wiped her hands on her apron and opened the back screen door. She called Grandpa to dinner by repeatedly striking a triangular iron dinner bell hanging on a nail, yodeling *To-nee, To-nee*. Grandpa and the rest of us would put aside our chores, wash up in a basin on the porch, then take our seats at the table.

Grandma was a wonderful down-home cook. Nancy, who had become interested in cooking since coming to live with us, eagerly helped Grandma in the kitchen. Being the tomboy, I preferred working outside.

That summer the rain, soil, and sun coalesced into a perfect growing season. The cotton in the surrounding fields stood bushy and tall. Uncle Willard, Grandpa's younger brother on the next farm over, had a bumper crop of cotton and said he could sure use any help we could give him. Farm wages were meager, but whatever money we made helped fill our family coffer. I would have done the work for free anyway.

I considered myself a good cotton picker and prided myself on my strength. I could drag the twenty-foot sack of cotton, the strap burrowing ever deeper into my shoulder, down a long row of cotton. Sweat ran off me in rivulets; a cotton field is nature's sauna.

"Would you look at that?" Uncle Willard clucked when I helped him hoist my cotton sack onto the scale. It weighed right around a hundred pounds. Uncle Willard had a little Tom Sawyer in him; he made me want to strive to pull even heavier loads.

Before leaving for the cotton fields that first morning, Grandma came at me with an old-fashioned, handmade sunbonnet as if she were trying to rope a calf.

I backed away, protesting, but to no avail. Grandma cornered me and muttered, *Jezis Maria, do you want to die of sunstroke,* and tied the floppy bonnet snugly under my chin.

The enchantment of working for Uncle Willard had a little something to do with his son Danny. Danny was my age and had an ease about him. A shock of brown wavy hair, high cheekbones, and freckles accentuated his face. When he smiled, so did his eyes. He was lanky and self-assured. Some boys might be nervous around a passel of girls, but Danny had a sister and seemed quite comfortable.

"Seems you're more interested in this crop of girls here than the cotton," Grandpa teased him one afternoon.

Danny blushed and studied his hands but, to his credit, Grandpa's teasing didn't keep him away. He must have enjoyed the attention we bestowed on him; six girls can be a powerful magnet.

Nancy once remarked that we older girls all took turns liking Danny during our summer vacations. I don't remember ever giving up my turn. I wanted to sit beside Danny on the porch swing; walk with him, barefoot, to the tank as grasshoppers whirred around us; hide with him forever, listening to the rain fall on the roof of Grandpa's car, where we escaped one afternoon to avoid getting wet.

Even though Danny qualified as my kissing cousin, we never kissed. But I had been kissed once by an older boy behind our trailer in Fort Stockton. The suddenness of his lips on mine had surprised me, but I didn't object, though I suspected Mama wouldn't approve. His kiss was soft, gentle. For days afterward, I replayed the kiss over and over in my mind, which confused me because I didn't particularly like the boy or want another kiss— just the delicious memory of that gentle press upon my lips.

The only physical contact between Danny and me was when

he casually held my thumb between his fingers one humid afternoon as we talked, sitting atop a cotton sack. I remember the
electricity I felt at the warmth of his skin next to mine.

But he held my thumb for a long while, I reasoned . . . *he
held it gently . . . he had not held Vicki's or Nancy's thumb . . .
he sought me out in the field . . . he . . .*

These thoughts kindled my imagination as I crawled beneath
my sheets on the couch that night. In the dining room where I
slept, the black and silver potbellied stove took a summer sab-
batical from heating the farmhouse. A glass jar of fresh-baked
sugar cookies waited for tomorrow on a ledge leading into the
kitchen.

I lay there, moonlight spilling through the window, listening
to the clock chime atop the china cabinet. I padded to the window
and looked out. Moonlight fell on the ladder resting against the
garage where we had been helping Grandpa replace the shingles.
Moonlight also fell on the old tractor, the one Grandpa taught
me to drive. Everything looked beautiful, awash in silvery light,
even the bloody axe cleaved into the tree stump where Grandpa
lopped off the heads of chickens for our noon meals.

When I lay back down, I raised my arms toward the ceiling in
the moonlight, rubbing them as if I had lathered on a silky moon
cream. I wondered if Danny might come tomorrow to help with
the roof, doubtful since it would be hard for him to break away
from picking cotton. Still, I pictured him arriving early, looking
past the stove to the couch where I lay. I began to make up my
own episode of the Nora Drake soap opera. If only I had a flowing blue gown the color of the porch ceiling.

In anticipation of Danny, I smoothed out my frizzy hair. I
eyed the distressingly flat place where my marble-sized breasts
hid under my shortie pajamas, patterned with rosebuds. I rolled

to my side and looked down. Nothing. I brought my elbows together and clasped my hands. I looked as if I were praying. Actually, I was praying—for cleavage. I hunched my shoulders forward to create a line that divided two pieces of flesh. From a distance, it might pass for cleavage. I decided to sleep in this contortionist pose all night, just in case.

I wanted Danny to swoop in the next morning to discover that the girl whose thumb he had held a day before was actually a woman in the making; the one true love of his heart. I awoke in the morning to the sound of Grandma making prune kolaches in the kitchen. I took note that I was on my stomach, one hand dangling off the couch and drool all over my pillow and hair.

Thankfully, Danny had not come.

"WHO WANTS to ride on the tractor to the mailbox?" Grandpa asked.

All of us jumped up. When I asked Grandpa if I could drive, he nodded and hitched the wood wagon to the tractor for the half-mile ride. Many a farm boy learned to drive a tractor as soon as his feet could reach the pedal. Grandpa wasn't sexist; he let me drive down the dirt road to the mailbox while he sat some distance away in the wagon with the rest of the girls. After we retrieved the mail, Vicki asked if she could drive back.

I swung out of the seat and stood upright on the axle beside her as she slipped in behind the wheel. I remained on the axle and held on to the tractor seat. Vicki steered straight down the dirt road without incident, grinning up at me. Nearing the farmhouse, we needed to bank left to stop in front of the garage. Vicki turned the wheel but failed to brake. We overran the garage and headed toward a large tree beside the fence.

I looked down at Vicki. She had stopped smiling. She gave no indication she planned on stopping. Her hands gripped the wheel, but she didn't move.

Grandpa sat too far away to help. I couldn't reach the brake. If I grabbed the wheel and swerved, we might miss the tree, but we still had the fence to worry about. Plus, I might flip the tractor and send us flying.

I suddenly saw my hand reach down and turn off the key. The tractor immediately rolled to a stop, only yards from the tree.

"Woo-wee," Grandpa said, "that was some fast thinking."

It amazed even me. When Grandpa told Mama and Daddy that I had saved us from crashing into a tree, I pulled back my shoulders and stood taller. I liked being a hero. But it had been, truly, a moment of grace. And *Grace*, being what she is, kept her mouth shut and let me take all the credit.

Vicki, however, wasn't so quiet. She told me she had pulled Grandpa aside to tell him she could have stopped the tractor by herself. She said Grandpa patted her shoulder and said, "I know you could have."

Grandpa was a farmer through and through. He knew what seeds needed cultivating—to help the cotton grow tall.

ONE MORNING near the end of our vacation, we climbed onto the roof of Grandpa's garage to finish removing the last of the decrepit shingles before nailing on new ones.

Daddy squatted on the high ridge of the roof, prying up shingles, the sun behind him. Mama and I worked side by side, down near the lower edge of the roof, our backs to the ladder.

I heard Daddy teasingly call, "Terry, lookie here."

I shaded my eyes and looked up at him. He smiled and held aloft a wriggling garden spider the length of his little finger. Then Daddy did what I least expected him to. He tossed the spider into the air toward me. I screamed and jumped backward off the roof.

Daddy looked stricken. Mama's face went white.

"Davy, how could you?" Mama shouted. She rushed down the ladder toward me.

Somehow, I landed on my feet in the soft dirt, shaken but unhurt.

"She's white as a sheet," Mama said, glowering up at Daddy.

I knew Daddy meant no harm; if he had guessed my reaction, he wouldn't have tossed the spider. But the incident did reveal his lack of understanding of just how much spiders frightened me.

Mama told me to rotate my ankles and shift my weight side to side. Satisfied that I had not broken a bone, she told me to go on off and *collect* myself; I had done enough work for the time being.

"He didn't mean for me to jump," I told her.

"Hell is paved with good intentions," she said.

That is how I came to sit in my oak tree, out by the barn, all alone, listening to the others go about their business. In the lofty arms of the ancient oak, I rested my back against the rough bark, sad to think summer was almost over.

I sat there a long while, as still as lichen; so still, in fact, I could almost feel the sap rising in me, almost feel my roots and the tree's roots intertwining as if we belonged to each other. She was my Great Mother, my Sistine Chapel, my Tree of Life.

Her massive limbs reach outward like a thousand-armed bo-dhisattva. From within her branches, a canopy of waxy leaves and dappled sunlight arch overhead. Long tresses of gray-green moss dangle from above. A lone ant traverses the furrows in the bark where my hand rests. I notice a tiny white wildflower blooming just outside her circle of shade. I think I must include the wildflower. If I can remember it juxtaposed next to her, I will never forget what it feels like to sit here, a slight breeze blowing, muffled voices coming from the farmhouse, utter contentment in every breath.

Looking up into her branches, I whispered the secret I had been carrying. "We're moving again."

I hardly reacted to the news when Mama told me earlier. I hadn't even asked *why*, only *when* and *where*.

"Before school starts," Mama said. "To Odessa, Texas."

Moving had become as commonplace as the changing of seasons. What use was there in railing against the inevitable? Our move to Ozona had been merely a summer sojourn, a place for Daddy to move the trailer to teach Mama a lesson.

"Why do we have to have winter?" I asked Mama. "Why can't summer last forever?"

My question took Mama by surprise. She looked at me oddly, like maybe the heat in the cotton field *had* addled my brain, despite Grandma's sunbonnet. But she saw I was serious.

"I don't know," she said thoughtfully. "Maybe we have winter so we can appreciate summer more."

I traced my finger along a crevice of the tree's bark, contemplating what Mama had said. It seemed to me I could appreciate a thousand summers without the help of a single winter.

Mama in front of our trailer

Odessa, Texas

IN 1932, COWGIRL Grace Hendricks roped a jackrabbit from
horseback in five seconds flat in the Odessa Rodeo, winning
against numerous cowboys. Even though the roping competition
took place three decades before I moved to Odessa (and my phi-
losophy leaned more toward freeing rabbits than roping them),

it was fitting that I moved into a town where a young cowgirl triumphed over a few cowboys.

You might say I found my courage in Odessa, in more ways than one.

My first day at Crockett Junior High, I couldn't locate the science room. I walked into class shortly after the bell rang. The teacher assumed I was lost.

"This is science," he informed me.

"I know," I said, looking for an unoccupied desk near the front.

He perused the class list. "What's your name?"

"Terry Vacha."

"You spell Terry with a *y*, like a boy?"

I nodded.

He rubbed his chin, looked out at the boys, and smiled. "Well, looks like we got us a girl in class after all."

The boys guffawed.

I quickly scooted into an empty seat and studied the rows of boys who wore collared shirts—school rules—tucked in. Not one girl in sight. Though I wasn't the first girl to enroll in science at Crockett, no other girls were assigned to this particular class. Maybe somebody knew something I didn't.

During the next several days, I smiled politely when the science teacher teased me about being the only girl. I didn't mind so much. I liked science, and the ratio of twenty-something boys to one girl made me feel almost popular. However, it was becoming increasingly clear that my science teacher thought I had breached some imaginary testosterone boundary. I kept up with the boys academically, but the teacher wouldn't let the matter rest.

Finally, one afternoon, he asked me point-blank, in front of my classmates, "So you think you can handle anything in this class a boy can handle?"

All eyes stared at me.

"I believe so," I said, feeling slightly uneasy.

"Even a paddling?" he asked.

I paused.

Was it a trap?

If I said no, I would be saying that boys were somehow better. But if I said yes, I could be setting myself up for a paddling. As Daddy often said, I was between a rock and a hard place.

Paddling was an accepted form of corporal punishment in those days, especially among boys who acted up in school. My science teacher had, evidently, reached the conclusion that my bottom, not my brains, could best prove my equality in the classroom.

It was 1961, the same year President John F. Kennedy established the President's Commission on the Status of Women. Gloria Steinem would not become a national icon for the feminist movement for another eight years. The game What Shall I Be?, offering young girls six careers to choose from when they grew up—teacher, actress, nurse, model, ballet dancer, or airline hostess—would not debut on toy-store shelves for another five years.

I hailed from a hardy line of women. Grandma Skinner held her own against any farmer in the field. Grandma Harless, Mama's mother, single-handedly remodeled her living room complete with built-in bookshelves. Even Mama tried her hand at repairing appliances, the most notable being the broken toaster. Granted, after Mama's tinkering, the toast popped a whopping three feet into the air, somersaulting across the kitchen counter, but we had toast nonetheless.

I had proved myself in the cotton field, tooled leather in another class filled with boys, and out-bull's-eyed an archery teacher. I liked math and science and was good at both. Yet none of this seemed to be enough.

Could I take a paddling in class?

I had no intention of backing down, so I agreed to undergo a paddling in front of the boys.

"Well, come on up here, then," the science teacher said, rummaging for his paddle in a cabinet beneath a row of windows. The boys in the class whispered and snickered.

"You sure you want to go through with this?" the teacher asked as I stood beside him.

I nodded even though my face had begun to flush. Usually, the boys received their paddlings privately, in the hallway, and not for *fun* but for misbehavior. Usually, the principal or another teacher stood nearby as a witness to the incident.

My witnesses would be my male classmates.

"Okay, bend over," the science teacher instructed.

This part humiliated me the most. Bending over, sticking out my butt. The boys squirmed in their seats. I think we all felt uncomfortable at this point, even the science teacher, but I had called his bluff, and unless I backed down, he wasn't about to.

The science teacher grasped the wooden paddle in both hands and smacked my backside. Just once. It stung, but not overly so. But my pride and dignity stung mightily. None of the boys in class had been asked to prove his legitimacy by submitting to a public paddling. I stoically walked back to my seat, feigning equanimity though I felt humiliated beyond belief.

I lasted through the bus ride home, up until the moment Mama walked into the trailer-house door. When I saw her face, I couldn't hold back my tears.

Mama listened in disbelief. "What a harebrained idiot!" she exclaimed.

The next day she stormed into school like a mother bear, looking to avenge her cub.

"You go on to your other classes," she fumed. "I'll take care of this."

All day long, I dreaded facing my science teacher. Obviously, I had failed his test; I couldn't take a paddling like a boy. I had run home and tattled to my mother. Mustering all my courage, I walked into the classroom. The teacher looked at me and motioned for me to approach his desk.

"I had a talk with your mom," he said.

I held my breath.

"I owe you an apology," he said. "What I did was thoughtless, even though I meant it only in jest."

"I shouldn't have agreed," I said.

"No. I shouldn't have singled you out. I'm sorry I embarrassed you."

He apologized again in front of the boys. I worried that my tattling proved his hypothesis until a boy named Roger looked at me and smiled in a way that said, "You deserved an apology."

After class, Roger asked if I planned to attend the formal dance coming up in a couple of weeks. I blushed and nodded, though I knew he wasn't inquiring about a date. The faculty had said no dates—they didn't want boys worrying about being turned down or girls about being asked.

The day of the dance, Nancy and I hurried through our chores so we could spend hours getting ready. That evening, thanks to Vicki, my frizzy hair had been tamed by rolling it onto orange-juice cans, then spraying it heavily with Aqua Net.

I glanced at the clock, then sniffed the flowery bouquet of Mama's Evening in Paris cologne on the underside of my wrist—Mama always perfumed the pulse points on her neck and wrists.

I smoothed down my gown again, admiring the gathers of pale green netting. No one at school would guess that Nancy's dress or mine had come from the thrift store; they both looked practically new.

I looked out the window. *One hundred fifty-one.* I thought surely Mama would have come home by now.

I hoped Roger would ask me to dance, especially after I overheard some girls talking in my Spanish class.

"You have to wait until a boy asks you to dance," one girl said.

"Yeah," another agreed, "and if you don't get asked, you're a wallflower."

One hundred fifty-two, fifty-three, fifty-four.

Vicki, who wanted to become a hairdresser when she grew up, also styled Nancy's fine, limp hair into soft, flattering curls. Vicki could work magic with a hairbrush, bobby pins, and hair spray. Nancy and I were quite pleased with the reflections smiling back at us from the bedroom mirror.

One hundred fifty-five.

Had Mama forgotten? Surely not. She had been so excited about finding our dresses at the thrift store. I imagined my girlfriend Michelle looking around for me at the dance, wondering why I was late, or if I was coming at all.

Mama could have had any number of reasons for being late: her part-time job as a cocktail waitress at one of the bars, which I did not brag about; the classes she took at Odessa College to become a licensed practical nurse (LPN), which I did brag about; and this could take the longest of all, her enjoying herself with a good ole boy, a bottle of beer, and a jukebox playing country-and-western songs.

One hundred fifty-six.

Mama was one hundred and fifty-six cars late.

I invented the Car-Counting Game in Fort Stockton, Texas, when I was twelve, the afternoon Mama dropped me off at the Laundromat with a mountain of laundry. Our washing machine had broken, so Mama handed me a fistful of change and waved good-bye.

"See you later, alligator," she quipped.

The Laundromat smelled of bleach. A coin clinked rhythmically in a nearby dryer. An old washboard, screwed to the wall, reminded me of wash day at Grandma and Grandpa Vacha's farm in East Texas, which Grandpa began by lighting a fire in the backyard beneath two black kettles of rainwater. Grandma scrubbed the dirty clothes against a tin washboard, then fed them into a wringer that Grandpa hand cranked. The memory of Grandma's ample underwear on the clothesline, waving to the cows, made me smile. Grandma wasn't one to flaunt her underwear.

Neither was I.

In the Laundromat, I discreetly folded our clean, warm panties and bras and tucked them into the bottom of the basket. When I finished folding the laundry, I set the heaping basket onto the floor near the door. After an hour passed, I dialed the pay phone.

"Hello." It was Vicki.

"Hi, it's me. Is Mama there?"

"No. Where are you?"

"Still at the Laundromat. Has she called?"

"No. I don't know where she is." I heard clanking and voices in the background.

"What are y'all doing?"

"Nancy's making fudge," she said.

"Well, tell Mama I'm done, if she calls. Save me a piece, okay?"

"Okay," she said and hung up.

I fed a dime into the Coke machine and pressed the cool glass against my lips. A Coke to drink by oneself was a rare luxury. Generally, after grocery shopping on payday, we lined up six empty jelly glasses along the kitchen counter. We poured three bottles of Coke into those glasses with the precision of aeronautical engineers preparing Alan Shepard for his first spaceflight. Then the trick was to make your portion last as long as possible without completely losing its fizz.

Still no Mama.

When I could find nothing else to occupy me, I came up with the idea of the Car-Counting Game. The premise was to guess how many cars would drive past the window before Mama came. If I reached the number I had guessed, I started over with a new guess. That day, I guessed over and over again until dusk. Finally, Mama screeched to a halt at the front door.

"Sorry, hon," she apologized, a faint odor of beer filling the space between us. "Time just got away from me. You been waiting long?"

Only hours and hours, I wanted to say. But I didn't dare.

"Yes, ma'am," I said.

AND NOW I was waiting for Mama again—so long that I had begun to think Mama had bought our dresses for nothing. Nancy gave up her lookout post and walked to the back bedroom. Just as I let go of the curtain, two headlights pulled in beside the trailer.

"She's here, she's here," I yelled to Nancy.

Nancy's heels clicked against the linoleum floor as she hurried past the picnic table. We slammed the trailer door behind us and skittered down the steps. I sniffed, but I couldn't smell any alcohol on Mama's breath. She handed over two corsage boxes, one for Nancy and the other for me.

"They're synthetic," Mama said. "Orchids made from wood pulp. You wear them on your wrist. It's not every day you girls go to a formal dance. I wanted you to have something special."

I didn't know if the tears I stifled were because I was touched that Mama spent precious money on our corsages, if I was mad that she was late, or if I was sad that I felt torn in two. I knew, upon our arrival at school, that I would exit our car and enter the gymnasium wearing Mama's corsage, pretending to be one of the happiest seventh graders there. The problem was that my outside didn't always match my inside.

Besides my friend Michelle, nobody at school knew about my home life—not Roger, my teachers, or my other classmates. I didn't want to be set apart. So I split myself in two. I thought of myself as School Terry and Home Terry. School Terry was carefree and her worries small—like what she should do for her science project or whom she should sit beside at lunch. Home Terry was much older and more responsible; she kept the home fires burning, cooked and cleaned, and watched over the other girls when Mama was absent, trying to keep them safe, even when things didn't feel safe.

One weekend, not long after the dance, Home Terry became concerned.

Mama had arranged for us girls to go away with Bud, Rose, and their two boys for two nights. Bud and Rose had moved their trailer from Fort Stockton to live beside us again in Odessa. Their young boys were playmates with Joni and Brenda, and the four of them were happy to be reunited. I liked Rose. She had taught us to cook enchiladas and protected us during the tornado, but she never stood up for herself, especially to Bud. I didn't trust Bud and had come to suspect that he knew Mama a little too well.

I was shocked when Mama told me she was sending us out of town. Besides needing to stay home and work on my semester science project, I didn't like the idea of traveling to another town to stay with people we didn't know.

"What are you doing?" I asked Mama.

"None of your business," she said.

I sighed loudly. Mama had left me in charge of the girls plenty of times; I couldn't understand why we had to go away to stay at a stranger's house. Maybe Mama wanted the trailer to herself. I half expected to see Dusty's tour bus parked outside our trailer when we returned.

Bud and Rose drove us through a decrepit oil town and finally turned in to a grassless yard overgrown with weeds. A rusted-out car chassis sat atop stacked cinder blocks. A mangy dog nosed through an overturned trash can. I felt inexplicably vulnerable. Later, lying on sheets that had not been laundered for a good long while, I grew furious with Mama.

How could she allow us to be taken to a place like this?

An endless stream of strangers wandered in and out of the squalid house. I spent that night and the next day pacing from one sister to the other, trying to make sure everyone remained safe. Warning bells kept going off inside my head. Years later, when Patricia confided that she had been molested by someone outside our family, my mind traveled back to that dreadful weekend. Could it have happened then? Could she have been spared? Maybe I had not been vigilant enough.

When we returned home, I marched into Mama's bedroom, mustering every ounce of my courage.

"Don't ever, ever send us somewhere like that again," I demanded. "I didn't feel safe. I didn't feel like I could keep the girls safe. It was an awful experience!"

Mama raised her eyebrows while I spoke. My forcefulness surprised even me. Amazingly, Mama apologized. But she had apologized to Home Terry.

On Monday morning, School Terry bounced into the classroom, pretending she had experienced the same weekend as everyone else—she acted as if she had gone to a friend's house to spend the night, maybe even see a movie. She wore the pendant Roger had recently given her, half a jagged heart. Roger kept the other half tucked into his jeans pocket. School Terry was adamant about one thing. She didn't want anyone to meet Home Terry—especially not Roger.

It was fairly simple to keep the two Terrys apart. Mama rarely allowed us to have friends in the house, and we certainly couldn't date. So even though School Terry and Home Terry shared the same body, they lived in two entirely different worlds.

SEVERAL WEEKS after the unnerving trip out of town, Bud knocked on our trailer door. I opened it to see him grasping the top of a clear plastic bag with a tarantula trapped inside. The tarantula was huge, hairy, and annoyed.

"Oh, my gosh!" I exclaimed. "Where did you find it?"

"On the Andrews Highway," he said, grinning.

Mama sat cross-legged on the couch with a syringe and needle in one hand and an orange in the other. She had been poking the orange repeatedly with the needle, pushing down the plunger.

"I can't believe you're the same girl who jumped off the garage roof," Mama said, motioning to the tarantula with her syringe.

It was true. I had decided to face my fear head-on. I thought studying spiders rather than running from them might make me more courageous. I had begun to realize that courage wasn't the absence of fear; it was a matter of forging ahead—despite my fear. So, for my science project, I had decided to collect spiders.

"Just a minute," I told Bud as I soaked a cotton ball in alcohol and dropped it into a Mason jar.

Bud waited, holding the bagged tarantula. He looked toward Mama. "What are you doing to the orange?"

"I'm practicing giving shots," Mama said. Her nursing books cluttered the end table in the living room. Mama had her ambitions; she liked to tell people she was training in the medical field. On the nights she didn't weave down the hallway from too much drink or from taking her headache pills, she usually studied in her bedroom. It comforted me to see her on the bed, reading her books while I researched and identified my spider specimens in a circle of light at the kitchen picnic table.

After I plunked down the Mason jar with the cotton ball inside, Bud handed me the plastic bag. I paused. Eight hairy legs waved about. Mama and Bud watched me as I gingerly grasped the top, then guided the tarantula onto the cotton ball inside the Mason jar. I didn't know I had been holding my breath until I screwed the lid on tight.

My eyes met Bud's. We both knew he had given me the

crown jewel of my spider collection. I thanked him again, but instead of leaving, he waited, looking toward Mama for some sign. She had set aside the orange and syringe and picked up a study sheet listing the bones of the human body. I had been helping her memorize the list earlier, making sure she pointed to the right places on her body as she rattled off tibia, fibula, and femur. Mama, intent on memorizing the different names, had tuned out both me and Bud.

Finally, he said good-bye and closed the door softly behind him.

My suspicions about Mama and Bud had begun the previous summer when Bud, Rose, and their sons went camping with us at the Pecos River. Wondering if I might see another meteor shower, I had lain awake late into the night, looking up at the stars.

Bud rose from his pallet and tiptoed into the bushes, away from the dim glow of the campfire. Mama soon followed. Rose and Daddy slept. The moon had time to travel behind the rock outcroppings before Mama and Bud crept back together. I raised my head and openly stared at the two of them. Their eyes traveled from me to each other. I suspected that Bud's marriage vows to Rose were either in jeopardy or had already been broken.

Mama turned her back on me, assuming I would hold my tongue. She kept upping the ante of my love. Bud, unsure of my silence, gingerly scooted underneath the blanket toward Rose. He stole another glance to see if I was still watching him. I was.

The tarantula may have been payment for my continued silence or yet another excuse to knock on Mama's door.

On the day my science project was due, I chose my favorite skirt and blouse, clasped Roger's jagged heart about my neck, and cautiously carried my large cream-colored gift box into school. I couldn't wait to see what my science teacher thought about a girl collecting spiders. The army of spiders looked even more menacing mounted on white cotton. Mama had had a nightmare about the tarantula crawling off the cotton to lurk in a corner of our closet.

"Is this your project?" the science teacher asked when I gently lowered the covered box onto the edge of his desk.

I nodded.

He leaned in close, casting a shadow onto the glossy lid. Then he paused, as if trying to guess the contents.

"What do we have here?" he asked in a tone I sometimes used to humor Brenda and Joni.

With his nose only inches away, he lifted the lid. When he saw the sheer mass and size of the spiders, he reared backward in his chair and gasped, "Holy shit."

SCHOOL TERRY loved the A-plus the science teacher gave her on the project, but Home Terry had more important things to worry about. Since Mama had marched into the science teacher's classroom at the beginning of the semester months earlier, things had disintegrated at home. Mama and Daddy were fighting more.

"What happened?" I asked Daddy at the end of the semester as he stood over the stove flipping pancakes. He sported a bruise and cut under his left eye.

"Your mom took off her heel last night and hit me," he said.

"Oh," I responded. Neither Home Terry nor School Terry wanted to know why.

A few days later, both of my worlds collided.

Mama picked up the hot iron she had been using to press her blouse and swung at Daddy. It was anyone's guess what started their dispute. She and Daddy yelled and began to wrestle. Suddenly Daddy had his hands around Mama's throat. He squeezed until she went limp.

I ran out the back door screaming for Bud. "Daddy's killing Mama, hurry!"

Bud sprinted out of his trailer barefoot and shirtless. He flew into our trailer while I waited outside with the girls. To my knowledge, Daddy had never raised his hand against Mama, ever. Not against any of us. He was patient and lighthearted, kind, and funny. I cried for whatever it was that caused him and Mama so much pain. It seemed to me that our family was on a downward spiral, pulling us into darker and scarier places than any of us had ever been.

"Your mom's going to be fine," Bud said, coming out of the trailer and over to where we stood in the front yard.

I looked out over the heads of my sisters huddled around me. I couldn't see all the way into the future, but I had begun to doubt whether Mama or our family would ever be fine. It seemed to me that we were trapped inside walls that nobody could see, like one of my spiders in the Mason jar.

Still wearing Roger's heart, I counted out the years on my fingertips. It was a new counting game: thirteen, fourteen, fifteen, sixteen, seventeen, eighteen. Six more years—that's all I had left until I was old enough to leave home.

JoAnn and Mama wearing blond wigs

Grand Junction, Colorado
Revisited

I SAID GOOD-BYE TO Roger and returned his heart pendant.
It didn't seem right taking it to Colorado; he might want to
give it to another girl.

Vicki and I had yet to start and finish a grade in the same

school since leaving Iowa. We had been in Odessa less than nine months.

"I'm sorry," I told Roger as I laid the pendant on his palm.

He quietly reached into his jeans pocket, pulled out his half of the heart, then hurled both halves onto the school roof.

A few days later, a truck towed our trailer almost eight hundred miles northwest to a trailer park in Grand Junction, Colorado. Upon our arrival, I timidly knocked on my friend Janet's door. Would she want to be friends again? We had been in fifth grade together, two years earlier. I worried that Janet's parents might remember Mama's comings and goings with Dusty, and, if so, they might frown on Janet's befriending me again. But when Janet's mom opened the door, I was greeted with warm hugs from both Janet and her mom.

The next day Nancy, Vicki, Patricia, and I transferred to new schools with less than two months left in the school year. Vicki headed off to sixth grade and Patricia to third. Joni stayed home with Mama and Brenda. Mama, now twenty-eight, had withdrawn from Odessa College's school of nursing and already called the registration office at Mesa College in Grand Junction to inquire about their nursing program.

I turned thirteen a few weeks after we arrived. Mama brought home a chocolate cake and decorated it with a ceramic figurine of a young girl wearing a yellow gown, and two small Siamese cats. Mama lit thirteen candles and she and my sisters sang an animated "Happy Birthday."

"How does it feel to be a teenager?" Mama asked.

Wobbly, I might have said if I had really thought about it, *like a new colt trying to stand on all fours.*

I made a wish that we wouldn't move anymore, blew out the candles, then licked the chocolate frosting from the bottom of the figurines before setting them onto the picnic table. Mama cut the cake into wedges and gave me the largest piece, with an entire yellow rose made of frosting.

I didn't know, as I dabbed the last crumbs from my plate, just how unlucky thirteen would be.

By the first frost, my hopes for a new start in a new place had withered on the vine.

One gray afternoon, I backed away from Mama in the living room.

"I don't want a shot," I protested.

The few shots I had seen Mama give herself left her alternately groggy, hyper, or moody.

"It's only a vitamin B-12 shot," she said. "It'll give you energy."

"I don't need energy."

"Teresa Eilene, get over here this instant!"

I huffed and stomped over to where Mama stood.

She jerked my arm in front of her. "Believe me, they won't take any lip from you at the convent," she said.

She flicked her wrist and thrust the needle into my arm. She withdrew the needle and dabbed my blood with a cotton ball.

I bet they don't make you get shots at the convent, either, I thought.

Recently, Mama had taken to pointing her finger into Nancy's, Vicki's, or my face and warning, "If you girls don't shape up, I'm going to send you to a convent."

I couldn't fathom how Mama had come up with this idea. We weren't even Catholic. I knew little about convents. In literature, King Arthur's wife, Guinevere, had taken refuge in a convent after being discovered with Sir Lancelot. In real life, I heard that nuns sometimes took care of orphans and wayward girls in convents—not always kindly. Somewhere along the line, Mama had conflated the chaste life of nuns with punishment.

I honestly didn't know whether Mama was bluffing. Her truths and nontruths were hard to discern. If anyone *could* arrange such a thing, Mama got my vote. She always got my vote. It wasn't beyond the realm of possibility to think that the pope or even the National Guard might acquiesce if Mama asked for help.

My biggest challenge since turning thirteen had been how to "shape up" to Mama's satisfaction. It seemed nearly impossible to please her anymore. So many things could go wrong. The girls minded me well enough, but there were always chores left undone, crumbs on the countertops, a dirty smudge on the linoleum floor, a rogue load of laundry still drying on the clothesline, or a forgotten rug dangling on the side-yard fence after we had beaten it clean with a broom. It seemed the harder I tried, the more Mama found wanting.

Certainly I had my moments of *not trying,* of sulking around Mama when we disagreed, or of letting her know I disapproved of her going out. But basically, we were good kids. We went to school and came home. We methodically checked items off her to-do list, made dinner, watched the younger girls, and did our homework. Our rap sheet was lackluster at best. Our most serious offense seemed to be growing up and asking questions. Should life be lived Mama's way or was there another way? Was the emperor—or the empress, in our case—in fact wearing clothes?

Mama's threat to send us to a convent was intended to scare us into submission. And for a time, it worked. I didn't take the possibility of separation lightly; it weighed heavily on me, like the cotton sacks I used to drag. Even though I planned to leave home at eighteen, I couldn't imagine my life now without Mama or my sisters. I remembered how forlorn I had felt kissing Mama's faded photograph in Iowa. So I did the only thing I knew to do: I tried even harder.

In our effort to shape up, Vicki, Nancy, and I came up with creative ways to make our chores more fun. Our family of eight generated mountains of ironing each week. We tossed the ironing into a basket in our back closet that sometimes reached Everest proportions, nearly touching the clothes bar at the top of the closet. One of our brainstorms was an ironing party to stave off the drudgery of ironing. In preparation, one of us made fudge while the others sprinkled the clothes, rolled them into tight balls, and wedged them into a basket.

Our late-night ironing parties would never make us popular at school—in fact, just the opposite. We knew that. Still, when Janet wanted to spend the night, I asked her if she could bring her mom's iron and ironing board. I thought the phone had gone dead.

After a moment of silence, she faltered, "Yeah, I guess."

I admit that the sight of Janet lugging an ironing board up our trailer steps did look odd. But the unorthodoxy of it all was soon forgotten as we unfolded the ironing boards in the living room, played vinyl forty-fives of rock-and-roll music, and danced and swayed as we took turns ironing.

Mama wasn't there. She still visited Timbuktu regularly when Daddy was out of town, which seemed to be most of the time now. I didn't know if Daddy's absence was by necessity or design. The night Janet came to our ironing party, we let the little ones stay up. Since Mama wasn't there, I decided to poke some fun at her.

Mama loved opera, and especially tenors. Every time she

played opera in our presence, we collectively groaned. The girls looked puzzled when I fished out one of Mama's Mario Lanza records and set the needle down on "Santa Lucia."

It wasn't until I picked up a spoon like a microphone and began to sing in my deepest, most off-key tenor voice, that they understood. Before long we were all singing our exaggerated versions of opera. Patricia and the little ones loved it. They danced and ate fudge until they fell asleep on the couches, whereupon we carried their limp bodies into bed. We continued ironing into the wee hours of morning, hanging crisp blouses, dresses, and skirts on every available knob and doorjamb. By the time we finished, we had listened to our whole stash of records and compared notes on every boy we fancied at school.

We folded up the warm ironing boards, maneuvered through the jungle of clothes hanging on coat hangers, and headed to bed. I turned out the lights and checked on the little ones—especially Patricia, who still sleepwalked on occasion. Only a few nights earlier, she had risen out of bed, walked past me in the living room, and gone straight out the front door, barefoot. I was so tired I might not hear her if she roused, so I locked the living-room door and left the back door unlocked in case Mama came home.

The next morning, I felt a sense of accomplishment when I saw the empty ironing basket. We had conquered Everest—at least for a week or two. Even Mama was pleased when she came home the next day, although she said her white shirt could have used a little more starch.

After the success of our ironing party, Nancy, Vicki, and I wondered if we could make cleaning the trailer on Saturdays more appealing, too. One Saturday, we came up with the idea of turning our chores into a game of chance. I wrote a list of chores on a sheet of notebook paper, Vicki cut the list into strips, and

Nancy and I folded and dropped each strip into a mixing bowl. During breakfast, we older girls took turns drawing the strips, one by one, as if we were drawing door prizes. Patricia, Brenda, and Joni were too young to do the work, but they wanted to be part of the game, so we let them draw on our behalf.

Our draws might include: *wash two loads of clothes, mop kitchen floor, clean out the refrigerator, scrub the toilet, dust the living room, change Mama's sheets.* If someone felt she had drawn an inordinate number of difficult chores, she attempted to barter with the other two. *I'll trade my "wax the kitchen floor" for your "oil the cabinets" and "take out the trash."*

I would always trade for "hang the laundry" because I loved being outside. Plus, I was strong and could more easily heft the wet loads of laundry. "Clean the oven" was my least favorite, but I think Vicki didn't mind it so much; she had the patience for detail work like cleaning out drawers and cupboards. Drawing for and bartering our chores gave us a sense of control, the way Monopoly money made you feel rich even though it wasn't real.

The three of us agreed to take turns cooking supper on school nights. That meant each of us could have two nights off to start our homework early. If we were going somewhere, we all pitched in. Surprisingly, Mama had recently allowed Vicki, Nancy, and me to go roller-skating at the local skating rink. This felt like a big deal for several reasons: Mama rarely allowed us to participate in extracurricular activities; she stayed home to babysit; and most of the oil towns in West Texas had been too small to support a skating rink. Moving to the largest city in the high-desert country of western Colorado had some benefits.

Another benefit was the pond across the street from our trailer park. Janet said it froze over in the winter and you could ice-skate on it. Nancy, Vicki, and I decided we wanted to learn to ice-skate. We asked for ice skates for Christmas after Janet told us her dad sometimes built a fire near the frozen pond to warm your hands. Not only that, but her mom carried over hot cocoa. The image of Janet's mother pouring cups of steaming cocoa made me think of Mama in the kitchen, long ago, making fudge when it rained.

FEW MONTHS separated Vicki, Nancy, and me—developmentally we had a lot in common. While we had our disagreements, the three of us were basically allies and had become friends almost by default. If an outside friend like Janet came over, she became a fourth to our threesome. But, in truth, it was rare to add a fourth. We didn't have much room in our daily routine or in our cramped trailer for outsiders.

Plus, outsiders noticed things—like how little Mama and Daddy were around. Mama watched Brenda and Joni on school days, unless she asked one of us to stay home. After the school bus dropped us off, Mama, having left a detailed note on the picnic table, hopped into our recently purchased Volkswagen van to drive to her job as a cocktail waitress, to one of her nursing courses, or to go dancing with men who liked the smell of rose water splashed on her skin.

On a really ambitious day, Mama might start supper by putting on a pot of pinto beans or throwing together her version of Texas hash. We didn't much appreciate the hash; it consisted of hamburger meat, cubed potatoes, and a can of green beans dumped into a pot to form a thin, watery soup that Mama said was good for us. In this case, healthy and tasty were mutually exclusive.

Still, Mama prided herself on knowing what a healthy meal comprised. She had learned about nutrition in one of her recent nursing classes. Afterward, she sat Nancy, Vicki, and me down at the picnic table to share what she had learned. A well-rounded meal, she instructed, should include a starch (any kind of potato or macaroni), a small portion of meat (chicken and ground beef were the cheapest), and two varieties of vegetables (we could heat up canned corn, green beans, hominy, black-eyed peas, or baked beans). Even though she and Daddy rarely ate with us, Mama insisted that we cook supper every night and feed the younger ones.

If Vicki was our hairdresser, then Nancy was our chef. Countless years of eating mustard sandwiches at the babysitter's house had ignited Nancy's desire to cook. She was always poring over recipes and opening up our spice cabinet to see if we had the right spices. She found a recipe for barbecue meatballs that became one of our all-time favorites; it could have won a blue ribbon at the state fair.

While Nancy enjoyed all kinds of cooking, she particularly liked to bake cookies, cakes, and gingerbread. She learned by trial and error. Vicki and I were once inspired to take an ice pick and poke a hole through one of Nancy's errors—a gingerbread that had petrified in the oven. We strung it up to the ceiling vent of the swamp cooler in the living room like a piñata. There we took raucous turns swiping at it with a broom. Mama wasn't home, but when she was, navigating her ups and downs was no easy task. Swinging a broom and breaking apart a gingerbread piñata was downright cathartic.

The small oasis of normalcy and nurture that year and a half in Grand Junction came at suppertime, when my sisters and I gathered around our kitchen picnic table. If we happened to think about it, Patricia, Brenda, or Joni might bless our food: "God is great. God is good. Let us thank him for this food." Then we spooned our bounty onto Melmac plates, passed a loaf of Wonder bread, and shared our day.

Usually, the six of us chattered about mundane things, like whose turn it was to make a wish on the wishbone. Sometimes we shared our dreams: *I'm going to live in a big brick house and go to Africa someday. Can we go, too?* Sometimes we attempted to explain the complexities of life: *No, this isn't "day after tomorrow." The day after tomorrow is always two days away—it never really comes.* Sometimes we questioned the unpredictable: *Do you think Mama would really send us to a convent?* Mostly, we bonded. Circled around that pine picnic table, we forged an indestructible ring of sisterhood that helped keep all of us afloat.

ONE SATURDAY, after we drew for our chores and cleaned the trailer, Freckles lay panting on the braided living-room rug. She had been acting strangely since her refusal the night before to eat our offerings from the supper table. I knelt down beside her and gently rubbed her tummy. She had gained so much weight during her pregnancy that she resembled a swollen tick, almost as wide as she was tall.

She struggled to sit upright but couldn't and began panting again. Then it hit me. Her due date had arrived. Very soon a perfectly formed puppy lay encased in a clear birth sac in a pool of bloody mucus near her stubbed tail. Freckles laid her head listlessly to the side. Her puppy squiggled in the sac.

"Come on, Freckles," I whispered.

That was the extent of my midwifing skills.

Freckles looked up at me, then laid her head back down again. Mama wasn't home and the younger ones must have been watching television in the back bedroom or playing outside, which was just as well. I felt uneasy. I had no idea what to do. Neither did Freckles.

Vicki watched as I lifted Freckles's head toward the struggling puppy, hoping her instincts would take over. Surely Freckles knew more about giving birth than I did. I wished I had watched Mama deliver Trixie's kittens when we lived in Alvin.

Freckles didn't respond to the squiggling puppy. Something told me to break open the sac. Yet I hesitated, teetering in that excruciating place between wanting to do something and fearing that no matter what I did, it would be the wrong thing. If I broke open the sac too soon, it might kill the puppy. The same way forcing open a cocoon would kill a butterfly.

Abruptly, the puppy's movements ceased. I leaned in closer and prodded the sac. Nothing. I started to cry. I knew the puppy had died.

I ran to the phone, my fingers shaking as I dialed the number of the Lori-Li Lounge. Mama could barely make out what I was saying between my sobs. She told me she would try to come home, but in the meantime, I needed to break open the birth sac of each puppy and towel his face. The puppy had suffocated, she said.

Freckles delivered a second puppy before I heard Mama clamoring up the metal steps. I tentatively broke open the gooey sac as Mama rushed into the trailer and knelt down beside me. I was still crying.

"It's not your fault," Mama said. "She must have mated with a larger dog and couldn't deliver them by herself. Look, another one's coming. They're going to be fine."

But I couldn't stop thinking about the black-and-white one that died. I wished over and over that I had trusted my intuition. When I shut my eyes to fall asleep, I saw the puppy struggling to free itself, and me sitting there, only inches away, watching it die.

MONTHS LATER, after Freckles's puppies had been given away, I stood at the ironing board in the living room, pressing a shirt I planned to wear to school that day. One of the girls accidentally knocked over her juice onto the picnic table where Mama sat, disheveled, dark circles under her eyes. Words flew back and forth between her, Vicki, and Nancy until Mama slammed her fist down on the picnic table and said, "You better shape up or I'm sending you to the convent."

Vicki and Nancy looked at each other and back at the empress. "Go ahead," they said.

Mama narrowed her hazel eyes into a steely stare. "I'm not bluffing."

Vicki and Nancy had no intention of backing down.

I stood aghast, watching the showdown, still holding the hot iron.

"I'd rather live in a convent anyway," Vicki said defiantly.

Nancy nodded in agreement. "Go ahead and send us," Nancy dared her.

I watched a fire rise in Mama that threatened to burn down the whole trailer. I had no idea how to put it out.

"You think you're so smart; get in there and get your jewelry to give away," Mama ordered. "They won't let you bring it with you to the convent."

Then Mama whirled around, looking wildly into my eyes. "You feel the same way?" she snapped. "You want to go to the convent, too?"

Vicki and Nancy had nothing left to give Mama. Her moods and rages had taken their toll on all of us. Mama's fury had become as bitter as the howling winds sweeping through an icy canyon. No matter how hard we tried, we constantly fell short. We didn't wax the floors right; we were too loud in the morning; we weren't grateful enough for the sacrifices she made. The list seemed endless.

But still, I didn't want to go to the convent. I didn't want Vicki and Nancy to go, either. I wanted . . . What did I want? I wanted to worry about what outfit to wear to school that morning. I wanted all the pain and craziness to go away.

"Please don't send us away," I cried. "I don't want to be sent away again."

"Okay," Mama acquiesced. "You stay here and watch the girls. I'm driving those two to school to check out."

There was no victory in what I felt. Vicki, Nancy, and I had been on the front lines together, taking care of the house and Patricia, Brenda, and Joni. Had I deserted them? Was I a coward for wanting to stay?

Vicki and Nancy got dressed, came back into the kitchen, and obligingly handed over their meager stash of chained necklaces, bracelets, and rings. They followed Mama out the trailer door and drove away.

I fielded questions from the little ones. *Why is Mama so mad? Where are they going? When will they be back?* Their questions were my questions, too. None of them were answered until Mama opened the trailer door less than an hour later.

"Get into the back," Mama shouted, herding Vicki and

Nancy into the back bedroom. I heard her in there hitting, slapping, spanking, and yelling, "This will teach you a lesson."

Afterward, Vicki and Nancy were sore and bruised—especially Nancy, who bruised easily. When Mama saw Nancy the next morning, she instructed all of us to say that Nancy had fallen at the skating rink and people ran over her with their roller skates. Nancy repeated the story exactly when a gym teacher saw her changing her clothes and asked what had happened.

Still, there was something oddly triumphant about Vicki and Nancy's demeanor. They told me Mama had pulled up in front of the building and ordered them to go to the principal's office to withdraw from school. They opened the door and began walking up the sidewalk, but Mama opened the car door and yelled at them to get back into the car.

At that point, they knew they had won. They called Mama's bluff and, to them, it was worth a pound of their flesh. I, too, benefited from their sacrifice. Mama never again mentioned the convent.

Unfortunately, there were other dragons to slay.

IN THE early years, Mama seemed fine 90 percent of the time. But since our move to Grand Junction, Mama's dark days had increased in number and magnitude. She hated nights more and more, as if she were afraid of the dark.

I observed her one morning after I had risen to see the thin light of dawn revealing itself through the kitchen window. From where I stood at the kitchen sink, I could see Mama still reading her nursing manuals from the night before. To keep herself company, she had slid a bottle of Mogen David wine under her nightstand. I watched her swallow some pills with the wine instead of water and turn off the light. It was as if she needed daylight to fall asleep.

If Mama did sleep, she often had recurring nightmares, like the one of me drowning. But the scariest thing Mama told me had nothing to do with nightmares. Not long after the morning I had watched her from the kitchen sink, Mama confided that she had been seeing little people at the foot of her bed—for real.

"They talk to me and won't go away, unless I turn on the light," she said, blowing on her cup of steaming coffee.

I stared at her in disbelief. A sickening dread filled me. *What did she mean, "little people"? Leprechauns? Fairies like Tinker Bell? She had to be dreaming. In order for her to be okay, she had to be dreaming! They couldn't possibly be real.*

Mama searched my face, like maybe I had an answer. The fear that flickered in her eyes was unfamiliar to me.

It didn't occur to me to confide in my sisters, laughing and watching television in the back bedroom. I wanted to be strong for them, so they wouldn't feel afraid. I wanted to be their oak tree, a place where they could find refuge when things spun out of control. So I buried Mama's confession safely away inside me, hoping her little people would go away.

Maybe if I helped out more. Judged Mama less harshly. Maybe I could do better at school, make her proud of me. I came close to confiding in my science teacher, Mr. Gilroy, the day he asked about the assembly.

"Are you excited about tomorrow?" Mr. Gilroy asked after class.

I stared at him blankly, trying to recall what was happening tomorrow.

"About your induction into the Junior Honor Society," he added.

"I don't know about it," I said.

He looked surprised. "I'm sure I saw your name on the list."

"No one said anything."

"Your grades are good enough," he said. "I was on the committee. At tomorrow's assembly all the Junior Honor Society students will be recognized onstage. Your mom doesn't know, then?"

I shook my head. I wasn't even sure Mama would come if she did know. I couldn't remember her ever showing up at school for a field trip, PTA meeting, class conference, or anything—except the time she talked to my science teacher in Odessa about paddling me in front of the boys.

"Let's go to the office," he said.

"Wait," I said. I realized I was alone with an adult who knew about things like molecules, atoms, and electricity. Things that were real, but you couldn't really see. Maybe . . .

Mr. Gilroy turned toward me, expectantly. What could I say? *Do you believe leprechauns can be real? If somebody thinks she sees leprechauns, is she okay?* I couldn't imagine where to begin, and my tiny window of opportunity disappeared.

I went home and ironed my favorite dress, trimmed with wide zigzag rows of dark brown rickrack. That night I went to sleep with rollers in my hair. I left Mama a note on the kitchen table asking her to please, please come to school the next day. Daddy was out of town.

Mama wasn't awake when I left the next morning. That afternoon, the student body gathered in the auditorium for the assembly. As my eyes adjusted to the darkness, I searched for Mama in the crowd but couldn't see her. When I heard my name announced, I walked down the dark aisle toward the stage.

I recognized the back of Mama's head; she had pulled her black hair into a stylish French twist. When our eyes met, I was astonished to feel tears form in my eyes. I hadn't known it was possible to cry with joy until that very moment. I stood tall onstage, smiling out at Mama. I didn't know if I was prouder of myself or of her for coming.

MAMA CALLED me into her bedroom. She did that a lot—called me into her bedroom to sit on her bed to talk. Not so long ago, I helped her wrap everyone's Christmas presents. She told me confidentially that Aunt Eunice had not sent Nancy a gift. Because of this, Mama bought an extra round of gifts for all of us girls, which she intended to say were from Aunt Eunice. I wasn't sure why, but Mama wanted Aunt Eunice's gifts to be wrapped the prettiest of all.

We covered the boxes in shiny blue paper decorated with brown pinecones. Mama cut strips of brown ribbon and showed me how to fashion large bows. For the pièce de résistance, Mama shook a can of fake snow and lightly dusted each bow with white flakes. I had never seen more beautifully wrapped packages.

On Christmas Eve, when we traditionally opened our gifts, Mama turned to Nancy and asked if she would like to pass out her mother's gifts. Nancy beamed as she proudly handed each of us a gift box with a lavish bow sprayed with delicate snow.

That's how it was with Mama. One moment I admired her more than anyone, and the next I wished she would become someone else. The last time she invited me into her bedroom to talk, it hadn't gone so well. I tried not to get upset when I saw

her rubbing rose water across her skin, or when she asked me to
zip up the back of her light blue dress that plunged into a deep
V in the front, revealing her cleavage. But Mama picked up on
my disapproval anyway and told me for the umpteenth time she
wasn't ready for a rocking chair and a shawl.

I couldn't imagine why she wanted me in her room again so
soon.

She sat shoulder to shoulder with me on the bed, which was
unusual. I felt her warmth through my shirt. She bowed her head,
her dark hair falling across her cheek, hiding her eyes from mine.
She took my hand. Now I was worried. Had the little people
been talking to her again?

After a long moment, she said softly, "I'm dying, Terry. I've
got a kidney disease."

I couldn't stifle my moan as I slid off the bed and put my
head on her knees. I don't know how long I sobbed there, feeling
her tears dropping onto my hair as she stroked it. After a while,
she pulled me up onto the bed beside her again.

"I don't want you to tell anyone for a while. Not even Davy."

I nodded.

She took my hand. "Especially not the girls."

"I won't." I sniffed. She didn't need to tell me that.

We sat there with our hands, mirror images of one another,
cupped together. Faint blue rivers ran just below the surface of
the skin on the undersides of Mama's wrists. I wanted to touch
her; to stop time, to hold on to her so she couldn't ever, ever
leave.

How could this happen? How could I survive without her?
What would happen to us after she died?

Her secret gnawed at my insides week after week. I watched
for the slightest change in her health, fretted over every head-

ache, and if she slept too late, crept to the door of her bedroom to make sure I could see her breathing.

The sharp edges of her impending death cut me at all moments of the day and night, at home and in school. At night, my cat Boots curled up beside me and I often cried into his fur.

I remember well the night Mama told me she was dying. What I don't remember well is the day I realized it wasn't true.

I may have become suspicious the day Mama and JoAnn bought their blond wigs. They planned to go out dancing in them. All I know is that I looked at Mama one day and thought, *This woman isn't dying.*

I felt angry and betrayed. *Is that why she had wanted me to keep it a secret? Because it wasn't true? Did she want my sympathy so desperately after the convent catastrophe that she would lie to me?* I should have been relieved. My nightly prayers had been answered. Mama was going to live! How could I be mad at her for *not* dying? I didn't know, but I was.

That was the miasma I stewed in when JoAnn came over one night and sat on the couch visiting with Mama.

"When I tell you to do something, young lady, you do it!" Mama snapped at me. "Do you hear me?"

I didn't respond.

"I said, 'Do you hear me?'"

"Yes," I answered.

"Yes what?" she asked.

"Yes ma'am," I said in a deliberate smart-alecky voice that caused Mama to fly off the sofa toward me and slap me across the face.

"Don't you sass me."

I covered my stinging cheek with my hand and walked to the back hall to rewash the clothes that had gone sour in the washing machine. Mama was mad because I had forgotten to take them out and hang them on the line.

JoAnn had five children of her own and knew something about being the mother of a large family. She had been aware of Mama's demands on us for a long time. I heard the concern in her voice when she asked Mama, "Jean, don't you think you're being way too hard on Terry? She's young; she can only take so much."

I didn't hear Mama's response, but I didn't need to. JoAnn's words tore open the smothering sac I had been struggling against. I had begun to wonder if Mama's dissatisfaction stemmed from something intrinsically wrong with me. JoAnn set me psychologically free. I wasn't flawed. Mama's displeasure wasn't my fault. I could finally lay down the burden of trying to make Mama happy; it was no longer mine to carry.

Mama with two rodeo horses

Denver City, Texas

HOPE SPRINGS ETERNAL.
   I sat up tall when we rolled into Denver City (population 3,500) on State Highway 83, seven hundred miles southeast of Grand Junction. This move coincided with summer—Nancy, Vicki, Patricia, and I had been able to complete an entire year of

school in one place. As we drove through town, Daddy pointed
out the high school where Nancy and I would be enrolling. The
school was surprisingly large and modern, with stadium bleach-
ers and a football field. Daddy said the high school football team
had won the Class AA State Championship three years earlier.
We would soon learn that the downtown merchants closed early
to allow people time to drive to out-of-town football games.

Towns like Denver City arose for various reasons in the
West—water, agriculture, cattle, gold, the railroad. Denver City's
genesis was oil. The city claimed to be the last West Texas town
created solely on the discovery of oil. Indeed, the tallest landmark
was the orange flame that burned day and night on top of the
Shell flare stack north of town. The wind blew southerly the day
we arrived, carrying the smell of sulfur all the way down to the
Dairy Mart on Broadway, where we ordered and ate our noon
meal. Daddy's company was covering our moving expenses, so
our meal was gratis.

"A round of chocolate malts for everyone," Daddy told the
waitress.

That alone could account for my feelings of optimism.

Every time we moved to a new town, we arrived with a
clean slate, a chance to start over. Sitting inside the Dairy Mart,
I felt almost at peace. We had no bad memories of this town,
no neighbors gossiping, and no present worry about Mama or
Daddy. Mama was downright perky. I had forgiven her for living, but not for lying. She had breached my trust. Even had I
wanted to, I couldn't unfry that egg.

I knew Mama would stay fairly close to home in the beginning. I watched her make honest attempts to try harder whenever
we first moved. Plus, it took her a while to establish herself at the
local watering holes. However, Mama would soon learn, none

too happily, that Yoakum County was dry. No alcohol could be sold. Not that banning the sale of alcohol stopped the locals from drinking. To the contrary, anyone wanting beer or liquor drove sober across the county line to Hobbs, New Mexico, then drove home intoxicated, trying to keep the car's headlight beams somewhere on the pavement. Outside of drunk drivers, jackrabbits were about the most hazardous obstacle on the sparsely traveled, straight-line highway between Denver City and Hobbs.

It wasn't long before Mama knew the route by heart.

I can only guess how the conversation went when Daddy told Mama we needed to move again. Not that anything had gone all that well in Grand Junction; even Mama must have realized she had been sucked into a quagmire of depression. But, for economic reasons, we had to follow Daddy. When the distance between Daddy's rig and our trailer became too great, the company no longer covered Daddy's traveling and living expenses. They expected him to relocate. If Mama wanted Daddy's full paycheck, the only option was to pick up stakes.

Daddy didn't care so much *why* Mama agreed to move, only that she agreed. If he wasn't blind to her faults, he was certainly tolerant of them. He continued to offer her enough love for the both of them. Though I saw little evidence of Mama reciprocating Daddy's love, I was grateful for Daddy's unwavering devotion. I couldn't imagine our world without him in it.

He handled our household of females with aplomb, joking that he wished he had stock in the companies that sold toilet paper and sanitary napkins. He was as dependable and comforting as my oak tree on Grandma and Grandpa Vacha's farm. Brenda and Joni loved to climb onto his back and ride him like a horse. Patricia often snuggled under his arm. Vicki, Nancy, or I might drape a casual arm around his neck while he sat at the

kitchen table. Daddy was as uncomplicated as Mama was complicated. With Daddy, you got what you saw—no dangerous un-
dercurrents, just a good man working long hours trying to make
ends meet for his family.

I was glad he was home the night I climbed back into bed
after rescuing one of our kittens from up a tree, only to feel
something with lots of legs scurrying down my arm. I instantly
grabbed it in the dark.

Got it!

It took a moment for me to realize my predicament. *Now
what?* Wriggling legs tickled the inside of my closed fist. Whatever I held was fairly good-sized. I was horrified but couldn't let
it go.

I screamed for Daddy, whose feet pounded across the linoleum as he ran a fifty-foot dash to the back of the trailer. He
barreled through the bedroom doorway and flicked on the light,
ready to fight whatever needed fighting.

I held up my hand. "Something's wiggling in here," I said. "I
don't know what it is. But it's big."

Vicki, fully roused from sleep, scurried to safety behind
Daddy.

"Just a minute," Daddy said, fumbling in the closet, looking
for a shoe. "Okay," he said, "see if you can flick it toward the
wall and I'll kill it."

The legs kept wiggling. I drew back my hand and opened my
fingers as I hurled it forward.

A golden-colored scorpion about three inches long struck the
wall. Daddy quickly killed it with the shoe and said it must have
climbed onto me while I was rescuing the kitten. The thought of
it crawling all over me sent shivers up my spine.

"I'll tell you what," Daddy said. "You must have grabbed

him just right, with his stinger still in the air. That thing could have given you a nasty sting."

"I didn't know what else to do. I couldn't see."

"You did the right thing." He tousled my hair and turned out the light. "Call me if you decide to climb any more trees tonight," he added. I couldn't see his face, but I knew he was smiling.

MAMA'S REASONS for staying with Daddy were surely more utilitarian than Daddy's reasons for wanting her to stay. The cold, hard fact was Mama couldn't or wouldn't raise half a dozen daughters by herself. Not many men in Mama's orbit were willing to take on a woman and her six girls. Plus, our prior moves had precluded Mama from completing her nurse's training; she still didn't have a profession. But she hadn't given up. On September 30, 1963, Mama enrolled in her third nursing program, at the Yoakum County Hospital School of Vocational Nursing.

Brenda and Joni were not yet in school, so Mama still needed child care. Mama decided that Brenda, at least, was old enough to start first grade that fall. The only *minor* problem was the state of Texas disagreed. Brenda was five, too young to attend first grade, according to Texas law; she just missed the cutoff date with her September birthday and had never been to kindergarten. Undeterred, Mama hunted through a box of keepsakes and located Brenda's embossed birth certificate, issued in Amarillo, Texas, in 1957. After carefully looking it over, Mama surmised she could change the seven to look like a six if she used the same color ink and some Liquid Paper.

We snapped a picture of Brenda before dropping her off for her first day of school.

Brenda stands at the rear of our Volkswagen van, holding on to the overhead door handle. The 1963 Colorado license plate reads NJ-2198. Brenda's head tilts to her left and she smiles widely toward someone off camera. Her hair has been cut and permed by either Mama or Vicki (probably Vicki, since it looks so nice). Brenda's pinafore is a Scandinavian design, something like Heidi might wear. Brenda holds a brand-new pencil box in her right hand (an item Mama bought for each of us every year before school started—until I told her I was too old to be slipping a pencil box into my locker). Brenda wears a watch and carries a small Easter purse in the same hand. Her lace anklets are neatly folded above her black Mary Janes. She is the picture of innocence—on the cusp of entering a wider world. She is proof that life continually sends up new shoots of hope. She is her mother's daughter, but mine as well. Our little girl is growing up fast.

Brenda entered first grade, and Nancy and I started high school.

Where are you from? What does your dad do?

I paused. Was I from an Iowa farm, southwest Kansas, Fort Morgan, one of several West Texas oil towns, Alvin near the Gulf of Mexico, or the largest city on the western slope of Colorado? Was my father a farmer or an oil driller?

"I've lived in a lot of places, most recently Colorado," I heard myself saying.

For the first time, I became acutely aware that my experience wasn't singular to a specific locale but, rather, an amalgamation of many. I differed from most of my peers in Denver City, some of whom still lived in the same houses in which they were born. My transience was confusing, but liberating, too.

I didn't identify with one particular school, group of friends, town, or state—I identified with something larger, more inclusive, the sum of many parts—like humanity instead of a particular person. My familiar landmarks had become, by necessity, overarching—the stars, sunsets, and moonrises. These were my constants. I knew the earth as mountain, field, canyon, desert, and sea. My roots weren't anchored to a particular neighborhood, yet they sank deep into the earth, like my ancient oak tree. Maybe that's what Africa represented to me: a return to the source, the mother continent, the cradle of civilization.

Though I came to understand this about myself, I found my revelation impossible to share. What could I say? *I am from everywhere and nowhere.* I feared this was a laughable response. My instinct for self-preservation warned me to keep this answer to myself, though it was the truest of all.

I told everyone my dad was a seismographic driller for oil. I had not had any contact with my natural father since Vicki and I left Iowa six years earlier. I recently asked Mama if she hated our father. She said "hate" was too strong a word but added that my dad forfeited his rights to us by not paying child support.

"If you want to look him up when you're eighteen, fine. But not until then," Mama said emphatically.

My eighteenth birthday was still four years away. I wasn't sure what I would do. I never wanted Daddy to think he hadn't been enough for me, because he had. He felt more like my father than anyone else.

I also recognized that my dad and his wife, Cathy, would have moved on with their lives. They had a child of their own, my brother, Lanny. Vicki and I had waved good-bye to Lanny before he was a year old. By the time I turned eighteen, Lanny would be ten.

It felt surreal to know I had a brother, one I wouldn't recognize walking down the street.

Mama relented on only one thing after we left Iowa. She let us correspond with Aunt Betty, my dad's sister, on the condition that Aunt Betty not send us pictures of our dad or talk about him in her letters. Aunt Betty made good on her promise; Mama saw to it by censoring her letters. I knew from Aunt Betty that Grandma Skinner remarried after Grandpa died, that the one-room schoolhouse closed down, and that the crops were attacked by insects or suffered from the drought. I didn't know if my father had had other children, if he still lived on a farm, or if he ever thought about me and Vicki.

Those answers would have to wait.

Nancy faced some of the same questions about her family that I did at school, plus one more.

So who's your mother?

By then Nancy had been calling my mom "Mama" just like my sisters and I did. I didn't see any difference between Nancy and the rest of us, but after learning our mothers were sisters, some classmates surmised, "So you're really cousins."

Nancy looked at me.

"No," I responded. "Nancy's our adopted sister."

Our new friend Leroy, who lived in the trailer next door to us, put it this way: "You sure have a mixed-up family!"

FOR A few precious months, we actually felt like a normal family. Daddy's presence steadied Mama like a rudder. I no longer saw her giving herself shots, and she removed the Mogen David wine bottle from beneath her nightstand. Her mood seemed upbeat and her headaches manageable. Daddy was home on the weekends, working on projects around the house and tinkering on his pickup truck. I even helped him under the hood sometimes.

I had a particular interest in cars since I had just acquired my learner's permit at the ripe age of fourteen. Daddy showed me how to check the oil and where the fan belt was. He showed me how to unscrew the carburetor cover and place my palm over the carburetor to create suction that helped the truck start when the engine flooded.

Unfortunately, not all of this knowledge translated to our Volkswagen van with its engine in the back. Daddy surprised me when he bought the van—especially since he loved the dependability of Fords so much. But whatever the Volkswagen lacked in horsepower and constancy, it made up for with an extra row of seats. Daddy showed me how to gas it up, change the tires, and use the stick shift. Both of us grimaced when I ground the gears, but Daddy assured me I would soon learn. And I did.

That fall, on November 22, fewer than four hundred miles away in Dallas, Texas, John F. Kennedy was assassinated. The announcement came over the loudspeaker at school as we changed classes. A minute earlier, we had been a hive of invincible teenagers. Kennedy's death exposed the fragility of life and hope. You could wake up in the morning with your life stretching forever in front of you and be dead by 12:30. I soberly took my seat in geometry while Mrs. Bingham comforted a burly football player who sat sobbing at his desk.

Six days later, Mama pulled giblets out of the cavity of a thawing turkey, boiled and chopped them, added tangy sage and poultry seasoning to bread crumbs, and showed us how to stuff a turkey.

Just before Christmas, someone Mama knew from nursing school dropped off a box of hand-me-down clothes. Mama gathered all of us into the living room and told us to strip down to our underwear. She unfolded various articles of clothing, doling them out according to size. I slipped into one dress and stood on the bed in the back bedroom to get a full-length view in the dresser mirror. It was cute, but what if it had belonged to one of my classmates? How many size-seven females could there be in Denver City?

Since store-bought clothes were a luxury we couldn't afford, and I fretted over the origins of my hand-me-downs, my plan was to make myself a stylish new wardrobe. Homemaking was a required course for girls and sewing was part of our curriculum. I learned to cut out patterns, set sleeves, and baste in zippers. But when I climbed back onto the bed to admire my handiwork, I noticed the dress hung too loosely and the waist puckered.

I tried being stylish in other ways. I began to twist the tops of my bobby socks in a swirl around my ankles just like the other girls, including my new best friend, Ada Beth, who was a year ahead of me. Ada Beth didn't mind that I was a freshman, that I wore homemade clothes, or that my hair refused to obey a can of hair spray.

The only problem was Ada Beth was actually allergic to my hair spray. As a matter of fact, Ada Beth had asthma and was allergic to just about everything—perfume, plants, chemicals, animals, the list went on. She couldn't spend the night with me because we had cats. Knowing this, Mama occasionally allowed me to spend nights with her, giving me a reprieve from watching the girls.

Ada Beth didn't live in a trailer (probably only a dozen families in Denver City did); she lived in a modest house on the outskirts of town. Her twin sisters slept on a fold-out couch in the living room because there weren't enough bedrooms to go around, and her dad worked in the oil fields like Daddy—only he didn't travel.

Ada Beth and I ranked about the same in the school's pecking order, which basically depended on where you lived or on what your dad or mom did—unless you were a star football player; then you could shoot straight to the top.

If your dad worked in the oil fields and you lived in a trailer, you needed the help of a football. Nancy, Ada Beth, and I joined Pep Club and cheered the football team, but so did most every other able-bodied girl in high school. Our circle of friends didn't include cheerleaders or candidates vying for homecoming queen, but it did include a group of girls who shared our same sense of excitement and expectancy about growing up.

Ada Beth and I found our worth and satisfaction in being diligent students and faithful friends who shared lunches as well as secrets. When I spent the night at Ada Beth's house, her beloved Chihuahua, Tiki, always curled up beside us during our late-night talks. I told Ada Beth more about my childhood than I had ever shared with anyone else. When I haltingly told her I was from everywhere and nowhere, she didn't laugh. When I told her I wanted to travel to Africa, she wanted to go with me. We secretly named each other Pickles and Peanuts for reasons I can't remember.

Our entertainment was limited in Denver City. We had a movie theater on Main Avenue, one drive-in movie off Highway 83 that Mama called the passion pit (we were forbidden to go there with boys), the bowling alley near the turnoff to Plains, and an abandoned house west of town that was supposedly haunted. Cruising the half-mile drag between Dairy Mart number one on Broadway and Dairy Mart number two on Mustang Drive was by far our favorite pastime—especially on Friday and Saturday nights.

Ada Beth's grandmother let Ada Beth borrow her automatic-shift car for cruising. I took note of how Ada Beth casually drove with only her right hand cupped over the bottom of the steering wheel. She balanced a cup of ice in her left hand on her left knee. Ada Beth and I often ordered cups of ice with two lemon wedges and a salt packet at the first Dairy Mart. Ice was cheaper than a cherry Coke and we felt unique squeezing lemon onto the ice and then sprinkling it with salt. Sucking on the cold cubes left a tart, salty taste on your tongue. Without realizing it, we had created virgin margaritas.

One afternoon, I was home watching the girls, hoping Mama might allow me to spend the night with Ada Beth again. I lay on my stomach on the living-room floor, flipping through one of Mama's magazines. My feet twirled in the air behind me. Three-year-old Joni leaned against me, peering at the magazine over my shoulder. The sun blazed outside. Joni and I had taken refuge in the trailer right beneath the humming swamp cooler. Cold air brushed our skin.

Daddy had been meaning to repair the water line on the swamp cooler. Recently, water had been leaking down the outside of the trailer onto our metal-grate steps. Ordinarily, the leak would have been little more than an annoyance. However, unbeknownst to us, the grounding wire from the breaker box on the trailer had not been attached to or had come loose from the grounding rods; grounding was the process meant to avert electrical shock.

As I flipped another page in the magazine, Joni stood up and said she wanted to play outside with Brenda.

"Better put on your flip-flops, hon," I said. "You might get a sticker."

"No, I won't," she protested playfully.

I didn't worry too much about the stickers. If Joni or Brenda stepped on a sandbur, she would usually let me know. *T-e-r-r-y, I have a sticker.* That was my cue to drop whatever I was doing, go pick her up, carry her to the metal steps outside the trailer door, and quickly yank out the prickly sandbur lodged in her dusty foot. I would then kiss my finger and rub it across the point of entry, which seemed to make everything better. I had culled hundreds of West Texas sandburs from my sisters' feet and my cats' fur.

That's how I remember Joni was barefoot that day when she opened the trailer door. Her feet touched the wet metal steps and her hands instantly froze above her head on to the metal door handle. She didn't scream or let go; she just dangled there. I knew instantly something was wrong, and almost as instantly that electricity must be traveling from the trailer, through her, and into the ground. Joni had become the grounding wire. I also knew that if I touched her, the current might freeze my muscles, too, and I would be helpless to free either of us. Reason told me to run to the back hallway for a nonconductive wood broom to pry Joni loose from the door handle; love and instinct told me she was too little to have this amount of electricity coursing through her body.

With as much momentum as I could manage, I lunged through the air like a receiver for our Mustangs football team trying to catch a pass before it hit the ground. My target was Joni's waist. My feet never touched the metal steps. The moment my arms wrapped around Joni, a jolting river of current rushed through me, scrambling my brain and petrifying my muscles into a flying embrace. I was three times Joni's size.

How can she take this?

The force of my running jump caused the door to fly open beyond the steps and the door handle to slide downward. Joni and I hit the ground hard, my arms still wrapped tightly around her. We no longer pulsed with current but I felt tingly. I looked into Joni's wide blue eyes—she was pale and in shock but very much alive. I kissed her forehead and then collapsed with relief.

Leroy's mother, Coco, showed me how to unplug the outdoor electrical wires until either Mama or Daddy came home. Daddy grounded the trailer and fixed the water line. Mama, feeling confident about her medical training, checked Joni over and declared she was fine. Then she told me I had a good head on my shoulders, and let me spend the night with Ada Beth.

THE NEXT May, we attended Mama's graduation ceremony from vocational-nursing school, held at the First Baptist Church in Denver City. When they announced Mama's name, she walked up to accept her diploma. At that moment, all Mama's past struggles receded into the background. As she stood wearing her nurse's uniform and starched white cap, I clapped long and hard. She looked so happy.

Maybe I could relax a little now. We practically had proof that she was okay. Mama had completed 1,424 hours of hospital experience and 528 hours of classroom instruction.

When Mama applied to take the vocational nurse's exam, she attached the required affidavit of her physical and mental health. Mama scored 90.8 on the exam; an examiner had written *high* next to her score. Everything pointed to her success. Maybe becoming a nurse was exactly what Mama and I needed to heal what was wrong with our life.

Or maybe not.

THE FIRST time I met Mr. Rodeo, he wore tinted glasses and flashed a big white smile. I drove Mama out to meet him at a place they called the Section, a house in the middle of nowhere, surrounded by acres of ranch land. Mr. Rodeo lifted off his cowboy hat and politely shook my hand. His chiseled features made him look as though the West Texas wind had carved him out of sandstone. His face was tanned, except for a white line running across his forehead where his cowboy hat usually rested. He was sinewy and strong just like the quarter horses he rode.

"He's a rancher, but he's in the rodeo, too," Mama chirped on our way to his place. "He ropes calves."

The longer we lived in a place, the farther away Daddy traveled to prospective oil fields. Being farther away, he didn't drive home as often. As Mama teased to a friend, "When the cat's away, the mice will play."

Mama was indeed a playful mouse, and I was the mouse's chauffeur. I was now fifteen and had my driver's license. When I showed Daddy my new license for the first time, he pretended to wipe dust from his eyes. Mama was happy, too. Not only because I could drive by myself now, but because I could do the grocery shopping, run errands, and drive her to her rendezvous with Mr. Rodeo. She often traveled with Mr. Rodeo to Ruidoso Downs in New Mexico to bet on the quarter horses, and to various rodeos in the region where Mr. Rodeo performed.

While Mama's love life no longer surprised me, it grieved

me in a new way. My naïveté faded with each passing birthday. In the past, I could feign ignorance when Daddy asked
questions about Mama's whereabouts. Now I knew not only
who she was with but the directions to his house. I had to
openly lie to Daddy, both on the phone and sometimes even in
person.

It never occurred to me to tell Daddy the truth and, in retro-
spect, I think he preferred the lies. They allowed him to preserve
his dignity; they kept his mirage of hope shimmering.

It wasn't until I saw Mama sipping from Mr. Rodeo's glass
real casual-like that I knew she had fallen hard for him. Mr.
Rodeo drove a white Cadillac with a trailer hitch soldered under
the back bumper to pull his horse trailer. His Cadillac also came
equipped with a drink holder in the front seat. I had never seen
a built-in drink holder before.

That particular day, Mr. Rodeo nestled a glass of bourbon
and branch, a fancy name for water, into the drink holder; the
ice cubes tinkled against the sides of the glass as he lifted it and
took a long draft. The sweet smell of bourbon filled the air-
conditioned leather interior as Mama reached over and took a
sip, too. Something about the way Mama lifted the glass—the
familiarity of her touch upon it, the assumption that it was hers
for the taking—made me sit up and take notice.

ONE NIGHT when Mama was out with Mr. Rodeo, James Ray,
a boy from our class, came over to visit Nancy. He and Nancy
opted to talk outside because privacy inside the trailer was non-
existent; besides, I had just made a concoction of soapsuds to
remove houseflies from the ceiling. If too many flies entered

the trailer during the day (we didn't have screens), we shook together soap and water in a jar in the evenings when the flies quieted down. We approached each fly one by one on the ceiling, holding the jar beneath them. The frothy foam acted like a fly magnet, practically sucking the flies into the jar.

I didn't worry about Nancy and boys; she was both shy and a bit awkward in their presence. Not that I was an expert. Vicki, Nancy, Ada Beth, and I determined that boys who smoked Camels or read *Playboy* magazine were *fast* and should, therefore, be avoided. This narrowed our playing field considerably. Stolen kisses were the extent of our wantonness, and I wasn't even sure Nancy had stolen one yet.

Mama, however, usually erred on the side of suspicion. That evening she returned home early before Nancy had stepped back into the trailer.

"Who've you been with?" Mama demanded when Nancy clicked the trailer door closed.

"James Ray," Nancy said.

"What happened out there between the two of you?" Mama asked accusingly.

It's possible that the impending train wreck might have been avoided had Nancy thought to censor herself, but she was never one for diplomacy.

She looked coolly at Mama and said, "Nothing happened. I'm not a whore like you."

The word *whore* struck with shattering force. Mama's unbridled fury sought only one thing: retribution. She cornered Nancy in the bottom bunk of the middle bedroom and delivered blows repeatedly to Nancy's body. Nancy fought back, kicking and punching until the two of them collapsed from exhaustion, Mama's wrath spent.

Nancy woke the next morning covered in bruises. She looked like she had been thrown under a train.

In addition to the driving and grocery shopping, Mama put me in charge of signing our report cards and writing notes for excused absences. I signed Mama's name so often the school would have questioned Mama's signature as the forgery. I wrote notes for our absences in the format Mama had taught me. In Nancy's case the note would have read:

To whom it may concern,
Nancy was absent due to the fact she was incapacitated.

Sincerely,
Mrs. Jean Vacha

If I had written the truth, the note would have read:

To whom it may concern,
Nancy was absent due to the fact Mama beat her black-and-blue and she was too sore to come to school.

Sincerely,
Terry Vacha

If Aunt Eunice had seen Nancy that day, she would likely have taken Nancy away from Mama. If child services had seen Nancy, we might all have been taken away. Mama knew she had crossed a line—she returned to Nancy's bunk crying and apologized. But Nancy turned her back. If Mama wanted absolution, she wouldn't find it in the eyes of any of her daughters—not even in mine.

*   *   *

IT WAS late Friday night; I wanted to finish my chores so I could have Saturday free. Ada Beth had introduced me to a boy named Darrel and the three of us planned to hang out together on Saturday and cruise the two Dairy Marts.

I was on my hands and knees scrubbing the kitchen floor when I spotted Mama's moccasins walking toward me. She pulled out a chair and sank down.

"Terry, I have something to tell you," she said. "You're not going to like it."

I stopped and looked up at her. So many things seemed possible.

She didn't look at me. She actually seemed nervous. Seconds seemed to tick by.

"I'm divorcing Davy," she finally blurted.

I felt the blood drain from my face and I braced my hand on the side of the bucket, dizzy.

"Why? After all these years, why now?"

She turned her eyes on me then.

"I want to get married again."

"To Mr. Rodeo?"

She nodded. "Don't you think we'll be happy together?"

I shook my head.

"Why not?" she asked indignantly.

How could she not see it? Mr. Rodeo was a maverick just like her. He was a man who gave orders, not one who followed them. He expected his horses, his field hands, and, I suspected, his women to take their cues from him. I had never seen Mama acquiesce to anyone.

"He's more strong-minded than Daddy," I said. "I don't think he'll let you have your way like Daddy does."

"I think we'll be happy," Mama said almost petulantly. "I'm

not changing my mind, so you might as well get used to it. And we won't be living in this trailer anymore, either."

My heart physically ached. I knew in my bones that Mama wasn't changing her mind. I sat there mute, watching my tears plop into dingy mop water. I couldn't fathom our life without Daddy. He had been a part of me for so many years. His love didn't have sharp edges; his love never hurt. Again and again he had forgiven Mama, hoping for the day she might love only him. But that day was like the day after tomorrow; it would never come.

Mama left me there to grieve and to finish mopping. It seemed appropriate somehow—scrubbing the floor with my tears. It was like penance for Daddy's pain. When I finished, I didn't know what else to do. I needed to stay busy. I ferreted out some liquid wax from under the kitchen sink and poured it onto the linoleum floor. I applied it in long, slow strokes to keep myself occupied, to keep myself from wailing, to keep myself from picturing Daddy wailing.

Later that night, I turned off all the lights and sat on the couch with my knees drawn up underneath my chin. Mama had left for the night and everyone else slept. The moon had climbed into the sky and was now shining inside the trailer window. I looked to where it spilled across the waxed linoleum floor, gleaming like the surface of a calm lake. I stared at it for a long while. How was it possible that moonlight on linoleum, washed with my tears, could be so achingly beautiful?

MAMA AND Mr. Rodeo married in Juárez, Mexico, on a weekend that I believe fell *before* Mama's divorce from Daddy was final—not that it matters all that much. Mama told Mr. Rodeo when they met that she was already divorced, so he wasn't too concerned with the dates.

Telling Daddy good-bye sent me into a state of shock.

I see myself in a fog, the hurt so deep that I can't let it out or else I won't be able to breathe. I clasp my arms around Daddy's waist and I feel my sisters' arms there, too. All of these arms and Daddy's tears, his telling us it will be okay, that we'll still see each other, that he will always love us.

According to the divorce settlement, Daddy acquired the trailer and visiting rights; he was also ordered to pay child support for Patricia, Brenda, and Joni. Mama took the six of us, the GE washing machine, the picnic table, the living-room sectional, the sewing machine, and the Volkswagen. In the blink of an eye, seven females moved into Mr. Rodeo's three-bedroom ranch on the other side of town. In that same blink, seven females disappeared from Daddy's life. He was left with the trailer and no place to sit or wash his clothes. For the first time, the ten-by-fifty-foot trailer he had proudly purchased in Fort Stockton was empty. We had shed it like a cicada shell, leaving only a tin husk of the family who once dwelt there.

TRUE TO form, Mama tried hard in the beginning. She wanted to prove to herself, to us, to anyone who thought otherwise, that she could indeed make a good life for herself, us, and Mr. Rodeo. To prove it, she bought a bolt of pink gingham material, western shirt patterns, threads, and snaps. Then she, Vicki, Nancy, and I pinned on patterns of every shirt size in the family—from Joni's little shirt to Mr. Rodeo's large one. We cut out yokes, sewed French seams, and pounded on snaps.

On the first day of the rodeo, we made our debut as a family. We put on our identical shirts (which was likely the first time Mr. Rodeo wore pink), climbed onto various horses, and rode together in the Grand Parade, in a circle around the ring. Mr. Rodeo led the way on his champion rodeo horse, beneath the flapping flag he balanced on his saddle. I can still feel the sun on my back, the wide girth of the horse beneath me, and the murmur of the crowd when they first saw us dressed alike. Mama had scored a home run.

Mr. Rodeo embraced his new role. He taught me how to saddle a horse, pulling the cinch strap through the cinch ring and rigging dee for a snug fit so the saddle wouldn't slide. It was important, he thought, for the Denver City Riding Club candidate for Christmas Queen (me) to know how to saddle and ride a horse.

I wasn't sure how I had been selected as a candidate, but the prospect of riding on a float in the Christmas parade wearing a formal gown thrilled me. All the candidates would be on floats—right along with the reigning Christmas Queen. It didn't matter if I won or not. Riding on a float would be about as close as I had ever come to being popular.

I helped Mama decorate little cans with my picture and we took them into local businesses to place beside their cash registers so customers could vote. People were supposed to vote for the candidates of their choice by stuffing coins and bills into the appropriate cans. Whoever tallied the most money would become the next Christmas Queen.

Once, when Mr. Rodeo and I went into a store, he stuffed some bills into my can and gave me a wink. He told me that a good many members in the riding club were supporting me, too. Mama and I talked about driving to Hobbs to look for a store-bought gown. *Move over, Loretta Lynn!*

Daddy seemed happy for me when I told him everything on the phone. We had visited him once since the divorce. We even stayed in the trailer again, which felt odd. The seven of us tried hard to pretend we were happy that weekend; I took off my sunglasses and propped them on Freckles's snout and Daddy snapped a picture of all of us sitting on the metal steps outside the trailer. But our unsmiling faces tell the real story. We still missed Daddy terribly. At least he had not been blotted out of our lives entirely; we could still see him from time to time.

Mr. Rodeo didn't try to usurp Daddy's place. He was more like a friend than a father. He refurbished an old blue Packard for us to drive to school. He even agreed to put a fresh coat of paint on the old cinder-block bunkhouse, not far from the main house, so Vicki, Nancy, and I could move into it. His eyebrows lifted when he saw our choice of paint color. Robin-egg blue was not your usual bunkhouse color, but it was perfect for three teenage girls who loved the Beatles. Though drafts blew through the bunkhouse and tiny piles of red sand built up underneath the door during every sandstorm, Nancy, Vicki, and I felt as if we had moved into a college dorm—something I actually hoped to do when I graduated from high school.

Sometimes at night, I climbed out of bed, pulled on my jeans, and headed for the giant haystack behind the metal barn. The haystack had become my refuge, much like Grandma and Grandpa's oak tree. I liked to lie on top of it, smelling the sweet grassy scent, as I communed with the stars and moon. I felt safe, anonymous, and peaceful there. I loved the bowl of sky over my head and the feeling that I was part of the land. Sometimes I listened to the plaintive cry of coyotes in the distance, or to a cow lowing to her calf.

Most of Mr. Rodeo's Hereford and Angus cows looked

after their calves just fine on the range. Sometimes the whole herd circled a calf to protect it from harm. But one mother cow, for unknown reasons, had recently abandoned her calf. Mr. Rodeo scooped up the struggling newborn and brought him home. He asked if we wanted to nurse him by hand. It was a unanimous yes.

We named our white-faced orphan Whibbles because he wobbled on his spindly feet. For weeks, the six of us took turns feeding him out of a nippled bottle, cooing and wishing we could keep him for a pet. The harsh reality was that someday Whibbles would become a steer, which meant he would be castrated and later sold for meat.

When Brenda and Joni asked me what would happen to Whibbles, I couldn't bring myself to tell them about castration or slaughterhouses. I let them believe Whibbles would live happily ever after in a field not far away from the haystack, forever grateful to the little girls who had fed and loved him.

AFTER SOME months, Mama's dream of living happily ever after with Mr. Rodeo began to crumble.

Mr. Rodeo would come to say three things of Mama: (1) She was the most creative person I ever met; (2) That woman had a way with a horse; (3) Everything was fine until she needed a fix; the dope did her in.

Mama's nursing career ended gradually, under a dark cloud of secrecy and suspicion. Mama had been dispensing medicines and pills to herself as well as to her patients. She had logged fifty-five hours of Administering Medicine during her internship. I had seen blank prescription pads in her possession. I had also noticed a plethora of prescription bottles from numerous doctors filled not only in Denver City but in the nearby towns of Plains, Seagraves, and Seminole.

Brief periods of calm in our lives were now overshadowed by long periods of fighting between Mama and Mr. Rodeo. Violent, dramatic battles were followed by tearful reconciliations. More than once, Mama woke us up in the middle of the night and told us to start packing our clothes. We obligingly removed clothing from our drawers, only to have her return to the room minutes later and tell us to put everything back.

Once, Mama locked herself in the bathroom and yelled to Mr. Rodeo that she had swallowed a whole bottle of pills. He forced open the door and found her lying fully clothed in the bathtub. She had taken some pills, but not the whole bottle.

Another night Mama bolted during a fight and drove a back road to a bar in Hobbs. On the way home, she flipped the Volkswagen. It was a dark and desolate road. A passerby called the police and reported, "People are lying everywhere." When the police arrived, they found Mama and lots of clothes strewn about, but no people wearing them. Mama's dry cleaning had been piled in the back of the van and scattered when the van flipped. Mama was sore and bruised, but she walked away from the accident—probably not in a straight line.

After another fight, Mama called Daddy and told him she planned to leave Mr. Rodeo. She asked if she could come back to him. When Daddy said yes, Mama told him to rent a U-Haul trailer for our things. A day later, Daddy arrived towing the U-Haul. I noticed an unmistakable spring in Daddy's step as he carried the sewing machine from the house into the back of the U-Haul. He couldn't hide his pleasure at nearly having his family back. After he had toted out several boxes of clothes, Mama pulled him aside and told him she had changed her mind; she wasn't leaving Mr. Rodeo after all. Daddy put his head on my shoulder and cried. I stroked his head like a child's. I cried, too.

"I'm so sorry, Daddy," I kept whispering. "I'm so sorry."

Daddy left and Mama limped on. She was like one of Daddy's Fords. She still ran even though she badly needed fixing.

For me, the climax came one night when Mama and Mr. Rodeo scuffled in the house. The girls and I took refuge on a single bed in the back bedroom. Their yelling became louder. We heard running footsteps and doors slamming. A few moments later we heard the unmistakable sound of gunshots in the night, possibly from the barn. Brenda froze, glassy-eyed. I drew her into the center of our sisters' circle, like a calf being protected by the herd.

I was overtaken by fear in that bedroom. I sensed danger all around us in a way that transcended logic. The bed became our life raft, adrift in an enormous sea. I felt as if sharks circled us and I had to keep us from being eaten alive. I didn't want anyone's feet or arms dangling off the sides of the bed. I tucked Joni's feet beneath my knee. I had no idea who fired the shots. Mama might be dead. Or she might be a murderer.

Which would be worse?

Eventually, the girls and I cautiously left the bed and crept out of the bedroom. The house looked in order. I didn't see blood. Both Mama and Mr. Rodeo walked away from their gunfight unscathed, at least physically. However, my radar had been switched to high alert. I surmised the battle had ended, but not the war.

It wasn't long before Mama called Daddy and told him she wasn't happy. By then, Daddy had moved to San Luis Obispo,

California, and rented a three-bedroom bungalow. In addition to making more money, Daddy had only his expenses to cover and his paycheck stretched a lot further. For the first time in his life, Daddy had money to spare. He told Mama that his house had a "genuine" fireplace and then he offered to move all of us to California to live with him again. He had divorced Mama twice and married her twice. Maybe three times would be the charm.

Mama had never been to California; she accepted his offer.

We checked out of school just before Thanksgiving. I was a junior and had moved well over a dozen times by then. The office staff at the high school wanted to know where we were headed.

"California," I said.

"Don't they have the Hells Angels out there, riding them motorcycles?" one of the ladies asked.

"I think so," I answered.

"I'm real sorry," she said.

I was sorry, too, but not because of the Hells Angels. I was sorry that Mama was such a mess. I was sorry for Mr. Rodeo, too. During one of their fights, when Mama wanted to take us to stay with JoAnn and had us packing in the middle of the night, I lined up the girls in front of Mr. Rodeo and asked straight-out if we could stay with him instead of following her. He said it wasn't possible since he had no legal rights. It wouldn't look right, either—six girls staying there alone with him. Like Daddy, Mr. Rodeo had once broken down and cried in front of me. He had envisioned a happy future and possibly even children with Mama—ones he would have a legal right to keep. After marrying Mr. Rodeo, Mama had her tubal ligation reversed. She was willing to have another child.

God help us if another child gets thrown into Mama's spin cycle.

I wondered what magnetism Mama possessed that caused so many men to fall in love with her only to buckle under the weight of that very love. I had compassion for both Daddy and Mr. Rodeo; loving Mama reduced me to tears many times. Again and again I had been brought to my knees. I doubted Mama would be any better in California, but there, at least, Daddy would be in our lives again.

Unfortunately, my boyfriend, Darrel, would not. I couldn't be sure what love was supposed to look like between a man and a woman, but I thought maybe I had stumbled upon it with Darrel. He had become even closer to me than Ada Beth. I felt safe in his embrace and finally understood, during one long kiss, what Mama meant when she once asked me if I ever felt *longings.*

In a fleeting moment of *what-if*s about our impending separation, Darrel threw out the possibility of running away to Mexico to get married. Many a Monday we had come into school only to learn that a couple of students had driven to Juárez over the weekend and gotten married without their parents' consent. I was sixteen. I didn't want to be separated from Darrel, but marriage?

Mama had such a dismal track record that I wasn't sure I ever wanted to get married—not even in my twenties. And for sure, I didn't want to repeat Mama's life. When I thought about finishing high school as Mr. and Mrs., I quickly knew how preposterous the idea of marriage was. Our best option, we decided, would be to write to each other—every single day. Darrel tenderly tucked his oversized red-and-gray football jacket around my shoulders.

"I want you to take this to California," he said, "to remind you of my arms around you."

The day we pulled out of Mr. Rodeo's driveway, headed west toward California, I thought of one other thing I was sorry about: my candidacy for Christmas Queen. I wouldn't be riding on that float after all.

Mama, my sisters, and me admiring the Pacific Ocean for the first time

San Luis Obispo, California

IF I THOUGHT boys who smoked Camels and read *Playboy* were *fast*, I was propelled into a whole new state of momentum and speed—one with six- and eight-lane highways. This was California in the mid-sixties. Hippies, free love, and flower children had begun their debut on the West Coast. *Bitchin'* wasn't a curse word but, rather, an expression coined by surfers. It meant "things are cool and groovy." The Beach Boys were bitchin'; boots were bitchin' (go-go boots—not cowboy boots); and girls with silken blond hair that fell like waterfalls across their shoulders were bitchin'.

The first day I walked up the steps to San Luis Obispo High School with my frizzy hair, wearing my swirled bobby socks, loafers, and Darrel's oversized football jacket hugging my thighs, I was not bitchin'.

A girl in my Algebra II class asked, "What gives with the jacket?"

I explained to her that in our high school in Texas, if you went steady with a football player, it was bitch-ing to wear his letter jacket to school. I think she crossed me off her list right then and there. Luckily, there were plenty of other girls like me, maybe not in football jackets, but also not part of the countercultural revolution. I had enough counterculture at home. Mama kept my hands full.

On one of our first outings, Daddy drove our family to a lookout along the California coast, where barking sea lions sunned themselves on boulders near a gleaming shore. I stood overlooking the grandeur of the Pacific Ocean, grateful to make its acquaintance. Mama oohed and aahed at the breathtaking scenery and the mountains rising from the sea, all products of the shifting tectonic plates along the San Andreas Fault.

"I'll tell you what," Daddy said, sweeping his hand from north to south. "That fault line runs almost the entire length of California. This here is earthquake country."

The possibility of the ground shifting beneath my feet and buildings toppling unnerved me some. But what California lacked in stationary plates, it made up for with a temperate climate, gorgeous vistas, and the bungalow Daddy rented on a street whose name I loved—Palm.

I fell in love with Daddy's house; it had archways, a fireplace, and a formal dining room. Even in December, the backyard was lush with thick grass, green hedges, and fragrant pink roses in full bloom. Bright yellow lemons weighed down the boughs of a lemon tree centered in the middle of the yard like the Tree of Life in our Garden of Eden. It was truly a paradise. I twirled around, taking in the blue sky and Spanish tiled roof. It seemed to me Daddy had struck it rich—at least by our standards.

After we unpacked and settled in, I couldn't wait to pick a bowlful of lemons from the lemon tree. I had never made lemonade so near Christmas. While I squeezed fragrant lemons in the kitchen, a six-foot artificial Christmas tree stood in a corner of the living room next to the fireplace. We had decorated the flocked boughs with shiny ornaments and carefully draped tinsel. Mama disliked clumps of tinsel thrown helter-skelter onto the branches. She wanted each strand to emulate a solitary glittering icicle hanging from the boughs of her beloved Colorado pines.

As I stood sipping lemonade and admiring our grand tree, it was hard to fathom the Christmas, seven years earlier in Ozona, when we had gathered around a squatty tumbleweed. Mama had sprayed the tumbleweed white because we couldn't afford a Christmas tree. Joni had been an infant.

Joni was six now and could hardly contain her excitement when Christmas Eve finally arrived. Daddy smelled of Old Spice as he proudly played Santa Claus, handing out dozens of gifts that took the eight of us a long while to open. We snapped pictures with Daddy's new camera, unaware then that those photographs would document our last Christmas together.

Daddy asked me to take a picture of him and Mama. They posed sitting on a blue chenille couch in front of cream-colored drapes.

Mama's hair is champagne blond; days earlier a hairdresser spent laborious hours bleaching her raven-black hair. Mama wears a new white faux-fur coat, a black dress with textured nylons, and bright pink lipstick. She looks remarkably like Marilyn Monroe. In each hand she holds up what looks to be a box from a jewelry store; Daddy may have given her another ring.

Daddy sits next to Mama, their shoulders touching. He wears black trousers, a white shirt, and a dark tie. His left leg is crossed casually over his right knee. He holds two sets of pajamas—one red-and-black plaid and the other white with red designs. His hair is cut short into a flattop. His expression exudes content-ment and his eyes look misty like the day I first showed him my driver's license. His expression says, At last! We're together again.

Mama's expression says, My God, what have I done?

ALMOST FROM the beginning, Mama acted like a corralled wild horse. She fidgeted and seemed displaced, aimless. During the day, all six of us attended school. At night I think she found the routine of dinner, dishes, and homework tedious. She shook out different pills from different bottles. We had been in San Luis Obispo little more than six weeks before Mama asked me to drive her to the emergency room to get a shot for her migraine headache.

Now, only two weeks later, I again pulled out of the San

Luis Obispo General Hospital parking lot onto Johnson Avenue. Mama cradled her head in her right hand, propped against the passenger window. I looked over at her from time to time as she massaged her left temple. Evidently, the shot had not yet taken effect. I continued down San Luis Drive to California Boulevard and clicked the left blinker to turn down Palm Street.

"Keep driving," Mama said when I braked to turn.

"Where?" I asked, surprised.

"Sierra Vista. I need another Demerol shot."

"You already had a shot," I said.

"It's not enough. I need another one," she said.

I ignored her and turned the Ford down Palm Street, toward our house. I reasoned that the shot had confused her and she didn't mean what she was saying. I knew she shouldn't double dose.

"I told you to keep driving," Mama said angrily.

"Mama—"

"I'm a nurse, for God's sake! I know what I'm doing," she said. "Turn around."

I braked and looked at her.

"Turn around," she hissed.

I fought the urge to remove the keys from the ignition and hurl them out the window. Why did I care if she took too much medicine? If she was stupid enough to do it and the doctors at the hospitals naïve enough to believe her, why should I care? I couldn't do anything about it anyway. It seemed her tolerance to prescription drugs was increasing.

I turned the car around.

"Slow down," Mama said.

She wouldn't let me go into the second emergency room with her. She didn't want to risk me blurting out that she had already been given a Demerol shot at another hospital less than twenty minutes ago. A half hour later, Mama emerged through a second set of glass doors. She had trouble walking a straight line to the car. She was quiet on the ride home and leaned on me as I walked her into her bedroom. I helped her undress, drew the drapes, and put her to bed.

SOMETIME IN late January or early February, less than three months after we arrived in California, Mama told Daddy she needed to return to Texas to divorce Mr. Rodeo. It would be easier to do in Texas, she explained. It shouldn't take long, maybe a week or two, to get the papers in order. She decided Brenda and Joni could miss a week or so of school and took them with her. Brenda was in third grade, Joni in kindergarten.

Mama left like she said; only she never returned.

After a month, Daddy, Vicki, Nancy, Patricia, and I came to a unanimous conclusion—Mama wasn't divorcing Mr. Rodeo after all.

She called finally to say that she, Brenda, and Joni had moved back in with Mr. Rodeo, and asked that I send the rest of their things. I can't remember if Mama asked whether we wanted to come back to Texas. I wouldn't have gone back. Life had become more painful living *with* Mama than living without her. What grieved me most, by far, was that our band of sisters had been severed. Since the time Brenda and Joni were babies, I had helped bathe, dress, and feed them. I felt they were partially mine. They had been on my radar for so many years that I wasn't sure how to orient myself without them.

When I heard Brahms's Lullaby playing on the radio a month after Mama's call, melancholy enveloped me. I sang that lullaby to Brenda and Joni dozens of times over the years, making up my own verses—telling them to sleep, telling them not to cry, not to fear, that I and the morning were near. Who was their buffer now?

I called them in Texas occasionally. They said Mama was doing well, and I tried to convince myself this was true.

Daddy, Vicki, Nancy, Patricia, and I lived in the Palm Street house peacefully for the remainder of that spring. Things were so calm, in fact, I felt sure something bad was bound to happen. Darrel and I continued to write each other almost daily, though our letters began to sound the same. There are only so many ways to say "I love and miss you."

By the end of the school year, Daddy's work had called him to Nevada.

"Do we have to move again?" we wanted to know. Nancy and I would be graduating from high school the following June.

"Not necessarily," Daddy said. "I could drive home on the weekends if you girls thought you could manage during the week."

That seemed like a perfect solution to us. We agreed we were self-sufficient enough to remain in San Luis with Daddy coming home on the weekends. Daddy would still pay the bills and give us money for groceries. He told the landlord and the neighbors across the street that we were on our own with his help and permission.

Daddy trusted us and we felt sure we would be fine. Why wouldn't we be? We had run a household for years. We continued to clean the house, grocery shop, and take turns cooking dinner. We'd curl up together on the couch to watch television in the evenings. Mama had accomplished what she once told JoAnn she hoped to do: she had enabled us to take care of ourselves should something happen to her.

San Luis Obispo was a tourist town. Quaint and charming motels lined numerous streets, tucked away in residential areas. Like some of our classmates, Nancy, Vicki, and I began to clean rooms on the weekends and during the summer. In addition, we babysat for two of the neighbors' children and cleaned an elderly man's house across the street. This garnered us extra money to go to the movies (where I experienced my first minor earthquake), to the roller-skating rink in Morro Bay, to a Mexican restaurant within walking distance, and to an ice-cream shop with hamburgers and malts.

We also drove to Avila Beach when our schedules allowed, rolling down the windows and turning up the radio. With our hair flying in the breeze, we sang along to songs like "These Boots Are Made for Walking" by Nancy Sinatra and "California Dreamin'" by The Mamas and The Papas.

The new living arrangement worked well for Nancy, Vicki, and me. We went to the same high school, had basically the same schedule, and shared most of the same friends, which allowed us to keep a watchful eye on one another. We were the checks and balances for one another.

The only one left out of this symbiotic arrangement was thirteen-year-old Patricia, who would be entering eighth grade in a few months. Patricia was too young to be part of our Rat Pack, and her age mandated that she attend a different school. We didn't know Patricia's world and couldn't help her navigate it or keep an eye on her.

Patricia wasn't particularly chatty when it came to telling me about her world, either. When I inadvertently found out she had gone to the movies with a boy instead of with a girlfriend, as she had said, I tried to have a frank talk with her. One thing was clear to me from that conversation—Patricia didn't think I had the authority to tell her what to do.

I may have dropped the ball years earlier when Patricia ran away from home and no one noticed, but I wasn't about to drop the ball this time. Patricia had grown tanner and taller, and her long blond hair cascaded, unlike mine, into a silken waterfall about her shoulders. She was, frankly, beautiful and boys took notice of her. I worried about her for that very reason.

Patricia seemed to stand at a different precipice. She was much younger, more isolated, and therefore more vulnerable. She felt oppressed by me. I feared she might be swept up by the countercultural revolution. Her only crime was sneaking off to a movie with a boy. But the fact was, she had no real authority figure living in the same house with her on a continual basis.

So I called Mama in Denver City.

I told her I thought Patricia was too young to be without parental supervision for weeks at a time. None of us dared act up when Mama was in close proximity; she had a way of putting the fear of God—or a convent—into you.

Mama listened to my concerns and said she had been doing some thinking of her own. Brenda and Joni had lost their four older sisters, and they missed us terribly. Later that week, Mama called Patricia and asked her if she would come back to Texas for the sake of Brenda and Joni. Patricia didn't want to leave California, but neither did she want to let down her two younger sisters. She had shared a room with them for most of their lives. She agreed to go back—not for Mama, but for Brenda and Joni.

And then there were three. . . . I missed Patricia, too.

BEFORE MY senior year began, Mama surprised Nancy, Vicki, and me by showing up on our doorstep, without notice and without the girls. She may have left Patricia, Brenda, and Joni under her mother's care. I suspected Mama's visit coincided with a fight with Mr. Rodeo, and that she hoped to find Daddy at home, but he was away working.

That first morning of Mama's visit, we had to work at the motel. When I finished cleaning my block of rooms sooner than Nancy or Vicki, I walked home alone to keep Mama company. I walked into the house to find her sitting on my floral bedspread with an open letter in her hand and dozens of Darrel's letters strewn about her. She looked up.

I expected to see guilt on her face, but what I saw was outrage.

"How dare he say these things about me?" she seethed.

I tried to remember exactly what Darrel had said about Mama. I knew he didn't approve of her. I remembered him writing something to the effect that he was glad I wasn't like her. I'm sure he questioned some of her decisions and behaviors, but he hadn't written anything untrue.

My hands started to shake.

"I don't want you reading my letters," I demanded. "They're private!"

"They're mush," Mama answered.

"Give them to me." I attempted to gather them up.

Mama grabbed some of the envelopes away from me.

"You know what I'm going to do," she said. "I'm going to move back here permanently and make sure you don't do anything but go to school and come home. And don't think you'll be reading any more of these, either." She waved a fistful of letters in front of me.

For the first time in my life, I said, "I don't care what you say. I won't do it."

Shock registered in Mama's eyes.

"Then I'll send you to reform school," she countered.

"Fine. I'll gladly go," I said. I didn't know anything about reform school, but I meant it. I knew I could never live with Mama again.

"Listen to me, young lady. I'll walk you to school and I'll be waiting for you when it lets out. I'll—"

"I won't do it."

"Then I'll send you to reform school."

"I'll do that."

Mama sat there looking at me, speechless for a long while. We both knew the ground had shifted under our feet. Within a few days, Mama repacked her suitcase and was gone—back to Texas. I had finally cut the cord that had been wrapped around my neck.

THAT FALL Nancy and I started our senior year, and Vicki her junior year. By then we had become regulars at the skating rink in the seaside village of Morro Bay, driving the fifteen miles to the rink most every Friday and Saturday night. We arrived when

240 Terry Helwig

the doors opened, retrieved our scuffed quad skates from the trunk of the Ford, and laced up our boots while sitting on the smooth wooden benches inside the rink. For hours, I practiced skating backward, perfecting my transitions and moving my feet quickly in a scissors step. I wasn't afraid to fall if it meant I would become a better skater.

One night, a particularly talented skater asked me to dance during the couples skate. He showed me how to lean into my turns, reverse directions together, and bend my knees low on the curves.

"You've got great rhythm," he said.

I beamed when he asked me to dance again later. *He must think I'm pretty good,* I thought. Our connection lasted only as long as the couples skates; we didn't talk or pair up off the floor. He was in his late twenties, too old for me, plus Darrel and I were still writing. But I loved the physicality of skating and dancing, how his movement and the music drew me in, as if we were water flowing across a streambed.

At the end of the night, Nancy, Vicki, and I were physically exhausted. It was hard to determine how many miles we skated in a single night, but it felt like a marathon. Mrs. Dickerson, who owned the skating rink with her husband, scooted out from behind the concession stand to hug us good-bye.

"Isn't skating just good, clean fun?" she asked.

"Absolutely," we agreed and waved good-bye.

"See you next week."

"We'll be here," I said, opening the outside door.

A cool fog had rolled in off the bay, creating a halo around the lights in the parking lot. We tossed our skates into the trunk and headed home, past the undulating hills toward San Luis.

* * *

IT TOOK me more than a week of peeking into our empty mail-box to realize that Darrel was about to break up with me. Just to give him the benefit of the doubt, I made a rare and expensive long-distance call to Texas to check on him. He was neither on his deathbed nor at home.

"No, he's feeling fine," his mom said awkwardly. I could tell she knew something I didn't. "Yes, I'll tell him you called," she said and quickly hung up.

Eventually a letter arrived saying he had found someone else. I moped for weeks before sending back his football jacket. I de-cided to keep the powder-blue knit jacket-and-skirt set he had given me the summer before, the one with two silver-gray but-terflies pinned on the jacket near the neckline.

THAT CHRISTMAS, Daddy drove home and we gathered around the dining table to eat a baked ham. Mama, Patricia, Brenda, and Joni were noticeably missing. Mama sent Nancy, Vicki, and me each a miniature Christmas stocking and had tucked inside a rosy-cheeked plastic elf—*our family gremlin,* she had said in a poem she wrote just for the occasion. After Daddy went to bed, I read the poem out loud to Nancy and Vicki. I had to pause several times to wait for the knot in my throat to loosen so I could continue. I wondered how Mama and the girls had celebrated their Christmas with Mr. Rodeo. I wondered if they missed me as much as I missed them.

* * *

"THE OFFICE wants to see you," my chemistry teacher informed me when I walked into class after Christmas vacation. I had an uneasy feeling in my chest as I headed down the hallway toward the office.

The secretary pointed toward the counselor's office.

"Have a seat," the counselor said.

Before sitting, I double-checked my skirt to make sure it complied with school rules; it couldn't be shorter than my fingertips with my hands at my sides. My fingertips touched well above the hem. I wore white go-go boots and for once my hair was straight. I recently learned that a number of girls at school ironed their hair on the ironing board; I feared I might need a steamroller, but the iron seemed to work fine—except where I burned my forehead when I tried to iron my bangs. I looked at the counselor. If my skirt wasn't too short, I couldn't imagine why I had been pulled out of class.

"I've just been talking to Nancy," the counselor said, tapping his pencil on some papers in front of him.

"Oh?"

"She tells me that the two of you and your sister Vicki live alone."

I wanted to shake Nancy.

"Well, we're not exactly alone," I stammered.

He leaned back in his chair, eyeing me. "She said you're in charge."

"That's true. When my dad's not home, I'm in charge."

"She said your dad lives in Nevada."

Good grief! Didn't Nancy realize that telling the school we lived by ourselves would invite scrutiny—maybe even the authorities?

"Our dad does work in Nevada," I backpedaled, "but he still

considers this his home." I didn't mention that Daddy was home only a few days a month.

"Nancy has chicken pox and we can't send her home because no one is there to take care of her," he said.

"I'll take care of her."

"You don't understand. The three of you are minors. Legally, you cannot live together without an adult."

"I told you my dad comes home whenever he can." I shifted my weight and leaned forward. "Look, it's been like this for months. Check our grades, check our attendance. We're good students, at the top of our classes. I do work-study for the business office. Wouldn't you say we're doing fine?"

He clasped his fingers and brought them under his chin, considering what I had just said.

I mustered every bit of my self-assurance and held his gaze.

"I should report this," he said hesitantly.

"Please don't. I'll be eighteen in a few months. We'll be graduating soon. We know how to take care of ourselves. I promise you, we're good kids."

He looked deeply into my eyes. Finally, he relented. "Okay," he said. "I hope I don't regret this. If there's any hint of any trouble—"

"There won't be," I interrupted. I jumped up before he could change his mind. I also wanted to retrieve Nancy from the nurse's office before the whole state of California became involved. If thirteen-year-old Patricia had still been living with us, I had no doubt the authorities would have been called. Vicki's being only sixteen was concern enough.

"What were you thinking?" I asked Nancy.

"What did I do wrong? The nurse said she needed to call my mom and I said, 'You can't—she lives in Texas.' Then she said,

'Okay, I'll call your dad,' and I said, 'You can't do that, either, because he lives in Nevada.'"

I shook my head. Nancy had told the truth all right, but the consequences seemed to elude her. Her chicken pox didn't stop me from chiding, "We'll be lucky if we don't end up in a foster home!"

WHEN DADDY brought Alice home to meet us, it had been almost a year since Mama took the girls back to Texas. I couldn't believe how much Alice reminded me of Mama. She had short black hair and Mama's twinkling eyes. She was vivacious and funny, but I didn't quite know what to make of her.

If you told her you liked one of her dresses, she said, "Really? You can have it." And she meant it. She gave Nancy, Vicki, and me several of her dresses. I was almost reluctant to pay her a compliment. When she looked in my closet and saw the blue knit suit Darrel had given me, she asked if she could wear it when she and Daddy got married.

A few weeks later, in front of the justice of the peace, wearing my blue knit suit, Alice said "I do" to Daddy. We girls signed as their witnesses.

Alice stayed on with us for a couple of weeks that spring. It was the dreary rainy season. She wore knee-high socks and kicked up the heat to a stifling eighty degrees. But for the first time in our lives, we came home from school to someone busily cooking in the kitchen. Delicious aromas met us at the door like warm hugs. Alice was a great cook, but she had rather expensive culinary taste. "I don't look at grocery-store prices," she said during one dinner. "I just buy what I want."

"That's a true story," Daddy said, nodding.

Alice taught us to play contract rummy and went shopping with us.

Once when she didn't call home to tell Daddy we would be very late, I warned her, "Alice, Daddy might get mad."

"Well, he's got the same boots to get glad in." She laughed.

I laughed, too.

Daddy seemed happy enough, though I surmised he must be feeling the pinch of maintaining two households. He recently bought a trailer for him and Alice to live in, in New Mexico. I imagined Daddy had to buy new dresses to replace the ones Alice so freely gave away, plus he continued to pay child support for Patricia, Brenda, and Joni. Daddy assured us girls, however, that his marriage would not change our living situation.

He said he would continue to pay rent not only until Nancy and I graduated in June, but until Vicki graduated the following year. Whoever agreed to live with Vicki could live rent-free because Daddy didn't want her to live alone. Based on our recent experience at school, we knew Vicki should live with someone at least eighteen years old.

I wanted to live on campus come fall, and my high school friend Linda and I had talked about renting student housing over the summer. Both Linda and I had applied to and been accepted at Cal Poly in San Luis. I chose it because I had been on campus numerous times, pretending to be one of the college students. I could see myself happily living in the dorm with Linda, driving to the ballroom in Pismo Beach to go dancing, and studying in the library.

Since I had other plans, Nancy offered to live with Vicki. But Nancy wondered, for several reasons, if Vicki would be willing to move to Morro Bay. First, Nancy loved walking the foggy beach near famed Morro Rock; second, she fancied a guy named Rick who happened to live in Morro Bay; and third, she had been promised a job at Rose's Landing, a restaurant overlooking the water where Rick's mom worked as a cook. Vicki readily agreed to the move—unaware that she would eventually marry Rick's younger brother Gary.

The living arrangements were settled, then: me on campus, Vicki and Nancy in Morro Bay.

Daddy and Alice drove back to San Luis Obispo for Nancy's and my graduation. Daddy told me that the blue Ford Fairlane would be my graduation present. I was thrilled.

The afternoon of the commencement ceremony, I squinted, searching the stadium seats for where Daddy, Alice, and Vicki were seated. I saw Daddy and waved. Daddy maneuvered through the crowd and walked down the steps to see me and Nancy before we lined up for the procession.

He hugged both of us and his eyes filled with tears.

"I'm so proud of you," he said.

I touched his face and kissed his cheek. How I loved his tender heart.

"Go on now," he said. "You'll miss the best part."

I wished Mama and the girls could be with us, too, to witness this milestone. Nancy's mother wasn't there, either. Aunt Eunice was still alive, but she was so jaundiced and sick that it never crossed our minds that she might travel all the way to California from Colorado. I told myself the day was about beginnings, not regrets.

I held my head high and marched across the stage with a smile as wide as the blue sky overhead. I felt buoyed by the current of life. I had attended twelve schools. I had made it through my eighteenth birthday. I had climbed a few hills, and now I felt practically on top of the world.

Meanwhile, a thousand miles away, Mama was about to make the darkest descent of her life.

Brenda and Joni in their Easter dresses

Odessa, Texas
Revisited

AFTER GRADUATION, I roomed with my girlfriends Linda
and Sam for the summer in a cute two-bedroom unit not
far from Cal Poly. Linda's mom helped me find summer work
at an electronics-parts supplier for computers and satellites. I

saved money that summer, but not nearly enough to cover tuition.

I began to realize that I might not be able to attend college. I didn't know about financial aid and student loans. I don't think Daddy knew, either. Surely my high school counselors knew, but I never confided in them for fear of inviting scrutiny into our living arrangements.

By the end of summer, I had adopted Plan B. I continued working while taking several adult-education courses at Cuesta College just outside of San Luis Obispo. The night classes were cheap and allowed me to work full-time. It wasn't my ideal scenario, because I wasn't matriculated, but neither was it the total collapse of my dream of attending college.

By late fall, yet another plan emerged. My roommate Sam and I embarked on a trip to Texas. The determining factor had been Mama's repeated phone calls, especially the most recent.

"I wish you'd move back," she slurred. "It wouldn't have to be Denver City, just someplace close by. So I could call on you. Things aren't going too well with Mr. Rodeo. And I'm not too good. I could really use your help with the girls. Please think about it."

I wondered what life was like for the younger girls now. Patricia was older, but Brenda and Joni were only in fifth and second grade. I could pretend Mama was doing better because I wasn't there to see her day in and day out, but her voice on the phone told me she was either drunk or drugged. It was hard to assess the situation from a thousand miles away. The simple fact was I still cared—deeply. How could I refuse?

"I'll go with you," Sam said, "to help you figure this whole thing out. I've never been to Texas."

Our lease was up on our rental and my classes had ended. We gave notice at work and here we were, on a desolate road with lights flashing behind us.

"He's pulling me over," I said to Sam.

She turned to see the red lights. We were literally in the middle of the Arizona desert. I pulled off the road, opened the glove compartment to retrieve my registration, and stepped out of the car.

A young highway patrolman approached, looked me over, and bent down to look inside at Sam. "You know what I think?" he asked, adjusting his hat.

"What?"

"I think you were speeding, saw me sitting back there, then slammed on your brakes."

"You know what I think?"

"What?"

"I think you're right."

My honesty seemed to catch him off guard. He smiled and asked to see my driver's license. I plopped my purse onto the warm hood. I wasn't about to confess that my speedometer had been pushing ninety, which sounded more reckless than it seemed on the arrow-straight road slicing through the cactus and yucca plants of the Sonoran Desert. We hadn't passed a car for miles— until the patrolman's car, that is, idling on a side road. Before I had time to brake, I whizzed past him like Road Runner leaving Wile E. Coyote in the dust.

The officer now stood, patiently waiting for me to produce my license, which seemed to have mysteriously disappeared. "It isn't in my wallet," I apologized. "Maybe it fell out into my purse."

I searched and fumbled more frantically. Finally, in despera-

tion, I dumped the entire contents of my purse onto the hood—
hairbrush, chewing gum, mirror, wallet, change, and tampons. A
tube of pink lipstick rolled off the hood and clanked against the
gravel.

The officer rolled his eyes. "I thought this happened only in
movies."

I picked through the contents of my purse but still couldn't
locate my license. "I can't believe it," I said. "I must have lost it
somewhere. I have one. Honest!"

"Where are you two headed?" he asked.

"Texas," I said. "My friend Sam has never been. I used to live
there."

He looked through the windshield at Sam. She smiled and
did a little wave with her fingers. He didn't quite know what to
make of us. We were either painfully innocent babes or frighten-
ingly smooth con artists.

"You've got California plates," he noted.

"I've been living in California the past two years."

He looked at my registration and back at us, trying to decide
what to do.

I returned the mound of items on the hood to my purse.

"I'm going to give you a warning this time," he said finally.
"But if I get back to the station and find out that this car is stolen, I'm coming after you personally."

"I promise you it's not stolen," I said and patted the Ford.
"This was my graduation present from high school."

"Well, slow down and live long enough to enjoy it." He
handed me my registration and casually closed my door as I
slipped in behind the steering wheel. "You two staying the night
in Phoenix?" he asked.

We nodded. He told us the name of a place to go if we were interested in dancing and nightlife. We thanked him and drove off, giggling with relief to have been spared a ticket.

It will be interesting to see Darrel again, I thought. It was his offer that made me choose Odessa, where he now lived. He called after graduation and said he still had feelings for me. When he learned Sam and I would be traveling to Texas, he asked his sister, Dola Jane, and her husband, Dick, if we could stay with them until we found jobs and a place to rent. I knew I could never live with Mama again and the eighty-mile buffer between Odessa and Mama in Denver City seemed just about right.

Sam and I thanked Dola Jane and Dick for the use of their guest room.

Once unpacked, we drove to Denver City to see Mama and the girls. Brenda and Joni squealed with delight when they saw me and came running to throw their arms around me. It felt so good to wrap my arms around their slender bodies. Patricia smiled and waved to us from the couch. Mama sat at the table eating stewed tomatoes over bread—her comfort food. She said she liked my hair lightened and asked Sam to have a seat at the picnic table, our same table from the trailer.

My first few visits to Denver City were unremarkable. I watched the girls occasionally. Mama still functioned most of the time, but her medicine chest and drawers were filled with prescription bottles. Then once, after Mama visited me in Odessa, Dola's pain medication disappeared from the medicine cabinet. Dola had had her wisdom teeth removed and was prescribed pain pills in case she needed them. After Mama's visit, Dola received a perplexing phone call from the dentist's office.

"If you're still having problems with your wisdom teeth, you need to come in."

Dola told them she wasn't having any problems. That's when we learned that a woman had called, saying she was Dola Jane. The woman also said she needed more pain pills. Both Dola and I knew Mama had made the call.

"I'm so sorry," I told Dola.

"It's not your fault," she said. "It's just sad."

"I know she has a problem," I said, "but I don't know what to do about it." Nobody seemed to know what to do about Mama.

By the time Mama stole Dola's pain pills, Sam had returned to California. She missed the beach and her boyfriend. Darrel and I, on the other hand, were officially history. Darrel's greatest gift to me would be introducing me to Dola and Dick. After I had found a job as a waitress at the Barn Door, Dick asked if I would stay on with them because Dola was pregnant. Dick drove a truck and didn't want Dola home alone when he was out of town. The living arrangements suited me, too. I couldn't have asked for two better roommates.

On nights I didn't come straight home from work, I went dancing with several waitresses who had become friends. I had, evidently, inherited Mama's dancing gene. I finally understood Mama's love for dancing and why one of her friends had described her as a "dancing fool." Mama liked all kinds of dancing—jitterbug, country-western, polka.

Dancing wipes away the past and the future; it exists only in the present moment. It's as if the whole world falls away and all that remains is the music. You become one with the notes, pulsing, twirling, dipping, and swaying. The body leads and the mind forgets. Rumi, a thirteenth-century poet, danced as a spiritual discipline. He wrote:

Dance, when you're broken open.
Dance, if you've torn the bandage off.
Dance in the middle of the fighting.
Dance in your blood.
Dance, when you're perfectly free.

In a roundabout way, dancing led me to my friend Larry, who visited me regularly at Dick and Dola's house. We played board games, talked, and hid ice-cream bowls under the couch—our own private joke. Larry was gentle, good-hearted, and kind—a lot like Daddy. I loved him as a brother, even more so after he helped me ferry Mama through her dark night of the soul.

Mama's call sounded urgent.

"I really need to talk things over with you," she said, "but I don't want to get into it on the phone. How soon can you come?"

I had to work that night.

"I'll be there in the morning," I told her. I figured I could drive back the next afternoon before my shift started at the Barn Door.

Eighty miles is a long way to drive with an uneasy feeling in the pit of your stomach. I didn't know if Mama was crying wolf or not. If she was, I needed to figure out how to handle her; if she wasn't, I would be walking into the problem without a clue what to expect.

Over an hour later, I pulled into the dirt driveway and parked near the old bunkhouse, the one Mr. Rodeo had painted robin-egg blue for us. I let myself in the back door of the main house and found the girls in the living room watching television. I sat and talked to them for a few minutes. Nothing seemed out of the ordinary.

"Where's Mama?" I asked.

Patricia pointed toward the bedroom down the hall. I walked into the bedroom and found Mama in bed. She looked awful. She had dark circles under her eyes, sallow skin, and tangled hair.

"What's going on?"

"Close the door," she said hoarsely. She propped herself into a sitting position and leaned against the headboard.

I clicked the door closed and sat down on the edge of her bed.

Her hand shook as she brushed aside her matted hair. "I'm not doing too well," she said. "I've . . . I've been thinking about . . . admitting myself to a psychiatric hospital."

I saw the look of defeat in her eyes, and tried to mask the relief in mine. A huge weight dropped from my shoulders. *Finally,* I thought. *She's finally admitting there's a problem.*

"I know I need help, but I don't want to go to Big Spring. I know what goes on in hospitals," she said adamantly. "I'll only agree to go to the Colorado State Hospital in Pueblo. A psychiatrist in Denver said he'd admit me, if I can see him first."

It didn't matter to me where she went. "I'm just glad you're getting help," I said evenly. I wondered how Mr. Rodeo felt about Mama going to a hospital so many miles away. "Where's Mr. Rodeo?" I asked.

"We're not together anymore." She exhaled as if the last bit of air had finally gone out of her. "That's why I called you."

She needs a ride to the hospital, I thought.

"I can drive you," I offered before she even had a chance to speak.

"No," she said. "It's more than that. We can't continue living here; this place doesn't belong to me. I want to know if you'll take Brenda and Joni to live with you until I get out."

Her request surprised me. Questions raced through my mind. *What about Daddy? Wouldn't he want his girls? How could I trump him? And, even if I could, would I be able to take care of them and still hold down a job?*

"What about Daddy?" I asked. "I'm sure he and Alice would want the girls. I've met her and she's really nice."

Mama shook her head. "If I lose them, I won't have anything to live for."

Her look begged me to understand.

"Patricia's not too happy with me right now," she confessed.

Patricia was in high school and I imagined she and Mama saw things a bit differently.

"She'll end up with Davy, I'm sure," Mama continued, "because she can't stay here, and I doubt she'll go with you." Mama hung her head. "But if I let all three of them go to Davy, he might not give them back. Then I'd have no reason to live."

I didn't know if Mama was right about Daddy. But true to form, she didn't consider what the law might have to say on the issue. I hated to go against Daddy after everything he had done for us. But neither did I want to jeopardize Mama's willingness to get help. I wondered if my tips from the restaurant would cover a rental for the three of us, plus expenses. It didn't seem likely that Daddy would send me child support. Why should he? To ensure I kept his girls away from him?

"If you don't say yes, I can't do it," Mama said. "I won't have anything to live for."

She kept using that phrase, "nothing to live for."

"I don't know, Mama," I faltered. The room seemed stifling.

"Let me think about it, okay? I'm going outside for a walk to clear my head."

I closed the door behind me and slipped outside. I stuck my hands deep into my jacket pockets to keep them warm. The cold February wind stung my face.

What should I do? I walked up and down the dirt road next to the fence, looking for guidance. *How long would Mama be in the hospital? Could I make it work for a while? Maybe if I got a second job. I didn't want to put Brenda and Joni in jeopardy in any way. I could try it and if it didn't work, I could figure out what else to do later. The important thing was to get Mama to the hospital.*

I turned and walked briskly back into the house. I had been gone no more than half an hour. I took off my jacket, draped it over a kitchen chair, and walked toward Mama's bedroom. When I opened the door, I saw a wide swath of blood soaking the white sheets. A dark crust of coagulated blood surrounded a deep gash in Mama's left wrist.

"What have you done?" I gasped.

Mama was pasty white. "I told you I wouldn't have anything to live for."

Then I saw she had sliced open *both* wrists with a razor blade. The sheets were growing redder and redder. The ranch was out of town—an ambulance was out of the question. I couldn't let the girls witness this; it would haunt them forever.

Flooded with adrenaline, I hauled a large dresser in front of the bedroom door so no one could come inside. I ripped off the top sheet and started tearing it into strips. I was furious. It was as if all the anger I had been suppressing my whole life suddenly surfaced.

"Why couldn't you wait? I told you I needed to think," I said angrily as I ripped another strip from the sheet.

"You were going to say no."

I bound several strips of sheet tightly around one wrist and then around the other.

"I just needed time to think it through. I can't believe you did this," I said, choking back a sob.

Mama cried and I cried. Mama looked like a mummy from her forearms down. I unbuttoned the sleeves of a long-sleeved flannel shirt so Mama's bandages wouldn't be visible. I helped her into a pair of jeans and slipped on her moccasins. In a matter of minutes, I had stripped the sheets off the bed and tossed them into a corner of the closet. I didn't want the girls to see all the blood, so I flipped the mattress, too. After I moved the dresser away from the door, I put Mama's arm over my shoulder and helped her walk down the hallway. She was woozy. When I saw the girls, I told them Mama wasn't feeling well and I needed to take her to the hospital. I told Patricia I would be back as soon as I settled her in.

Only in our house would taking Mama to the hospital seem mildly alarming. The girls watched wide-eyed as I folded Mama into the passenger seat.

Mama didn't want to go to the hospital in Denver City. Instead, she begged me to drive her to Seagraves, to a physician she knew there. I worried about Mama losing too much blood, but when I checked her bandages, they seemed to be stemming her bleeding. I had tied them tight. Seagraves wasn't that much farther. I turned right onto the county road and gunned the accelerator; my speedometer climbed toward ninety.

The nurse in Seagraves helped me bring Mama into the back

office. The doctor unwound the bloody strips of sheets from her wrists.

"Looks like you meant business," he said. He turned to me. "Why don't you step out?"

Mama grabbed my hand and asked the doctor. "No, can't she stay?" Then to me she said, "Please. Will you stay and hold my hand?"

The doctor looked up at me. "You okay with this?"

Though I felt weak and nauseated, I nodded and willed myself to be strong for Mama's sake. I tenderly held her bloodied hand with its gaping wound while the doctor sutured her other wrist.

"You're lucky you didn't bleed to death," the doctor told her.

I held her hand firmly, the way she must have held mine all those years ago through the slats of the crib.

"Things can't be this bad," the doctor continued.

I watched a single tear travel down Mama's cheek. "God has to be more merciful than life," Mama whispered. She was thirty-three.

I bent over and kissed her forehead. I was eighteen.

Before the doctor released Mama back into my care, he gave her a sedative and something for her pain. He told me she definitely needed psychiatric help. I explained that she had agreed to admit herself into the Colorado State Hospital in Pueblo, and that I planned to take her tomorrow. We would be meeting with a psychiatrist who could refer her. Evidently, you couldn't just show up at a state hospital as if you were checking in to a motel.

"It's imperative she gets help," he said gravely. "She's at risk and might try to commit suicide again." His eyes looked into mine as if to make sure I knew the gravity of the situation.

"Her wounds were deep," he reiterated, "deep enough that she could have bled to death. She was lucky."

The word *lucky* seemed oddly out of place.

Mama dozed on our drive back to the ranch. I put her to bed and called Larry. When I heard his voice, I slid down the wall onto the floor, sobbing.

"I've handled everything life's thrown my way," I told him. "I just don't know if I'm strong enough to handle this one alone."

"You don't have to," Larry said.

Within hours, Larry arrived. He had taken his vacation time and withdrawn money from his checking account. He helped me slide Mama into the backseat of his car and the three of us headed northwest toward Denver.

As we sped through New Mexico, each gouged-out place in the landscape reminded me of the wounds on Mama's wrists. All I could see were deep canyons and fissures where blood flowed. In my mind, I kept opening Mama's bedroom door to find her lying on blood-soaked sheets. I didn't know how long it would take for these vivid images to fade away.

After we left the psychiatrist's office, we drove Mama straight to the hospital and parked the car.

"I'm not sure about this," Mama said, hugging herself with her bandaged wrists and pressing herself farther into the backseat.

I reached in and grabbed her firmly by the arm. Larry hefted her bag out of the trunk.

"It'll be okay, Mama," I reassured, knowing it took every bit of her courage to walk toward that hospital door.

Mama stopped and looked around.

"You can do this, Jean," Larry said and held open the door for her.

Mama walked hesitantly across the threshold. I felt a surge of relief. The woman in admissions was gentle and reassuring. A bouquet of red roses sat atop her desk; it was Valentine's Day.

Larry and I said good-bye to Mama. She hugged me for a long while.

Mama wrote in her diary that first night:

February 14, 1968

My first day in the wards, and what a terrible feeling of terror. Windows are barred, doors are locked, and I'm so full of tranquilizer that the depression is smothering me with horror. I realize that I have placed myself here. Will I ever walk free again?

After Larry and I dropped Mama off, we drove back to Texas together, mostly in silence. I looked over at him guiding the steering wheel. He returned my gaze and smiled. His presence helped calm me. For the first time in my life, I understood what it might feel like to have an older sibling, one to help carry the load. I loved Larry the way I imagined I would have loved my brother, Lanny, had I been given a chance to grow up with him.

I had been thinking a lot about Lanny the past few weeks, ever since Aunt Betty's letter arrived with the shocking news that Lanny had brain cancer. He was eleven years old. The last time I had seen him, he was an infant.

My eighteenth birthday had come and gone and I still had not contacted my dad. Dad and Cathy had not heard from me since the summer Vicki and I waved good-bye from the backseat on our way to Kansas with Mama and Daddy. I always wondered what I might say to reinitiate contact. I never guessed it would be under such dire circumstances.

I was so saddened and sorrowful to hear about Lanny that I

sat down that night to write my dad and Cathy a letter, hoping to offer them some small solace, to tell them how sorry I was.

I received two answers right away, one letter from Dad, the other from Cathy. Dad said, "When I got through reading your nice letter I was so happy my eyes were full of tears. I missed you girls many times during the last ten and three-fourths years." He said he had hoped and prayed I might someday write and even come for a visit. Cathy said they heard from Aunt Betty that we were in Texas and then California. "We wanted very much to see you and to write, but we talked it over, and decided under the circumstances maybe it would be best to just leave you alone."

On another page Cathy said Lanny had the worst type of cancer possible and the prognosis wasn't good; he was undergoing cobalt treatments. She ended her letter, "You didn't mention your mother. Where is she now?"

I didn't plan on telling them about Mama—at least not now. My dad didn't go into detail about Lanny, but he wrote:

Life is hard to understand at times. The next few weeks or months are going to be very hard on us. Like you say we got to have faith no matter what happens. It is going to leave an awful hole in my life, but I must remember I have Cathy and Robin [Lanny's baby sister and, therefore, mine as well]. You got in touch with me now and maybe Vicki [will], so I still have a lot to live for.

Dad was right. Life *was* hard to understand. He, Cathy, and Lanny were fighting to hold on to life, and here I was driving with Larry because Mama tried to bleed hers away.

"You okay?" Larry asked.

I nodded. I was shell-shocked and unsure how long Mama

might need to stay, but I wanted, more than anything, to rise to the occasion. I wanted to be a good mother to Brenda and Joni. I didn't want them to feel abandoned the way I had, ever. They were too young to lose Mama. I wanted Mama to live for them, for herself, for me, for all of us.

I wanted Lanny to live, too.

Upon our return, I told Brenda and Joni that Larry and I had taken Mama to a special hospital, a place where she could get some rest, a place that would help her to feel not so sad.

"You're two very special girls," I said. "Nothing that's happened is your fault."

When I told them I would be taking care of them until Mama got out, they hugged me long and hard.

I told Patricia, Nancy, and Vicki the distilled, bloodless version of the truth. They were sorry but not surprised. Mama had threatened to harm herself before.

Patricia wanted to remain in Denver City with Mr. Rodeo, but that wasn't an option. She was sent to live with Daddy and Alice in New Mexico, though Daddy continued to work out of town. I couldn't bring myself to talk to Daddy personally, afraid he might insist that Brenda and Joni come, too. I felt guilty for shutting him out—he didn't deserve that—but he hadn't been the one to find Mama lying in her own blood. He didn't know how high the stakes were. Brenda and Joni had become Mama's lifeline.

I had to consider Brenda and Joni, too. They had been through so much. They didn't know any of the gory details but knew something was amiss. I understood when they hugged me hard, after I said I would take care of them, that they needed me to step in. They needed an anchor. I could moor them for a while; they had always felt safe in my care.

After Valentine's Day, I withdrew them from their Denver City school and Larry helped me move them to Odessa, where I had a job. I informed Dola and Dick I would be looking for a place to rent, now that I had two sisters in tow.

Without pausing, Dola said, "You'll do no such thing."

Though Dola had just given birth to Diana, my new god-daughter, Dick rearranged the bedrooms so that Brenda and Joni could have a room of their own. I found a second job at a fast-food restaurant that allowed me to be home with Brenda and Joni after school for a few hours before my night shift at the Barn Door. I hoped my two jobs would cover our expenses.

I wasn't so sure the afternoon a letter came from the Colorado State Hospital. My mouth dropped open when I read, "We hope we can be of help to you in arriving at the most reasonable charge for the hospitalization of your relative." I hadn't even considered the cost of hospitalizing Mama, nor did I imagine I would be approached financially for her care. But Mama didn't have any assets, was in the middle of a divorce, and had no insurance. I was her next of kin, her contact, the one who helped her check in to the hospital.

I couldn't afford to pay more than a few dollars toward her hospital bill. I nervously filled out the questionnaire they sent and included a copy of my most recent income-tax return. I worried the whole arrangement might fall through. Time would tell.

I enrolled Brenda and Joni in a nearby school and took off work to attend parents' night. Brenda and Joni held my hand and proudly showed me around their rooms, pointing out the artwork and stories they created. They were so resilient and hopeful—despite all they had been through.

I read them parts of Mama's letters, especially when she wrote about how much she missed and loved them. Three letters helped me track Mama's progress:

February 28, 1968

Dear Terry,

Received your lovely letter. I do hope that all of you are happy. I know it's hard to work and be saddled with two little ones at your age; but I do know that you love them and will take good care of them. God willing, it won't be for too long and I can take care of them myself. Let me know how you are managing. . . .

I'm keeping a diary and am going to send it to you. Read it if you want but put it in a good place. Don't be shocked and don't discuss it with everyone. Remember this is a mental hospital. A world entirely its own. Someday, I'll write a book. The stitches are out and my arms are healing well. I will have some terrible scars. Reminders, I guess. . . .

Send me some heels and a few of my nice things. Not too many. Just a couple of complete outfits (something to dance in). . . .

Be sure to let the little ones know I love them dearly. When you write Patricia, tell her I love her and hope she'll find it in her heart to write me someday. Do let me know if you have financial trouble. I'm not that delicate.

Well, Pumpkin, it's time that I made my nightly entry and got to bed. Thanks again for all your understanding. Tell Larry hello and to look out for all of you until I'm well again.

All my love,
Mama

I didn't bother Mama with my financial concerns other than to say I had taken on another part-time job. Luckily, when the Colorado State Hospital realized I was only eighteen, and the primary caretaker of my two youngest sisters, they didn't want Mama's stay to be a financial hardship for me. I would not be charged for her care. I breathed a sigh of relief. I packed up and mailed Mama a couple of outfits and heels so she could go dancing.

Mama's Diary Entry

I miss my girls much and evenings are always my low. . . . Everyone is so quiet at night. . . . no sleep last night . . . Wish the doc would prescribe Doriden — not a narcotic or a barbiturate — [just] good old restful sleep. Damn the nights.

As long as I could remember, Mama hated the night.

I didn't hate the nights; they were just too short. Whatever social and individual time I had came after ten at night. During the days and weekends, I tried to spend as much time as possible with Brenda and Joni. I took them for picnics at Dennis the Menace Park and showed them prairie-dog town, a live colony of prairie dogs that sometimes tunneled outside the fence designed to protect them. Brenda and Joni delighted in the prairie dogs' cavorting as they popped in and out of their mounded burrows, making high-pitched squeaks timed to the twitch of their tails.

Whenever I drove Brenda and Joni anywhere, they begged me to call Dick and Dola on the CB radio. To them, it was a toy. Long before the era of cell phones, I often picked up the CB mike and said, "KOVO514, mobile to base, come in, please."

"KOVO514 base to mobile, go ahead." It would be Dick's or Dola's voice crackling over the radio.

"We're meeting Larry at Whataburger for lunch," Brenda told Dola over the CB mike one day after leaving prairie-dog town.

"Sounds great," Dola said. "Can y'all stop by the store and pick up some diapers and a can of sliced pineapple on the way home? I'll make a pineapple upside-down cake tonight."

"Ten four," I said.

"I'll make sure she remembers," Brenda piped in. She loved pineapple upside-down cake.

Joni grabbed the mike from Brenda. "Over and out," Joni said, giggling and covering her mouth.

March 25, 1968

Dearest Terry and Little Ones,

It was so nice to hear your voice on the telephone last night. I was afraid to answer at first because I thought that it might bring bad news. It was quite a relief when I heard all of you. Joni and Brenda sound real happy, Terry. You must be doing a real fine job. . . .

There is a new girl in my dormitory that is only eighteen. She does not even know what size dress that she wears. Her mother has always done everything for her until she just couldn't take it anymore. I was thinking that maybe I pushed you girls to learn too much and maybe I did. Now I see that it can also work two ways. I could not stand for one of you to be in here. Better me than you. . . .

Terry, I may have a chance here to brush up on my schooling. What do you think? The girls sound as though they have made such a good adjustment that I hate to move them out of school until the summer vacation. If the opportunity is offered to me, should I take it? Of course, I may not have any choice. Even though I am a voluntary patient — they can commit me if I try to leave before they agree to it and at this point I really do not know what the doctor has in mind. . . .

It is odd how many things are changing for me as I have time to think of them. I did not realize how much I was tied into knots. I find that I had put up several mental blocks as a defense. I forget some things that I would rather remember. It must have been a habit I formed to hold myself together. What a tight rope I must have been walking for a long time — years.

The psychiatric technicians (educated fools for the most part, ha) want me to talk, talk, talk. And I have formed such a habit of keeping so much to myself for so long that we are really clashing. How in the world do they expect me to be able to talk to these kids who are not yet dry behind the ears about a life that has covered as many miles as mine? They are supposed to be objective about it all, but most of them have not yet lived in a broad enough world to be objective about anything.

Hugs and kisses to all,
Mama

P.S. They listen to the telephone conversations so I feel under a strain to talk too personally

It sounded like Mama was doing much better and gaining some insight. I felt a twang when I read that she wanted to brush up on her schooling. I knew the feeling. I told myself I still had time. It made sense to let the girls finish out the school year. They were happy and we were doing well together.

Mama's Diary Entry

Ray is drawn to me and me to him. . . . he has little faith in women. It must be that he senses in me something akin to himself. I don't trust men. He seems intelligent enough to realize that the closeness of our situation and my role in his life (and his in mine) are part of a temporary arrangement.

When I read this entry, a little warning bell went off in my head. Mama was in the hospital to get well, not to get involved with another man.

April 2, 1968

Dearest Terry,

How is the little mother? Now you can see why it is nice to have children while you are young. You have the energy to keep up with them. . . .

I really do want to go back to school if I can and even if it is not possible, I am finding myself and I think that I can not only make a new life for myself, but one that I will be happy in. Not bragging—just realized that my IQ makes it impossible for me to be happy in most situations. I am overly sensitive because I am overly perceptive to other people. I am continually amazed at the amount of intelligent [patients] in this place. . . .

Ray was discharged two days ago. He is job hunting in Denver and asked me to call him when I got out. I may do that. . . . He helped me as much as anything because his was my own situation in reverse. Complicated? This place is that!

Do you know that I really did not think that there was anything that anyone could do that would make me want to live again? I really thought that I would be wasting everyone's time.

How wrong I was!!!! Just the rest and the time to think have brought about more changes than you could dream of. . . .

I am taking aptitude tests at the rehabilitation center this week. Will you please pick out some of the dresses that I will be able to use in an office job and send them to me? Hope to be out of here in about a week and a half. . . .

Meanwhile, just keep smiling. It won't be too long before I will be able to take care of the girls again. Bye now.

Love,
Mama

I boxed up more of Mama's clothes. Over the course of several months, I had sent most of her clothing. It sounded like she was headed for Denver and Ray. I had an uneasy feeling, but I told myself everything would be fine.

In the meantime, I decided to give Brenda and Joni the best Easter they could imagine. I put two Easter dresses on layaway, a white eyelet dress for Brenda and a blue ruffled dress for Joni. I had been saving my tip money to buy the dresses along with ruffled bonnets, lace socks, and new white shoes. The night before Easter, I proudly laid out their outfits. I positioned two large Easter baskets in the hallway outside their bedroom door.

Brenda and Joni awoke on Easter morning chattering and jumping with delight to find a stuffed Easter bunny and jelly beans inside their baskets. Dola and I hid colored eggs, Avon eggs with decals, and chocolate eggs in her mother's backyard for the Easter-egg hunt. I helped Brenda pull her dress over her head, then helped Joni thread her slender body into hers. Both dresses fit perfectly. I combed their long hair, tied on their bonnets, and handed them their baskets for our Easter-egg hunt. If a day can be perfect, that one was.

Mama had been out of the hospital for four days but apparently had no plans of coming to Odessa anytime soon. In fact, we weren't sure where she had gone. Possibly Denver, as her last letter suggested.

Dad and Cathy spoke to Vicki in California and learned about Mama's suicide attempt and that I was taking care of the girls. Since I had been writing them regularly, Vicki assumed I had told them. I hadn't. I still kept most things to myself. Besides, I thought Dad and Cathy had enough to worry about with Lanny. The cancer had spread to Lanny's spine. He was in considerable pain.

Whenever he could manage it, Lanny drew pictures for me. Dad wrote, "Lanny drew you a rat fink—whatever that is." I unfolded the picture and easily recognized the Rat Fink cartoon character. When I received Lanny's school picture, I wrote back saying I couldn't believe I had such a good-looking brother. Cathy said Lanny loved to read that and couldn't wait to walk to the mailbox to see if there might be another letter from me. When he received the books I sent him, he immediately stashed them in his treasure chest. "Only his greatest treasures go in there," Cathy said. When Lanny heard I had taken the girls bowling, he told Cathy to tell me he thought he could beat me at bowling. Cathy said he scored 136 once and thought he was a great bowler.

For my April birthday, Lanny sent me a Snoopy card about zooming across the miles to wish me a happy birthday. He had written in cursive. "Dear Terry, I really do wish I could zoom down there to see you. Love to my sister on her birthday. Love, Lanny."

I propped his card up on top of my dresser.

Dad and Cathy had hoped they could bring Robin and Lanny for a visit after Lanny had shunts inserted to take some of the pressure off his brain. The doctor said a slow, easy trip to see me in Texas, and Vicki in California, might be possible. But, too soon, Lanny's headaches returned with a vengeance. It broke my heart to read, "He screams from the pain."

May came.

When Mama finally called, I asked where she was staying. She said she was moving around and staying with different people in Colorado. I asked when she thought she would be coming back.

"I'm not sure," she said. "I do miss the girls, but if you could keep them just a while longer . . . If you need me, you should be able to reach me at this number for a while."

She didn't sound depressed or irrational, just untethered.

Before school let out, I bought Joni's and Brenda's class pictures.

Brenda sits in the front row of her class with her hands folded. She will be going into sixth grade come fall. She looks like me. Joni stands in the second row of her class and smiles. She will be entering third grade. Joni looks like Daddy. Both Brenda and Joni look happy and well-adjusted.

As I looked at their pictures, a wave of sadness washed over me. These two girls were precious in every way. I knew suddenly I was at a crossroads and had a choice to make. I could put my life on hold and try to raise them until they were grown. Or I could call Mama and tell her this was a good time for them to transition into a new place with her. They still wanted and needed Mama.

I held their pictures a long while. I had been Joni's age when I was in Iowa, waiting for Mama to come back before the end of summer, as she had promised. And here I was, all these years later, waiting for her again.

Only this time, I wasn't helpless. I had just turned nineteen. I was old enough to nurture and protect what was precious to me not only now, but what had been precious to me as a young girl watching Mama drive away.

I knew what I had to do.

I DROVE with all the windows down, toward the setting sun. The waxing moon climbed into the desert sky. I was headed west toward California for Vicki's graduation from high school. Mama wouldn't be there. I knew it for a fact. She had the girls now. I had called her and told her I thought it was time. I would miss Brenda and Joni and they would miss me, but I would always see to it that their dresses were never too big.

The girl in me who had been waiting her whole life was in the car with me now, her hair flying in the wind. She couldn't stop smiling.

Epilogue

UNBELIEVABLY, IT'S HAPPENED again. I know I'm in the general vicinity, but here I am walking up and down the rows, unable to locate Mama's grave. A worker riding a droning lawn mower observes me from beneath his baseball cap. The air smells of newly mown grass.

It's been almost twenty years since you were last here, and thirty-five years since she died, I tell myself. This is supposed to assuage my feelings of exasperation for being unable to locate the grave, though I have the lot and block numbers in hand. It's purely coincidental that my visit falls so close to Memorial Day. I have flown into Colorado for a few days before returning to

South Carolina. My husband, Jim, returned home without me, and my daughter, Mandy, returned to Boston, where she now lives.

The three of us flew to California days earlier for my niece Kim's wedding. My sisters, along with our husbands, children, and grandchildren, filled numerous pews on the bride's side of the church. Over the years, our extended family has grown into a small village. Within it, Nancy, Vicki, Patricia, Brenda, Joni, and I are known simply as The Sisters.

The Sisters—it's our collective identity. Though we live apart from one another, in four different states, The Sisters have never been closer. We have a reunion almost every year. Invariably, when we gather, the six of us pile atop a single bed—just the way we used to, growing up—to talk, share, and remember.

Over the years, our children have joined us cross-legged on the floor and implored us to tell them stories about our childhood, which we did with great relish. Ours has been an oral history for many decades. I turned sixty. Joni, the *baby*, will be turning fifty in November. I know Joni wishes I would forget this fact, the way I seem to have forgotten the location of Mama's headstone.

Frustrated, I tromp to the caretaker's office to see if someone there can help me. I have an agenda of sorts. I have come to read, out loud, part of my book manuscript over Mama's grave. I have chosen this location to ask for her blessing on my book before I send it out into the world.

A graying man and younger woman greet me inside the office.

"I'm looking for my mom's grave," I say. "I have her name and both the lot and block numbers."

"What is it?" the woman asks.

"Carola Jean Vacha," I say. "Lot 398, Block 10."

She begins flipping the ledger.

Before I have a chance to tell them the history of her headstone, the man says, "I believe they changed that headstone some years ago."

My eyes widen in disbelief. Incredibly, he must be the same caretaker I spoke to almost twenty years earlier. "I'm the one who ordered the headstone back then," I tell him. "How can you possibly remember that?"

"It's a curse," he jokes. "If I'm here when something happens in this cemetery, I remember it. Even if I don't want to."

I'm amazed someone can have a photographic memory of a cemetery. He rises and, for the second time in my life, leads me to my mother's grave. As we walk, I scribble a note to myself telling me *exactly* where I can locate her grave should I ever come back. *Almost the last grave on Maple. To the left of the cemetery road.* In my arms, I carry the working manuscript of *Moonlight on Linoleum.*

It must look odd, I think, *visiting a grave site with hundreds of typed pages in my arms.* I open my mouth to tell the caretaker I have mentioned him in the prologue of the book I am writing. I think this might please him, but then I stop myself. I decide I want privacy instead. I didn't travel nearly two thousand miles to chat.

A wild rose balances atop the manuscript pages I carry. I spotted it earlier growing alongside a cement sidewalk near the florist shop where I planned to buy Mama a store-bought variety. It struck me that a *wild rose* better suited Mama, so instead of entering the florist's, I plucked a bloom from the bush and walked back to my rental car.

The caretaker leaves me at Mama's grave. I kneel and place

the rose atop her pink granite headstone. I feel as if I am making a pilgrimage to a shrine.

"Hello, Mama," I say as I deposit the manuscript beside the rose. "I've come to ask your blessing on this." I pat the pages. I pause; so many thoughts tumble in my mind.

I have been working on the manuscript for the better part of two years. Sometimes it felt like Mama rose from her grave and wandered on and off my pages. My sisters have undertaken this journey, too, for my benefit. They answered my questions and visited painful places to tell me how it was for them. While all of us lived in the same household for many years, we remember different things, and sometimes we remember the same things differently.

Memory is something more than a set of facts. It can be colored by age, perspective, expectations, and disappointments. A strong emotional charge can cause a memory to be carefully stored in the vault of one mind and not another. I am lucky to have the collective memory of The Sisters. In our case, one memory often sparked another.

This was never more evident to me than when my sisters and I rented a van and drove to several Texas oil towns where we once lived. I wanted to revisit them as research for my book. Vicki couldn't join us because she wasn't feeling well enough to travel. Joni didn't want Vicki to feel left out, so she made a cut-out doll we nicknamed Flat Vicki. We took Flat Vicki everywhere we went. Nancy and Brenda designed T-shirts for the trip imprinted with THE GIRLS' COMEBACK TOUR.

I asked each sister to bring the single amber bead I had given her as a gift when I returned from Africa. (Yes, I finally made it to Africa.) Amber is fossilized tree resin that sometimes hardens around pieces of seeds, soil, and insects. Each bead carries a piece of Africa inside it. *What could be more fitting, I had reasoned, than holding a piece of Africa in the palm of your hand?*

For our trip through Texas, I strung our amber beads together to make a single necklace of sisterhood. We hung the necklace from the rearview mirror, where it swayed back and forth for fifteen hundred miles. It swung mightily the day the van bounced and shuddered down a rutted, unpaved road toward the Pecos River. Miraculously, we found not only the river but the exact place we used to camp.

We traveled to East Texas to hug the old oak tree on Grandma and Grandpa's former farm; to Fort Stockton to pose for a picture sitting atop the giant roadrunner Paisano Pete; to Ozona to descend again into the Sonora Caverns; and to Odessa to gather around Mama's old friend JoAnn in her living room.

At one point during the trip, I pulled out a CD.

"This song's for Mama," I told the girls.

After an expectant pause, Mario Lanza's deep tenor filled the van with a passionate rendering of "Santa Lucia." As we listened reverently, an unexpected dust devil blew across our path and shook the van. Our sister necklace swayed back and forth. We commented on the uncanny timing of the wind to the music.

Almost every sentence out of our mouths that week began with "Remember when . . . ?" No doubt our trip down memory lane would be a huge gift to me as I worked on the manuscript. For old time's sake, I bought each sister her own chocolate malt. Naturally, I took a sip of each to make sure it wasn't poisoned.

* * *

WE LOST Mama in 1974.

She lived another six years after being released from the Colorado State Hospital. I wish I could say Mama's life turned around from that point forward. It didn't. She continued to despise the nights until she died. Her death certificate says she died from an accidental drug overdose, from oral and hypodermic consumption of meperidine, a narcotic pain reliever similar to morphine. Brenda remembers Mama more than once crushing tablets with a teaspoon, mixing them with water, then drawing the liquid into a hypodermic needle.

It was during this time that Mama married twice more and surprised everyone by giving birth to another child— a son named Jeffrie Joel, whom she called Jodie. A month before Jodie's second birthday, he found and swallowed Mama's sleeping pills. He was rushed to the hospital and later died of pneumonia, a complication from having his stomach pumped.

Jodie's death haunted Mama. She wrote the following note after he died.

My Son,

Your time with me was so short — and so loving. There were moments when you lived that I longed for peace and quiet. But not this silence which now engulfs me. How I long to hear the chatter of your voice and how it does hurt to see the cars with which you busily putted away your days. . . .

I know that you lay in sleep until resurrection. I am very unsure that I shall be worthy of that day. God be merciful and grant that someone care for you.

I have loved you dearly. I long to feel your arms about my neck

*and rock you one more time. Another could never take your place.
Each child has his own. My heart is so hurt. My arms are so
empty. . . . The ache is so deep. . . . I loved you so. . . .*

Mama

Eight months after Jodie's death, Mama died.

There were other tragedies, too. At the age of fifty-four, my biological father loaded a shotgun, held it up to his head, and pulled the trigger. "Life is hard to understand at times," he had written when Lanny was dying of brain cancer.

Life is not without its tragedies. But neither is it without its points of radiance. I believe joy and sorrow rest together, the two sides of love. I have repeatedly uncovered places of joy inside my own heart, tucked within the folds of sorrow. The love for my sisters comes to mind.

I can't imagine my life without them. They are the amber beads of my childhood. I also can't imagine my life without Jim, my husband of forty years, or my daughter, Mandy, whom I named Amanda Jean after Mama. I'm sure part of my motivation for earning a master's degree in counseling psychology was to help me sift through the joys and sorrows of childhood.

One thing I know for certain—I am largely who I am because of my life with Mama.

I subtitled my book *A Daughter's Memoir* thinking it would be primarily about life with Mama. It wasn't until I began writing that I came to realize how much Daddy was the glue that kept all of us girls together under one roof for so many years. His devotion never wavered. I was Daddy's daughter every bit as much as I was Mama's. He helped shape me, too.

After I left home, Daddy started his own business, married a third time, and fathered another family. He finally found the stable home life he always wanted.

IN ONE of Mama's letters from the state hospital those many years ago, she wrote, "Someday, I'll write a book."

"I wrote this book for both of us," I whisper over Mama's grave.

I pick up my manuscript and begin reading aloud, beneath the blue Colorado sky.

Selah.

Sisters' Texas Trip 2008
Front L to R: Terry, Brenda, Joni; Back: Nancy, Patricia, Flat Vicki

The "real" Vicki and Terry

Acknowledgments

TO MY DEAR and treasured friend Sue Monk Kidd, my love and thanks for encouraging me to write my story. To Claudia Ballard, my agent at William Morris Endeavor Entertainment; Becky Nesbitt and Holly Halverson, my editors at Howard Books; Jennifer Walsh and Jordan Pavlin—I am grateful to you remarkable women for your support and keen insight. To the entire team at Howard Books, under the thoughtful guidance and expertise of Jonathan Merkh, many thanks for your overwhelming support and hard work on behalf of this book.

To my sisters who grew up with me—Nancy Matulich, Vicki Hess, Patricia Fleming, Brenda Guichu, and Joni Knauer—my love and gratitude know no bounds. To my youngest sister, Robin Shaddy, who didn't grow up with me but who once took me to show-and-tell to prove she had a big sister, my love and thanks.

To my mother, Carola Jean, Daddy, my father, Don Skinner, Ruth and Guy Skinner, Daddy's parents and sister, Cathy Skinner, Grace Harless, Betty Dyke, Dixie Deitchler, Gerald Skinner, Helen Reafling, Dodie Oleson, and W.W. for your love and care. To Eunice Black and Gaylen Simmonds for loving my mother and your sister. To my newly found cousin Bonnie Magnetti, who pieced together the roots of my mother's lost family tree. To JoAnn Lane, Dola Jane and Dick Woodson, and Larry G. Harding—you were bright stars in my dark sky.

While it's impossible to name all the people who have given me inspiration, I wish to recognize the friendship and loving support of Trisha Sinnott, Curly Clark, Sandy Kidd, Ann Kidd Taylor, Carolyn Rivers, Henk Brandt, Susan and Trenholm Walker, Molly and Rob Lehman, Carla Riffle, Carol Graf, Alex Beard, Donna Farmer, Lynne Ravenel, Cindy Hope, Barbara Curry, Betsy Chandler, Diana Crookes, Eirin Connelly, Ginny Agans, Laurie Steinberg, Anne Foyle, Linda Hardesty-Fish, Denise George, Kareen Kimsey, Mary Cameris, Lila Cruikshank, Debbie Haas, Linda Warren Norris, and Ada Beth Cogburn. Thanks, too, to the many wonderful people I met through The Thread Project and TriLumina.

I especially want to acknowledge my husband, Jim, and my daughter, Mandy: without your support and love, I could not have written this book. In addition to reading every word many times, you encouraged me to tell my truth, believing in the healing power of story—especially my story.

Q & A with Terry Helwig

1. **Was it difficult for you to relive any of the tougher memories while writing this book? Were there a lot of emotional ups and downs?**

   I remember telling several friends how hard it was, at times, to relive some of the more painful moments of my childhood. I likened it to being in the basket of a hot-air balloon as it descended into an abyss. My friends offered to hold the tether lines as I descended. I liked picturing myself enclosed in a basket because it provided a sound boundary between the past and the present. I kept reminding myself that I could surface whenever I needed a break or a change of scenery, although I felt in close proximity to my mom and the early years of my life the entire time I was writing.

2. **Sue Monk Kidd (author of *The Secret Life of Bees*) is a great champion of your work and encouraged you to put your story on paper. How did you two become friends? Did she offer you any valuable writing advice?**

I met Sue twenty-seven years ago, through a mutual friend, when Sue was visiting Louisville, Kentucky, where I lived at the time. On another visit, three and a half hours after ordering breakfast, Sue and I asked to see a lunch menu at the same restaurant. We knew then that we saw something special in each other. Over the years, we have formed a deep and abiding friendship that mirrors sisterhood.

The most valuable writing advice Sue has shared with me is that she allows herself to write badly. This stunned me because Sue's writing is so spectacular. Sue assured me that not all of her sentences flow out of her perfectly polished the first time.

I now give myself permission to write badly. It takes the pressure off. The key, of course, is to burnish, polish, edit, and rewrite until you have said precisely what you want to say in the best way possible; I call this process "wordsmithing."

3. **In Kidd's foreword she writes that you had thought about writing this story for a long time but you weren't sure whether the world needed another memoir. Was there a particular event that cemented your decision to finally write the book? While visiting your mother's grave with your manuscript, you tell her, "I wrote this book for both of us." Did her unfulfilled desire to write her own book influence you?**

I believe I inherited my love of writing from my mother. I remember reading a spiral notebook of her poetry when I was ten years old and feeling as if I had glimpsed her inner world through a window. Fingering her notebook, I decided I wanted to write, too.

In my memoir, I mention the "novel" I wrote in fifth grade called *The Lost City of Enchantment*. Fifty years later, I still have those yellowed pages, along with one of my mother's spiral notebooks. When I began writing poetry in high school, Mama encouraged me. So, yes, standing over my mother's grave, I felt as if I had written *Moonlight on Linoleum* for both of us.

As far as the defining moment of my decision to write the book, I have to think about that. It may have happened during a family reunion with my sisters as we stood in the kitchen cooking together. Vicki teasingly asked if I wanted to taste the spaghetti sauce to make sure it wasn't poisoned. We all laughed because we knew the childhood story behind her question. Our children even knew that I used to taste-test all of my sisters' malts to make sure they weren't poisoned just so I could have a few extra sips.

As I observed us in the kitchen that evening, working side by side, I was extremely proud of the women we had become—either in spite of our childhood or because of it. I thought about Mama, about how she had given me life and these sisters. Maybe it was time for me to tell exactly what Mama's gifts had meant to me.

4. Near the end of the book you write of your sisters: "They were so resilient and hopeful—despite all they had been through" (page 265). Clearly this passage applies to you, too. In her foreword Sue Monk Kidd writes that there is a "mysterious transaction in the human spirit that I marveled at where Terry was concerned. . . . Well, there are no explanations for

that, there are only stories" (page ix) What do you think? Is there any explanation for the "mysterious transaction" of how you and your sisters were—and are—so resilient?

I believe young children are incredibly resilient. Think about the number of times a baby falls down before he or she finally learns to walk. It never occurs to them to give up. Unfortunately, as we mature, our resiliency may be compromised for one reason or another. It's hard to know why the same set of circumstances affects people differently. We are all so complex. Even though my sisters and I grew up in the same family, we have different reactions, different memories, and different beliefs. I can speak only for myself as to why I never gave up hope.

First, I always felt connected to something larger than myself. I didn't feel alone. Maybe I was a child mystic—whatever that means. I found solace in my world by petting a purring kitten, sitting quietly outside under the big sky, climbing the limbs of an ancient oak, or watching moonlight stream through my window.

Second, I always had my sisters. Taking care of them gave me a great sense of purpose. I knew they needed me, and I felt confident I could meet their needs. We were called "the girls" growing up. Our circle of sisters was a whole greater than the sum of its parts.

Do these things account for resiliency? I don't know. But they come to mind when I'm asked about it. Maybe it goes back to the major theme of the memoir. No matter what happens to us, we should never abandon ourselves. That's a choice we can always make, to stand up for ourselves, no matter what.

5. *Moonlight on Linoleum* reads almost like a novel in many sections. How did you reconstruct these long-ago scenes in such vivid detail? What steps did you take in re-creating the dialogue?

Millions of moments encompassed my childhood. Why did I remember some things vividly and others not at all? What makes experience memorable? As I began to write, I noted that my memories were often attached to an emotional charge—love, abandonment, awe, disgust, fear, excitement, bewilderment.

Revisiting my childhood feelings helped open my memory bank, as did perusing old photographs, researching the different places we lived, interviewing family and friends, and rereading old letters. As an exercise, I wrote my most vivid memories on sticky notes and arranged them in chronological order on the inside of a closet door. This exercise helped me discover the narrative arc connecting these memories.

Occasionally I compressed time to spare the reader. Instead of delineating four separate driving trips through the Southwest, I forged several memories—taking pictures by a state sign, visiting a pueblo, discovering Durango, Colorado, and driving on the Million-Dollar Highway—into a single section. Memoir writing demands that endless hours of experience be edited without altering the truth of those experiences.

Two things helped me with dialogue: For years, my sisters and I orally recounted many childhood stories, incorporating dialogue. Plus, I'm an auditory learner; I remember by hearing. A number of my yellow sticky notes included bits of dialogue, idioms, and speech patterns. Still, life is not accompanied with a set of transcripts. Conversations from the distant past were related from memory. The *imperative* of dialogue is to make sure it's true, even if it isn't verbatim.

6. **You mention that you had help from your sisters and other family members in piecing together your history. Can you talk a little more about this collaboration and how you pulled all of their memories together?**

I am extremely grateful to my sisters for embarking on this journey with me. They helped me flesh out many events and scenes. We spent countless hours talking on the phone, writing e-mails, ferreting out old photographs, and debating differences of opinion. It became clear to me, as I pieced together our family puzzle, that, if given an opportunity, every sister would write a very different memoir. A happy memory for one might constitute a painful memory for another. Our perspective, our birth order, our emotional charge around an event—all impacted us uniquely.

I came to believe memory was more than a set of facts; it was also the interpretation of facts—even with something as concrete as a floor plan. When I drew up a floor plan of our trailer house from memory and e-mailed it to my sisters, a debate ensued about the existence of a wall in a small middle bedroom. Some vividly remembered a wall in place and others swore it was not there. Eventually, one of us remembered Daddy removed the wall. Both opposing memories turned out to be true.

Even before the mystery was solved, I wasn't concerned—in fact, just the opposite. Whenever our discussions digressed into minutiae, it usually meant we agreed on the larger issues. Not one of us ever questioned that we had lived in a trailer with a tiny middle bedroom.

7. **There has been quite a bit of focus in the media lately on the issue of accuracy in memoirs. Was this on your mind as you wrote your book?**

I thought a lot about accuracy as I wrote. What events should I include? As a child, how could I accurately portray the complexity of the adults in my early life? What if I misunderstood personal motivations or the causality of events? How could my life and the lives of my sisters be accurately distilled into two hundred pages? What if someone took exception to what I said?

These were the dragons I faced.

Memoir differs from autobiography in that it is a reflection on one's memory. While the story must be true, emotional truth differs among individuals. Ultimately, I had to recognize the authority of *my own* emotional truth. Only I knew how it felt to grow up inside my skin, trying to interpret the world in which I lived. I tried not to impose my emotional truth on others, but memoir necessitates looking through the lens of the author.

8. **After 9/11, you founded The Thread Project (www.thread project.com). The resulting tapestries were exhibited at the United Nations and St. Paul's Chapel, across from Ground Zero. Can you tell us more about the project? Did your childhood have any bearing on this work?**

As a young girl, I clung fiercely to the slimmest threads of hope, even in times of despair.

After 9/11, I felt the world hung by one of those slender threads. Having learned from moving around so much in childhood that people are really more alike than different, I invited people worldwide, via the web, to send me a single thread, representing hope. Those early threads were woven into *Hope Materializing,* the first of seven world tapestries.

I received tens of thousands of "threads"—guitar strings, cloth strips, fishing line, electrical wire, lace—the variety seemed endlessind People identified their threads—a tattered fiber plucked from the Killing Fields in Cambodia, a strip cut from a marker flag in Antarctica, a ribbon sent by a 9/11 family, a lace pulled from the tennis shoe of a murdered son. I was both humbled and inspired.

Forty-nine weavers, in fourteen countries, set up looms in their communities to weave the collected threads into the tapestries that hung in the United Nations and St. Paul's Chapel. Now, ten years later, I hope to gift this *fabric of humanity* to an interested organization that promotes peace, tolerance, and compassionate community.